CHEROKEE PROUD

SECOND EDITION

by

Tony Mack McClure, Ph.D.

A Guide for Tracing and Honoring Your Cherokee Ancestors

PUBLISHED BY

CHUNANNEE BOOKS

SOMERVILLE, TENNESSEE

First Printing
1999

. . . my father is proudly watching his grandson suck his breakfast from his daughter, the baby three quarters Cherokee, more than enough . A few drops of Cherokee blood were required, that was all, to give him a place in the family, full citizenship in the nation, this blood kin of Attacullaculla, the high chief. . .

From "Trail of Tears-The Rise and Fall of the Cherokee Nation." by John Ehle

Respectfully Dedicated to the Memory
of My Cherokee Great - Grandmothers:
Lucy Briant (Bryant)
Who Resided at Chu-nan-nee, Old Cherokee Nation, Georgia
Prior to the Trail of Tears . . .
Katy McClure of Texana, Oklahoma (Indian Territory)
. . . and to
the Thousands of Cherokee Men, Women
and Children Who Died So Needlessly Along
the Paths of that Merciless Journey.

Chunannee Books
P. O. Box 127, Somerville, TN 38068

Library of Congress Catalog Card Number: 98-73506

ISBN: 0-9655722-2-6

Cover painting, "The Cherokee Trail of Tears," provided by the kind generosity of respected Cherokee artist Laverne Elliott, a native New Mexican whose ancestral heritage includes a full-blood Cherokee great-grandmother. Mrs. Elliott has studied the culture and customs of Indian tribes throughout the United States for many years and is well known for her contributions toward preserving and sharing these traditions through more than 200 published prints of her highly acclaimed works. She has served on the Visual Arts Council of Eastern New Mexico University and 30 of her paintings are included in the Marbridge Foundation Collection of Austin, Texas. For additional information on obtaining Mrs.Elliott's prints, contact Elliott Art & Gifts, 1020 W. 21st St., Clovis, NM 88101. Phone (505) 769-0064; Fax (505) 769-9050.

Cover background art by Gerry Crist.

Printed in the U.S.A.

Graphics© 1994 by RT Computer Graphics, Inc. 602 San Juan de Rio
Rio Rancho, New Mexico 87124.

Acknowledgments

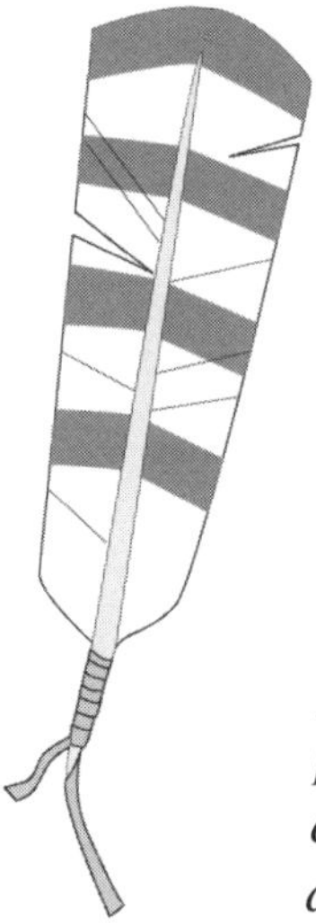

Every writing that I undertake involving Cherokee roots and history involves the work of many to whom I must express sincere gratitude. My maternal grandfather Paul McKinley Argo always made sure that I was fully aware of my Cherokee heritage and taught me all that was passed down to him from previous generations. My mother, Marian Argo Haley (Adudalesdi Adawelagisgi), in continuing that tradition, has always gently, but surely, nudged me back to the path of remembrance when I have strayed. My paternal grandfather, Aulie Floyd McClure, left me a legacy of love and truth, and aunts Myrtie Hughes and Louise Jackson, the encouragement to realize it.

For almost 150 years, numerous family members have spent countless hours, days, years, indeed - even small fortunes, to insure that our family archives are as complete and accurate as possible, and I draw from these regularly, regardless of the nature of the work. Among the more recent of these kin: Raleigh Robinson, Betty Robinson, Jere Robinson Cox, Fred Braden , Edith Manor, Lillian Rowe Steele, Ann Tabor, Jean Tabor Benz, Billy Sherrill, Paul Belew, Iva Argo Morales, Beth Argo Beardslee and Brent (Yanusdi) Cox.

To Lee Sultzman, Marijo Moore, Laverne Elliott, Prentice and Willena Robinson, Marvin Plunkett, and again to my cousin Yanusdi, I am deeply grateful for permission to include their excellent published works. Accolades are due computer gurus Shane Bell and Wayne Carey who kept my machines running smoothly; to Angel Harden for her typesetting expertise and valuable insights; to Patti Hunt and Peggy Havener for being my postmen; and to my Cherokee sister Sue Morrison who helped keep my sanity intact during this endeavor.

A very special thank you is due the late Mr. Virgil Talbot of the Talbot Library & Museum, Colcord, Oklahoma. During his life-

time, he helped countless families discover their roots and this author can be counted among them. My Cherokee brother, Tommy Wildcat continues to be my soul mate, travel mate and teacher; his entire family has given freely of themselves to make their world my world. Noted historian Don Shadburn continues to inspire me and his friendship and advice are valued. Kathy Huber at the Schusterman-Benson Library in Tulsa and Wally Waits, keeper of the Grant Foreman Room at the Muscogee, OK Public Library have graciously lent their support as have staff members and volunteers of numerous other archives and public service institutions: The Indian Sections of the National Archives in Washington, D.C. and Fort Worth; Oklahoma and Cherokee Historical Societies; Georgia Department of Natural Resources & Indian Affairs Commission; Alabama Indian Affairs Commission; the Cherokee Nation of Oklahoma and Eastern Band of Cherokees, and Smithgall Woods - Dukes Creek Nature Conservancy.

I express gratitude to friends Van and Debbie Hailey who are always helpful and supportive and genuine love to Angie Freels, a cherished, adopted brat who always takes excellent care of her surrogate mom, Poppa and Bouncer, whether they are near or far.

Finally, my wife, Robin McClure (Golanv Adanhdo Unole), deserves special recognition, not only for her assistance, support and understanding, but especially for condoning my profusion of temperamental moods and general neglect. She is truly one of a kind.

Contents

Introduction

The first edition of Cherokee Proud was almost instantly successful as judged by the remarkable number of testimonials received advising it had served the intended purpose. This surprised no one more than me because, while I knew there were scores of people with family traditions of Cherokee blood, I had no idea there were so many who did not have a clue about how to verify it, nor that the interest reached virtually from coast to coast. Hopefully, this fully revised and greatly expanded second edition will continue to provide help to all still involved in the search as well as those just beginning.

If you have read edition one, you will notice that most of its contents have been incorporated into this new edition, yet most sections have been augmented with new information. There are new chapters, appendixes, and photographs; more document and census roll samples. Additional sources of materials are included; the segments on cultural and historical enlightenment have been enhanced. And just for good measure, we brushed in a swath of color to brighten the way.

There is an internal view, a geography of the conscience and soul; we search for its delineations throughout our lives. Those who are fortunate enough to find it ease like a gentle breeze over a placid mountain stream, causing only a faint ripple and are - for the most part - contented. For some, the quest is of a contemporary nature - we seek intimate impressions of those living: a spouse; a child; perhaps a lover. For others, it is a search for obscure roots; a knowledge and better perception of our forebears from whose blood we inherited much of who and what we are.

In the world of the Cherokee, this is not always an easy task, but I have been most fortunate in that regard. Since I was a small boy, my mother, my grandfather, and grandmothers and grandfathers before them instilled in each succeeding generation not only a knowledge of our Native American ancestry, but inherent pride in that unique family legacy.

It would be dishonest of me not to say that, with the exception of my mother, Marian Argo Haley, there have been periods when most of my family members have strayed from acknowledging these inherited hallmarks, even to the point of hiding them completely. In times past, mixed-blood Indian descendants would never have been fully accepted into the mainstream of the predominantly white communities where we always lived, regardless of blood quantum. And the desire to be like the majority seemed to always take precedence over honoring the hopes and memories of our beloved ancestors. For the part of my own life when I shared that attitude, I am truly ashamed.

To borrow words from the Honorable Jim Pell, Principal Chief of the state recognized Cherokee Tribe of Northeast Alabama: *"There is no such thing as "part-Cherokee." Either you're Cherokee or you're not. It isn't the quantity of Cherokee blood in your veins that is important, but the quality of it . . . your pride in it. I have seen full-bloods who have virtually no idea of the great legacy entrusted to their care. Yet, I have seen people with as little as 1/500th blood quantum who inspire the spirits of their ancestors because they make being Cherokee a proud part of their everyday life."*

I must forewarn you that throughout this work, I occasionally stray from what critical reviewers might consider normal journalistic standards. By sheer necessity of conscience, opinions occasionally emerge which I find totally unavoidable. In suggesting ways for you to honor your Cherokee forebears, it is impossible not to point out examples of the horrors they suffered, especially when some of their exploiters continue to be immortalized today as "valiant." In those instances, if it seems that my intentions are to indict, you are quite correct. Poor Andrew Jackson. Perhaps the devil stood behind him and delivered him successfully to evil. Nevertheless, his deeds speak for themselves. My words serve merely to inform, but I do sometimes indulge in saying what I think. Such is a privilege of self-published authors.

You also will notice that this book has an unusual format and style - not by omission, but choice. To me, reference books by their very nature tend to be boring. One can take just so much relentless how-to, therefore in relating how to find your ancestors, I have interspersed the sections on honoring them with bits of history and candid anecdotes from which people new to the Cherokee culture might learn.

You may never have the desire to become fluent in the Cherokee language. You may never participate in a Cherokee spiritual stomp dance or come to prefer our traditional music over that of more renown. But trust me my friends, you cannot truly venerate the memories of those you seek unless you make a concerted effort to learn at least the basics of their existence.

If you are an English professor or strict librarian, you may be disconcerted to find that I write as I speak . . . again it is by choice, and for this I make no apologies. Although I have spent many years of my life with my nose buried in books, to this day I cannot outline a sentence and see little need to do so. The definition of a *dangling participle* escapes me and for that I am thankful. Flowery, puzzling words are irritating; nothing frustrates me more than to run across *fortuitous* in some piece I've just begun to enjoy reading when *lucky* would have fit just as well. So, in the few places you find the needless hype here, please recognize that it is only because the Grammatik checker in my computer betrayed me.

Obviously, my primary goal in preparing this text was to guide you to an area of the forest where the proof of your ancestry lies hidden in the undergrowth waiting to be discovered. Suffer me, please, detours along the route to express ribbons of feelings. This is, after all, an Indian's story, not a white man's story. Since you are reading this book, I know that you have a genuine interest in learning about your Cherokee ancestors. With that comes a responsibility of knowing their pain and listening to their hearts. I consider it a rare privilege to be one of the vehicles to that end, and wish you the best in this endeavor. If the pursuit is successful, you'll have the extreme pleasure of realizing just what it really means to be *Cherokee Proud!*

Was Your Grandmother Really a Cherokee Princess?

Airings of such popular and colorful Native American movies as *Dances with Wolves, Lakota Woman, and Crazy Horse* always seem to inspire a rush of new interest in Native American genealogy circles. I've seen this phenomenon often, and each time questions to my family increase dramatically from people who know us as mixed-blood Cherokee descendants. I'm always happy to take the time to assist people who have a genuine interest in *Tsalagi* culture, but I have to admit I get somewhat tired of hearing that hilarious old axiom *"My great-grandmother was a Cherokee Princess."*

While there are literally millions of Americans who do have Indian blood, it seems that virtually everyone who wears shoes has been told at one time or another that their great-grandparents were Cherokee, Chickasaw, Creek or whatever. In the Cherokee culture, especially, this is so prevalent that we jokingly say Adam and Eve must have been Tsalagi! I must alert you that in some cases, these are simply myths that have no basis passed down by family members for whatever reasons. One thing you can be absolutely sure of is that no one's grandmother was a Cherokee *"princess,"* because there has never been any such title in Cherokee culture (at least not since Columbus was discovered on our shores). In fact, it might also surprise you to know that in the old days, there was actually no such thing as a *"chief"* in Cherokee or other Native American hierarchies. In more recent times, many tribes have adopted the word "chief" as a designated title, but originally it was a term used primarily by white men to describe *high priests, elders or headmen*. In early Cherokee communities, leaders were known by these names and the titles closely approximated what we would know today as a mayor. Europeans may have referred to our headman's daughter or other endeared female as *princess*, and modern tribes sometimes bestow the title in beauty pageants, but no such adaptation was ever recognized by the early Indians.

It is important, however, to stress that you should not become discouraged and give up your search for native roots simply because you may have always been told there was an Indian *"princess"* somewhere in your lineage. In your European ancestor's view and language, "princess" may have been the best descriptive available to characterize the unique relationship they saw between headmen and their biological or adopted female family members.

Richard Pangburn, well-known and respected author of the popular *Indian Blood* series found in most libraries, was kind enough to point out to me that *"nay-sayers of the princess tradition"* often cause people to feel rebuffed and they immediately abandon their quest for Native American roots. That result is certainly not my intention.

There are many misconceptions that seem to permeate people's understanding of the Cherokee. To most people, the term *Indian* conjures up images of dark complexions, black hair, painted faces, loin cloths or other traditional dress of deerskin, beads and feathers. True, there was a period in history when the Cherokees fit this stereotype, but there has always been a vast difference between these original Smoky Mountain inhabitants and the plains Indians out west.

For the most part, early Cherokees were woodland hunters and farmers and they began to adopt a variation of white man's dress during the Revolutionary War period. Also, because the vast majority of Cherokees are of mixed blood, only a handful now look anything like plains Indians. The number of enrolled people in both federally and non-federally recognized Cherokee tribes today approximates 235,000 and not more than 15,000 can properly be called "full-bloods."Yes, you still will see many dark-skinned Cherokee people with jet black hair, but except for a few distinguishing inherited traits, the majority look very much like any other average citizen you encounter on the streets. Mixed-bloods have a tendency to be dark under the eyes and very few (whether dark or light) have the stereotypical high cheek bones of other tribes. Some even have blond hair, blue eyes, fair complexions and every other unexpected combination of traits you can imagine, but they are Cherokee descendants, nonetheless.

If you either know or sincerely believe that your ancestors were Cherokee, you might wonder if the work necessary to substantiate and document it is worth all the effort. Be assured that the culture remains very much alive, and most who successfully complete the task find it both interesting and culturally rewarding to take an active part in this rich heritage. No one understands this better than my trusted friend and fellow author CJ Adair-Stears of the Cherokee Nation of Oklahoma. CJ has an admirable way with words and she once said to me, *"the rewards derived from searching for Cherokee roots extend far beyond one's own biological family. New friends that I've met along the way have always strengthened my Cherokee soul, my Cherokee mind, my Cherokee spirit."*

Although I doubt that she has ever had to actually search for her own native genesis (CJ is of homegrown *Adair* stock, one of the oldest and most respected family names in modern Cherokee history), this amiable and benevolent lady has spent the better part of the last twenty years preparing an extensive and authoritative new Cherokee family reference text designed solely to help others recognize their own unique origins. The future release of her definitive work *"Cherokee Trails"* will be a highlight for me personally, not only because she is my Cherokee sister, but because I know it will be of great value to everyone involved in *Tsalagi* genealogical exploration. Watch for it!

From a purely personal and impassioned standpoint, it is very important to insure that the Cherokee people never perish from this land where our dead lay buried. The downright savagery inflicted upon the indigenous native peoples of Tennessee, Georgia, Alabama, North Carolina, and other southeastern states deserves to be remembered and fully understood if we are to insure that atrocities like the infamous *Trail of Tears* never happen again.

It has always been my family's view that our ancestors who were so directly and pitifully affected by these actions deserve to be perpetually honored for their sacrifices. Making this proud heritage an important part of our daily lives is how we accomplish this venerable task and helping you to do the same is what this book is all about.

Cherokee descendants today have every type of unexpected physical feature you can imagine - from dark skin and jet black hair to fair complexions, blond hair and blue eyes, but they are Cherokees nonetheless. Here, Jill Davis, a 1/16th blood Cherokee from Rome, Georgia poses with her good friend Mr. Tom Webber Wildcat, a full-blood from Tahlequah,OK.

The Search Begins

There are many places to look for Cherokee ancestors. The best place to begin is at home, talking to your parents, the elderly, and friends of the family. Listen carefully to every old story, regardless of how ridiculous it may seem and make a written record of every word that is said. Make a copy of old family documents or photographs and watch for notations on these i.e., photographer's stamps, handwritten dates, names, places, etc. If there are no documents, don't let this dampen your enthusiasm - it is not unusual. Be sure to attend family reunions and take along plenty of film or videotape, writing materials, and an audio recorder.

Attempt to determine where ancestor(s) lived and approximate dates. Learn about any unusual old customs, habits, distinctive dress or traits that anyone can remember. A minuscule of information may seem unimportant at first, but could later prove to be the key that unlocks the mystery.

Recognize that many of our Native ancestors lived through generations of suppressed pride and persecution so they found it very difficult to hold on to Native American traditions, especially if they lived in mostly white communities. Don't be surprised if some of your older relatives are not overly excited about exploring the details of that part of your family's genealogy. There can be some heavy memories here, so be sensitive to their feelings.

Mrs. Edith Manor of Brazoria, Texas, the author's eldest maternal Cherokee relative in 1998.
Photo by Van Hailey

Old wills are often important finds and if your family does not have copies of them or even know if they exist, check the courthouse in the counties where the ancestors lived. These documents sometimes list family names that your current generation did not even know about or variations of names or facts that failed to be passed down or remembered.

Cemeteries where your ancestors are buried can be very important sources of data, provided you can find them. I have been searching in Oklahoma for the burial sites of my paternal Cherokee great-grandparents, James and Katy McClure, for years. Although I still haven't found them, I will stop looking only when I succeed. Some of the old family plots where my Tennessee and Kentucky ancestors were buried are now soybean fields, so expect some similar disappointments while continuing to carefully research in those you can find.

Gravestone inscriptions can reveal important details and it is not uncommon when visiting family sections to find the graves of relatives you never heard of. This can open some meaningful doors for later exploration, so be sure to take photographs or make paper traces or sketches of all markings. Even if you are unable to add to your stores of close family info, it's a good way to pay respect to those who came before, and the visit can often result in other valuable learning experiences.

Visiting a small Cherokee McClure family cemetery overlooking the Canadian River near Briartown, Oklahoma, I hoped to find the graves of my great grand-parents; instead, I discovered the stones of several other distant cousins including that of Robert L. McClure who gained some notoriety in the late 1800's by fathering the granddaughter of Belle Starr, the famous six-gun toting female outlaw. I knew this well recorded bit of family history, but actually standing there in the cemetery among family, regardless of how distant, always puts everything in an entirely different perspective. Like many First Americans, I believe the spirits of those gone before still walk the land. I can feel an ancient presence anytime I am near their burial sites, meeting places, old ceremonial grounds and homeplaces. I expect revelations and often discover them.

Later that same day, my wife Robin and I called on our good friend, Miss Lucy West, one of the oldest living members of the Cherokee Nation of Oklahoma, who lives nearby in the small town of Porum.

The subject of cousin Robert's grave came up and this inspired Miss Lucy to reveal that one of her own great-grandfathers had actually started the McClure cemetery. It was from her family that the first McClures who migrated to Indian Territories from the Old Cherokee Nation in Georgia had acquired their improvements (houses, barns, etc. on communally owned tribal land). Several of her ancestors were the first buried there, including her grandfather, Frank West, also a Cherokee of some renown. He was the man who killed outlaw Sam Starr, Belle Starr's husband, at a barn dance in December, 1886. In fact, West also was killed by a shot Starr managed to get off as he fell dead. This account has been published many times, but has a particular significance when heard firsthand from a friend who is a family member of those involved.

So, what's the importance of all this? Simply that cemetery's contain history because history is made by people. The time you spend in burial grounds researching your own family roots can pay big dividends if you record all you see and ask questions of anyone you can find who either knew or descended from other people buried there. Longtime friendships can ensue, therefore the benefits continue.

My first meeting with Miss Lucy West was arranged by a distant cousin, Jean Jones of Porum, Oklahoma. I learned of Jean through a benevolent lady named Pat Smith in the same town when I was asking questions regarding the cemetery. Miss Lucy introduced me to the caretakers of the McClure cemetery, Luther and Leroy Brashier whose grandparents also are buried there. From each of these kind people, I learned something about my own family that I did not know. Now, we stay in touch and there is no question that if something of importance regarding my ancestors there should turn up, I'll hear about it posthaste.

For locating cemeteries and listings of people buried within the Cherokee Nation, a 12-volume set entitled *"Our People and Where They Rest,"* by James and Maxine Tyner and Alice Timmons is invaluable. These booklets are available from the Cherokee Nation gift shop in Tahlequah, Oklahoma and other outlets listed later in recommended "Book Sources."

Locally produced cemetery and burial records may be available at your local libraries and churches and microfilm records from limited counties in several states can be found in the National Archives or from the American Genealogical Lending Library, listed in appendix one. The Association for Gravestone Studies, 46 Plymouth Road, Needham, MA 02192 has a listing of helpful books and pamphlets about cemeteries and gravestones for researchers.

Author and his mother, Marian Haley at Maternal Family Marker, Poplar Springs Cemetery near Skullbone, Tennessee.

Gravemarkers in some old Cherokee cemeteries are inscribed using Sequoyah Syllabary, so if you cannot read it, be sure to bring a camera along to record the inscription for later intepretation.

Robert L. McClure gravestone in Cherokee McClure family cemetery at Briartown, Oklahoma.

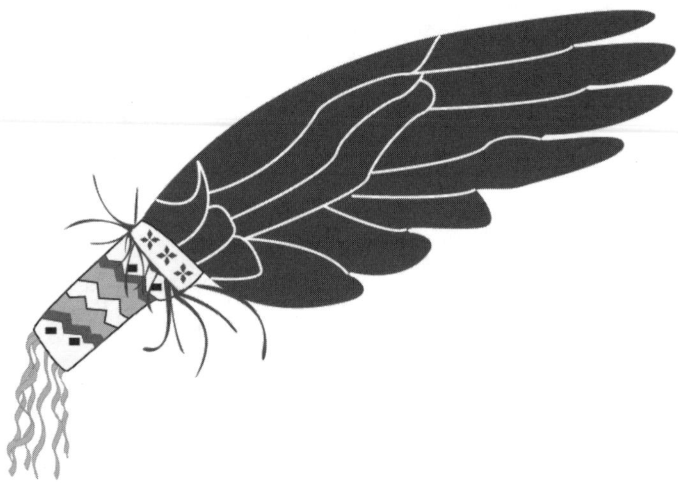

Searching the Cherokee Census Rolls

Originally, Native American Indians were to be included in the vital statistics records of each state when states began to keep records, but because they were spread out in large areas, complete registering was not done for many years.

The original Cherokee Census & Roll records are located in the National Archives, Washington, D.C., the Fort Worth Federal Record Center, the Oklahoma Historical Society in Oklahoma City and a few other Regional NARC Centers. Most are available on microfilm, but a few are available only to researchers who actually visit the depository. All Bureau of Indian Affairs records are a part of National Archives Record Group 75. Microfilm publication identifiers for each record or roll (all part of Record Group 75) listed throughout this book are shown in parentheses immediately following the listing. Because some contain more than one roll of microfilm which may be of interest, I recommend that you review a copy of *"American Indians: A Select Catalog of National Archives Microfilm Publications"* at your local library or available from the National Archives, 7th and Pennsylvania Ave, Washington D.C. 20408. An alternative publication, *"A Guide to Records in the National Archives Relating to American Indians," (order # W100004)* is available for $25 from the National Archives Book Store. This can be ordered by telephone, toll-free at 1-800-234-8861. Additional information on records available from the National Archives is included throughout this book.

Recognize at the outset that traditional methods of conducting family research do not always work when looking for American Indians. Cherokees sometimes took orphans, homeless people, widows or other strays into their home and called them "brother, sister, aunt" etc... when there was no blood relationship at all. It was also an accepted practice to use the mother's family surname and she is often listed on documents as head of household. To further complicate matters, when Indian names are encountered, they generally do not offer a clue as to whether the person is male or female.

Many Native Americans were missed completely when the census rolls were taken because of distance, lack of communication and understanding of the language and customs. Others did not want to admit they were Indian and some simply refused to report because they wanted nothing whatsoever to do with white "authorities."

As very few natives could read or write, names were often recorded like they sounded to the person taking the census. (Bryant could be recorded as Bryan, Briant or Brant). Another obvious problem was that many Native Americans had only one name (such as "Crow"). If you have ever been involved with any traditional genealogical surname searches, imagine tackling that one! Many had given and surnames so different from what the record takers were accustomed to they often did not understand them, much less know how to precisely record them. They simple wrote down whatever came to mind in such cases. This, coupled with the fact that enrollees sometimes gave an Indian name and at others gave an English name, resulted in the same person appearing on different rolls with a different name.

During research, I have often seen occasions of Indians making voluntary name changes for themselves or their children at the time of enrollment. The old document on page 13 serves as a good example of what to watch for in this regard. This is a copy from microfilm in the National Archives of a Dawes enrollment application made on June 2, 1902 by Mr. William Webber for the enrollment of himself, his children and grandchildren. We'll discuss the more important significance of Dawes applications like this a little later in the text, but for purposes of illustrating such a random name change, review this document now and note the particular area of the questions referenced by the black arrow. Mr. Webber states through an interpreter to the commissioner that his daughter Sallie Webber has a young son named "down Watt" but that she wants his name to appear on the roll as "Jim Smith." It seems that the name was simply selected at random; nevertheless the agent complies and it is so recorded.

Imagine now that it is 1999 and you are a fourth generation descendant of "Jim Smith" attempting to locate your ancestors. Of course, if you are fortunate enough to find this application which explains the name change or someone still living in your family knows of the change and tells you, there will likely be no problem. But consider

Department of the Interior,
Commission to the Five Civilized Tribes,
Muskogee, I.T., June 2, 1902.

In the matter of the application of William Webber for the enrollment of himself, his children and grandchildren as citizens of the Cherokee Nation. The said William Webber being first duly sworn testified through interpreter Joshua Ross as follows:

COMMISSION: What is your name? A William Webber.
Q. How old are you? A He says about - he don't know, but about 52 I reckon, he was a soldier.
Q What is your postoffice address? A Campbell.
Q Are you living in Illinois District? A Yes, sir.
Q You are a full-blood Cherokee are you? A Well yes, he is part Nochee and part Cherokee, full-blood Cherokee.
Q Do you apply for the enrollment of anyone besides yourself; have you a wife or children? A Well he wants him and his children put down, his wife is dead.
Q What is the name of your oldest child? A Well she's living to herself, the oldest one.
Q She's married now; tell him I only want those that are home living with him? A Sallie.
Q How old is Sallie? A 23 years old.
Q Well is she married or single? A Yes, sir, she's living with him, but she's got children.
Q She's not got a husband has she? A No, she hasn't got any husband.
Q She's never been enrolled? A No.
Q Now what is the name of the next child, your own child now? A John.
Q How old is John? A About 14 he says.
Q Next child? A Ollie.
Q How old is Ollie? A 12.
Q Now the next child? A That's all of his.
Q Now that's all of yours; now are these all named Webber, do you want them all enrolled under the name of Webber? A Yes, sir, put them Webber, that's the name.
Q Now you say Sallie has some children has she? A She has three.
Q The name of the oldest one first? A His name is down Watt, but he wanted to change the name.
Q What name does he want him enrolled under? A He wants it down Jim Smith.
Q Jim Smith? A Yes, sir.
Q How old is Jim? A Jim is five years old.
Q What's the name of the child is it? A His name is written Watt before on the roll I suppose, and they said they wanted to name him Jim Smith.
Q All right; tell him we will enroll him that way; now the name of Sallie's next child? A Squirrel.
Q How old is Squirrel now? A Three.
Q Now is Squirrel's name Squirrel Smith? A They don't know.
Q Well if he doesn't know the father's name tell him he had better enroll that child as Squirrel Webber? A You had better put it that way because he don't know the father.
Q Doesn't know the father of the child? A Well put it Webber.
Q Now what's Sallie's next child? A Wahleah, about three months old, that's all he says.
Q Does he know who Wahleah's father is? A No, he don't.
Q Well then tell him we will enroll that child as Wahleah Webber? A That's all right he said.
Q Now are those all the people now you want to enroll? A Charley.
Q Charley who? A Charley Webber, well he's living by himself, he can enroll.
Q Well he will have to enroll himself tell him. Now this includes

This Dawes Roll application illustrates a random name change that sometimes occurred during the enrollment process.

what a brick wall you will encounter in your research if you're not so lucky! Watch for changes like this in all old roll documents - for that matter any type of documents - and be particularly observant for interchanges of European and Indian names mentioned earlier. The Indian name "Buzzardflopper" or "Buzzardflapper," for example, is often used interchangeably with the name "Martin." The popular Cherokee name "Watt" or "Watts" is often analogous with "Watie" and also "Christie." Early ancestors of Cherokees whose surname is "Boudinot" will also be found to be "Watie" or Oowatie." (Young Buck Oowatie, took the European name "Elias Boudinot" as a gesture of respect for a man of the same name who made his formal education possible at Cornwall. He later became editor of the first Cherokee newspaper, the Cherokee Phoenix).

When researching Indian rolls, you can save time by starting with any "knowns" and working backwards in time from there. First, check the most recent rolls for your parents and grandparents. If you determine that neither were enrolled on these as Cherokee citizens and you know the birth and death dates of any generation of your great- grandparents, calculate the time frames when they would have been living and check all rolls that cover that period. Keep working backwards through several generations (and cross your fingers that if there is a "Jim Smith" in your line, someone has told you about it).

To fully understand the significance of the various census rolls, it is necessary to understand why they were taken and this requires knowing a bit of history about the movements of various tribal groups. Most rolls were recorded by the U.S. Government to document some payment or other transaction between the government and the tribe.

The Cherokees were once known as the mountaineers of the south. When they first saw the white man (Hernando DeSoto about 1540), their territory included over 130,000 square miles covering parts of eight present-day states: North Carolina, South Carolina, Georgia, Alabama, Tennessee, Kentucky, Virginia and West Virginia.

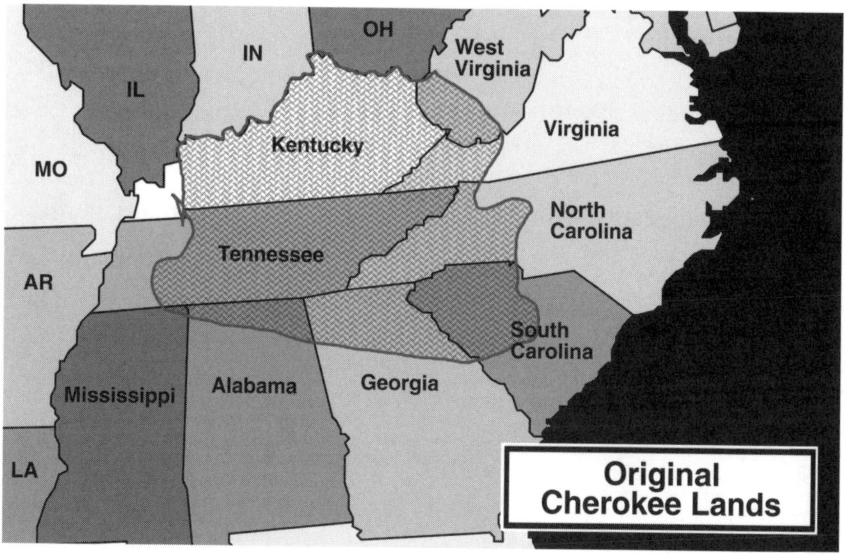

By the end of the Revolutionary War, the Cherokees had lost over half of their vast land holdings.

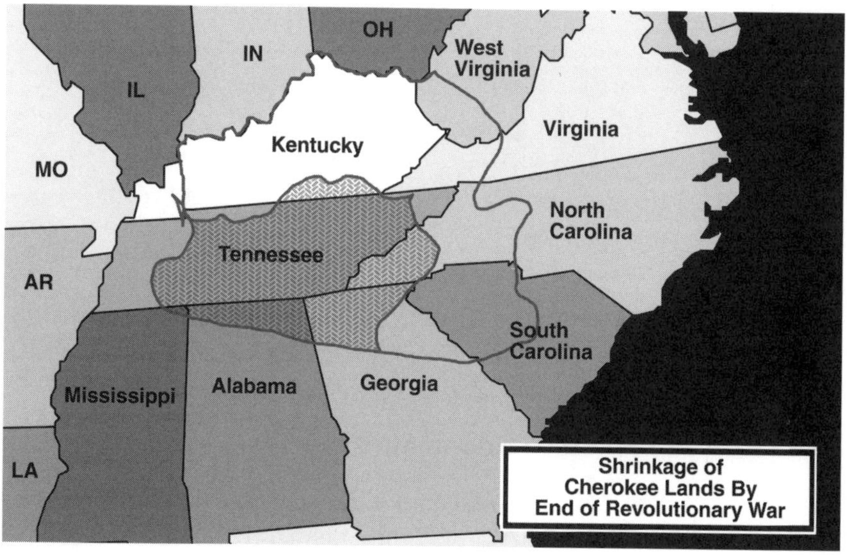

Between 1785 and 1835, Cherokee lands had shrunk to a few million acres.

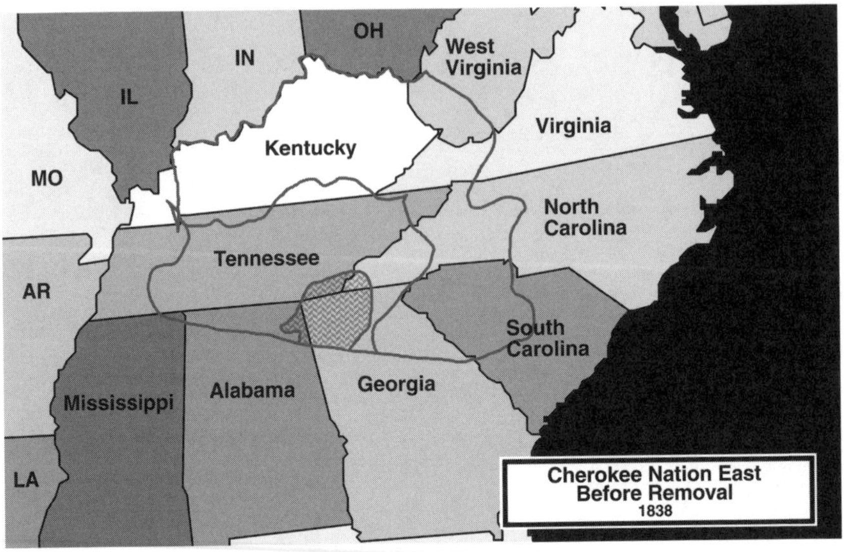

By the treaty of New Echota in 1835 (See appendix 3) all lands east of the Mississippi River were ceded to the United States Government.

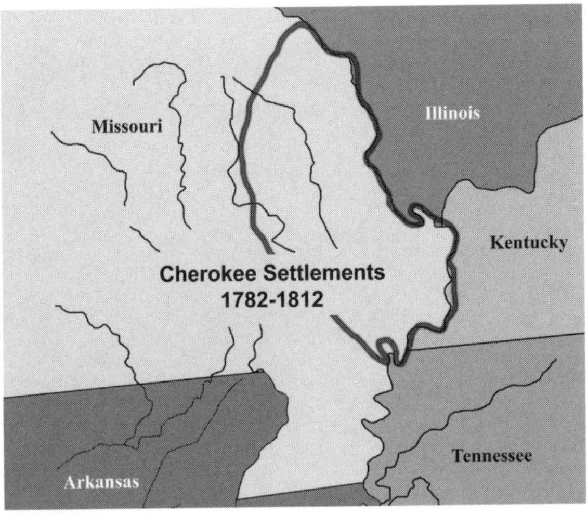

As early as 1782, a group of Eastern Cherokees who fought with the British in the Revolution petitioned the Spanish for permission to settle west of the Mississippi. When permission was granted, a band moved into the St. Francis River valley in present-day southeastern Missouri.

It is probable that there were already Cherokee settled in that area. Records of exactly how many people moved west are limited. Due to the New Madrid earthquakes and flooding in the Missouri bootheel in 1811-12, most of the Cherokee in Missouri moved into present-day northwestern Arkansas. A few remained and the state recognized "Northern Cherokee Nation of the Old Louisiana Purchase" tribe listed later is likely made up primarily of their descendants.

In the "Turkey Town Treaty of 1817" (see appendix 2) the Cherokee made a land cession and during the next two years about 1,100 of them removed from their ancestral lands east of the Mississippi to areas in Arkansas Territory. The Cherokee agreed to exchange 1/3rd of their lands in the East for equal acreage located between the White River on the Northeast boundary and the Arkansas River on the Southwest boundary in what was then Arkansas Territory.

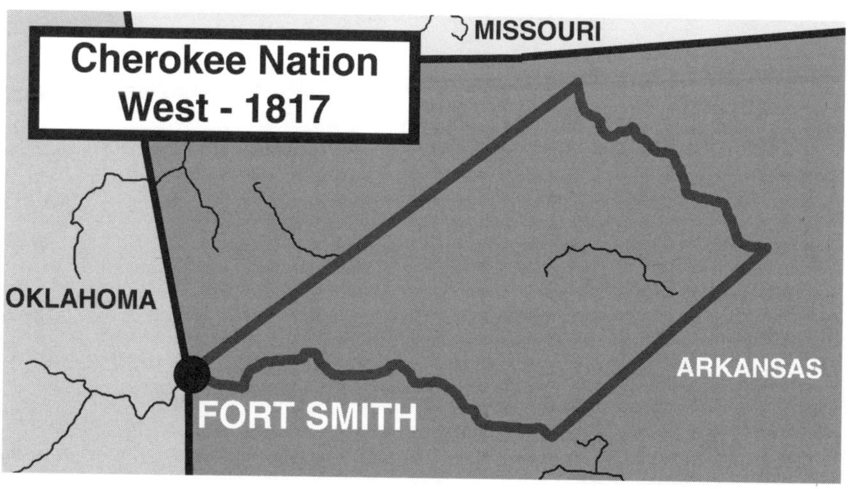

In this treaty, the Cherokee had a choice of two alternatives: They could either enroll to move to the traded land in Arkansas or they could relinquish their Cherokee citizenship and file for a reservation of 640 acres in the east on lands where they already resided. This would revert to their children upon their death or to the United States if the property was abandoned.

The first Cherokee roll you will encounter is known as the **Reservation Rolls of 1817** (M-208, and associated records, M-217 and M-218), (A-21) a listing of those Cherokees desiring the 640 acre tract (mentioned above) in the east and permission to reside there. A total of 311 "heads of households" are listed.

Because this particular roll includes the name of my maternal great-grandmother Lucy Briant (7th generation), it will be used at this point to illustrate a few of the records my family was able to obtain from the National Archives as a result of making this discovery. This will also demonstrate another of the name spelling discrepancies, so often encountered in Indian records.

Grandmother Lucy's name was actually "Bryant" and the certified copy of the original roll from the National Archives shown on page 19 indicates it as such, but a later version (also from the National Archives) erroneously lists it as "Briant." (See page 20). Most printed versions of today use "Briant." This is also true for some of her other records, and the same variation was noted for two other people on the same roll whose first or last name was either Bryan or Bryant. Lucy was granted reservation plot number 91 known as *"Chunannee,"* the land where she was then living, located in what is now known as "Smithgall Woods," a nature conservancy near Helen, Georgia.

The document on page 19, believed to be the original handwritten roll taken by the census taker in the field, was received from the archives with a note stating *"Original document from Record Group 75 Badly Faded and Torn."* The original had been folded vertically and microscopic examination revealed other important information not readily visible here. The entry to the immediate right of her name in the same column actually says *"A Widow."* A third column to the right (cropped here because it appears only as black when printed) has the entry *"Proxy of B. Rogers."* These entries can be read in the transcribed version on page 20.

Looking again at the top of the roll on page 19, you will note that B. Robert Rogers is the fourth name shown, himself a reservee, in right of his wife. For over 100 years, members of my family have attempted to determine the relationship between our grandmother and B.Robert Rogers, but today it remains a mystery.

Perhaps worthy of mention, however - and this serves as a good example of just how much you can learn if you are persistent in your research - we have gleaned more information on Mr. Rogers and others listed on this roll than we ever have on Grandma Lucy. From several records, we learned he was a white man married to a mixed blood Cherokee named Elizabeth "Betsy" Harnage, whom he later

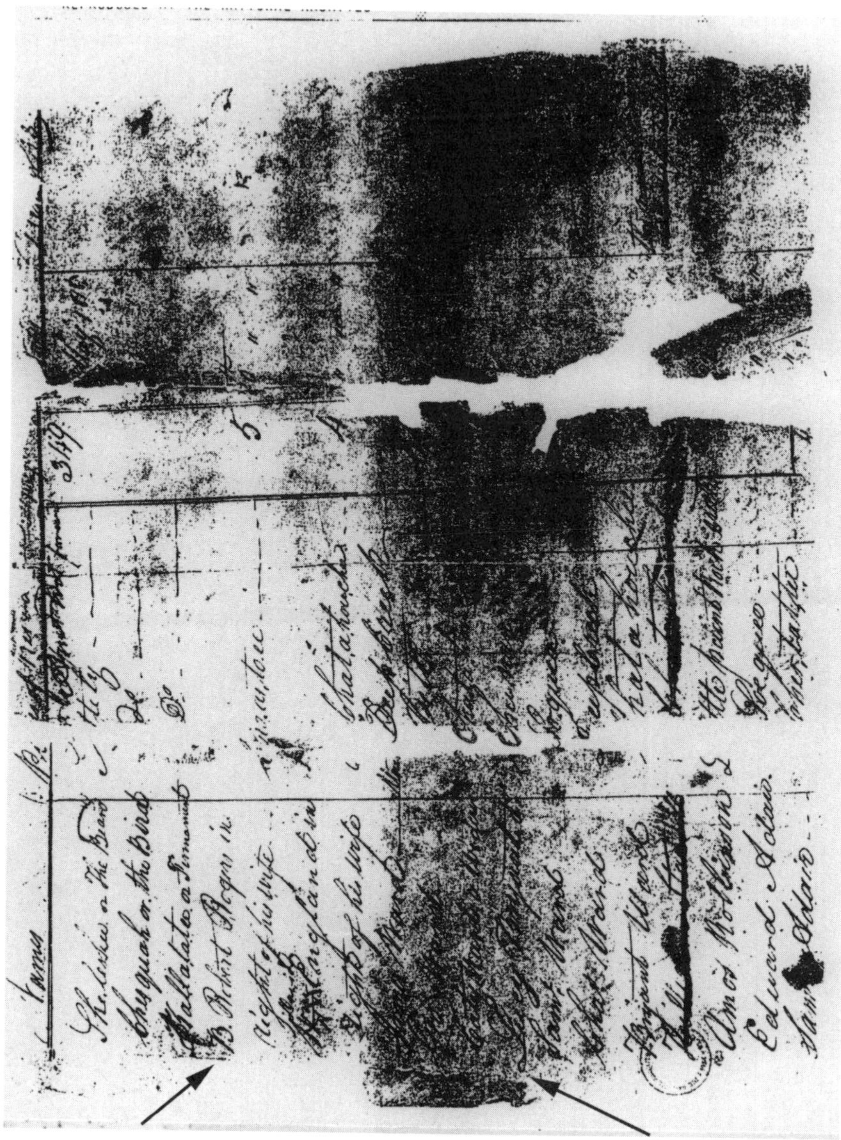

Page from original handwritten Cherokee Reservation Roll of 1817
as received from the National Archives.

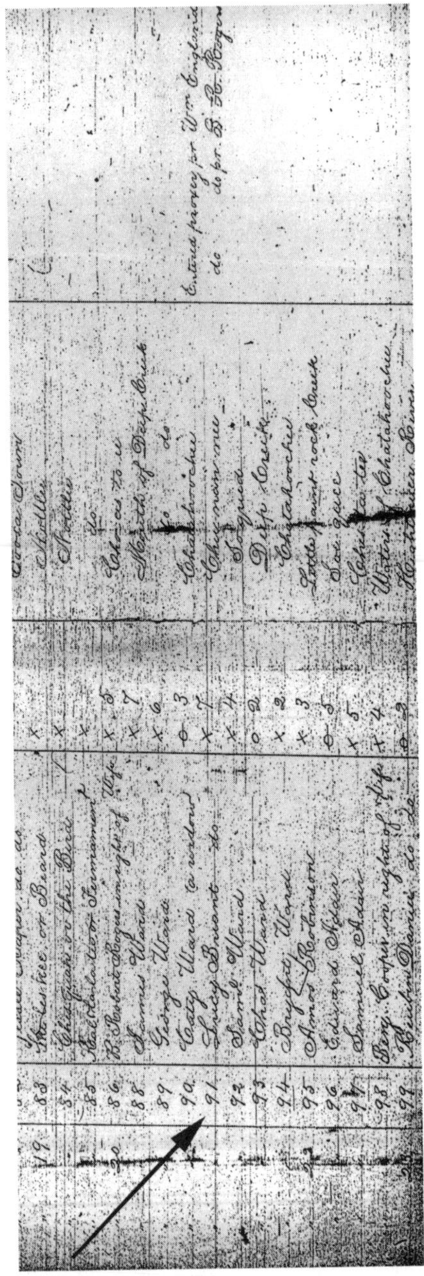

Section of page from another version of the Cherokee Reservation Roll of 1817 received from the National Archives. Note spelling of the name "Briant" here as compared to "Bryant" on page 19.

abandoned.

Caty Ward, (nee Catherine McDaniel) also listed as "a widow" immediately above Lucy Bryant on these roll pages was the step daughter-in-law of Nancy Ward, historical Beloved Woman of the Cherokees. More on Caty Ward later.

Much to her dismay, Grandma Lucy learned the hard way that the "abandonment" rule, mentioned earlier, often was vigorously enforced against reservees who left their property for any extended period, even if they planned to return.

Chu-nan-nee Falls located on old Cherokee Reservation # 91, original home of the author's maternal great grandmother Lucy Bryant. Some experts believe it was here on Duke's Creek near the town of Helen, Georgia that gold was first discovered in the late 1820s, an event that contributed greatly to the removal of Cherokee citizens on the Trail of Tears. Today, Chu-nan-nee is a part of Smithgall Woods - Dukes Creek Conservation Area, a 5500-acre wooded area acquired by the state of Georgia as a gift-purchase in 1994 from noted conservationist and businessman Charles Smithgall, Jr. Governor Zell Miller dedicated it as a Heritage Preserve, ensuring this spectacular tract will remain protected for future generations. An historical plaque at the trail head leading to the falls commemorates the property as the former home of Cherokee widow Lucy Bryant.
Photo by James Owens.

National Archive records confirm that around 1826 - 1830, Lucy left her land in the custody of another Cherokee to care for it until she returned from the "west." A few months later, he was dispossessed of the land by a white man under the laws of Georgia.

How do we know all of this? Family information passed down over several generations indicated that our great-grandfather, John Bryant, a Native American Cherokee (son of Lucy Bryant) came from the old Cherokee Nation, Georgia to South Carolina in the early 1800s. From there, he migrated to Lauderdale County, Alabama where he lived for two years. Eventually, he joined a group of families headed by Davy Crockett, who lived in adjoining Lawrence County, Tennessee, to become one of the early pioneer settlers of Gibson County, Tennessee.

Oral family histories also indicated that grandmother Lucy had lived on reservation land in Georgia in the early 1800's which she later lost. Sometime around 1880, a family member verified that her name was indeed listed on the original 1817 reservation roll shown earlier. A later generation family member requested any additional information available about Lucy Bryant from the National Archives and received the following transcript which reflects an attempt by her in 1845 to be compensated by the U.S. Government for improvements made to her dispossessed land:

Lucy Briant, widow, reservation Chunannee, May 20, 1818, states that the reservation was taken for her by B.R. Rogers as her proxy, that it embraced the place on which she lived at the time & for eight years afterwards & that she abandoned the reservation when she removed with her son to this country. She was not forced to abandon it. She never sold or made any disposition of it in any way. She left a Cherokee on the place to take charge of it until she returned and he was dispossessed by a white man under the laws of Georgia. She states she had about 30 acres of cleared land & three small log houses & a stable & a crib. The man she left in possession was dispossessed in a few months afterwards and in about one year after the dispossession she left the Cherokee Nation East and emigrated to the West. She never received any compensation for the improvements, nor is she aware that they were ever received.

The above statement was made before me this 8th of July, 1845.
E.C.Washington,
Comm.

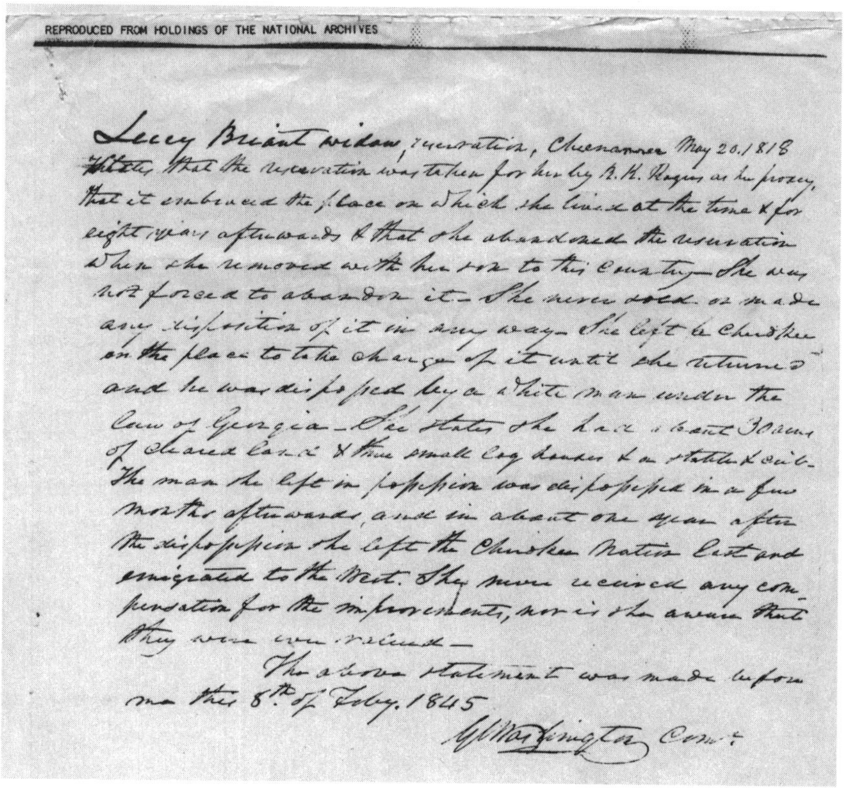

Lucy Briant widow, reservation, Chenanowee May 20.1818
States that the reservation was taken for her by R.K. Hagus as her proxy, that it embraced the place on which she lived at the time & for eight years afterwards & that she abandoned the reservation when she removed with her son to this Country — She was not forced to abandon it — She never sold or made any disposition of it in any way — She left a Cherokee on the place to take charge of it until she returned and he was dispossessed by a white man under the law of Georgia — She states she had about 30 acres of cleared land & three small log houses & a stable & crib. The man she left in possession was dispossessed in a few months afterwards, and in about one year after the dispossession she left the Cherokee Nation East and emigrated to the West. She never received any compensation for the improvements, nor is she aware that they were ever valued —

The above statement was made before me this 8th of Feby. 1845

G.W. Washington Comm.

Copy of actual handwritten document from the National Archives

Over two years later on July 20, 1847 her claim was rejected as reflected by the two brief archive documents that follow:

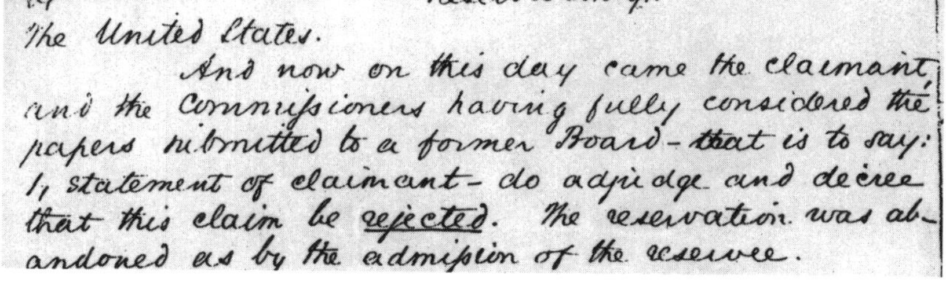
[redacted]
vs Reservation 91.
The United States.

And now on this day came the claimant and the Commissioners having fully considered the papers submitted to a former Board - that is to say: 1, statement of claimant - do adjudge and decree that this claim be rejected. The reservation was abandoned as by the admission of the reservee.

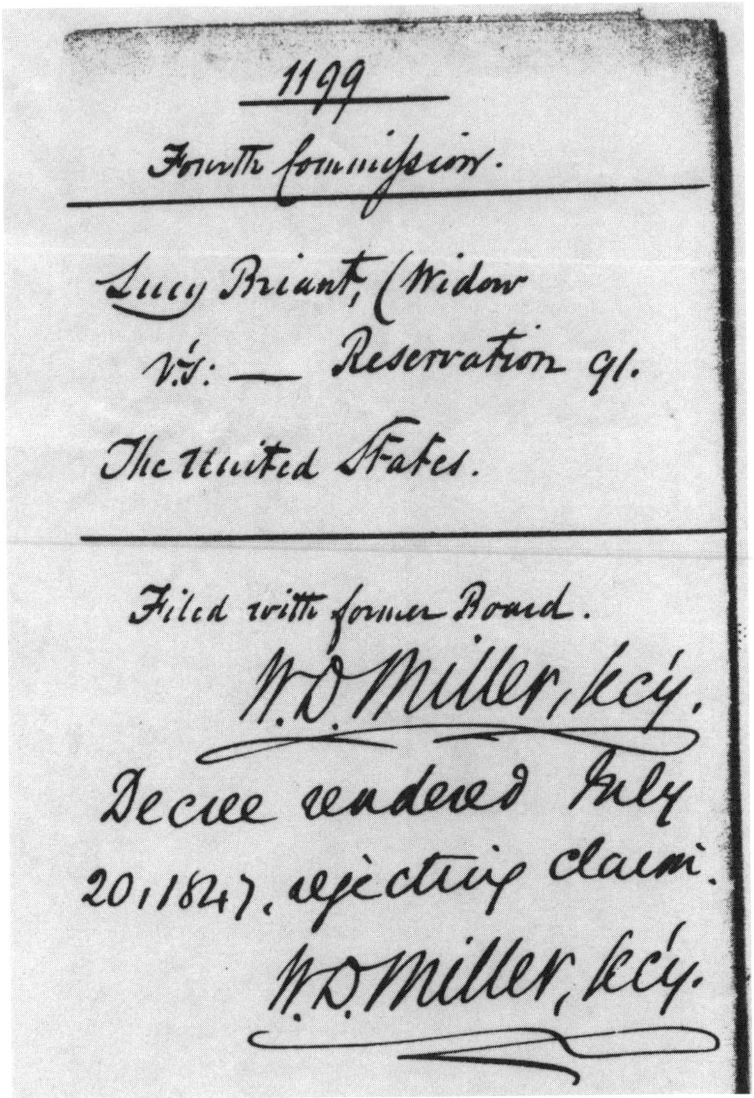
1199

Fourth Commission.

Lucy Briant, (Widow
vs: — Reservation 91.
The United States.

Filed with former Board.
W. D. Miller, Secy.
Decree rendered July
20, 1847, rejecting claim.
W. D. Miller, Secy.

To encourage removal by the Cherokees, the 1817 treaty promised *"to give all poor warriors who remove a rifle, ammunition, blanket, and brass kettle or beaver trap each, as full compensation for improvements left by them."* It also promised to pay the full value of any improvements that added real value to the land, to provide transportation and subsistence for those who would agree to remove. Several hundred Cherokees took advantage of the offer and emigrated west in the years 1818 -19. Some were induced to go look at the new land in the west by unscrupulous Cherokee agents who were bribed by the U.S. Government. Upon their return, they found their "abandoned" reservations taken over by white people.

The Cherokee Emigration Rolls of 1817-35 (A-23) lists Cherokees who voluntarily enrolled themselves as emigrants to the Arkansas country and relinquished all rights, titles and claims to lands within the limits of the Cherokee Nation east of the Mississippi River. This group is also known as the "Old Settlers." It should be noted that many who put their names on these rolls to go west never actually went. Separate muster rolls were kept of those that did actually emigrate. No record exists of the 2,500 or so Cherokees who emigrated to Northwestern Arkansas before 1817 without enrolling.

In 1828, at U.S. Government insistence, the Cherokees ceded their treaty acquired lands in Arkansas under a new "treaty" for land farther west in Indian Territories (later to become Oklahoma). Here, once again, heads of Cherokee families that still remained east of the Mississippi River were offered *"a good rifle, a blanket for each member in the family, a kettle, five pounds of tobacco, and the promise of being compensated for all abandoned improvements if they would remove to the west."* The U. S. Government was to pay removal expenses, subsistence for one year thereafter, and each head of family taking four persons with him or her was to receive $50.

By 1835, the total number of Cherokees west of the Mississippi was thought to be about one-third of the entire Cherokee population. These people became known as the "Old Settlers" and since no actual census was made until 1851, the emigration rolls noted here provide the only roster of them prior to that time.

The fraudulent *"Treaty of New Echota,"* 29 Dec 1835, (See Appendix 3) represented the final cession of all Cherokee lands east of the Mississippi. A census known as the **Henderson Roll, 1835** (T-496), intended as a final enumeration of Cherokees to be removed to the west, was taken of the Eastern Cherokees before they were forced to move on the infamous " Trail of Tears" to Oklahoma. In the three years between 1835 and 1838, however, no records seem to have been kept of Cherokee Indians who were born, died before they left or along the way, (4000 of them), never left their homes, or initially reached the new territory in the west. Also, it includes a large number of Cherokees who somehow avoided the removal and omits many who

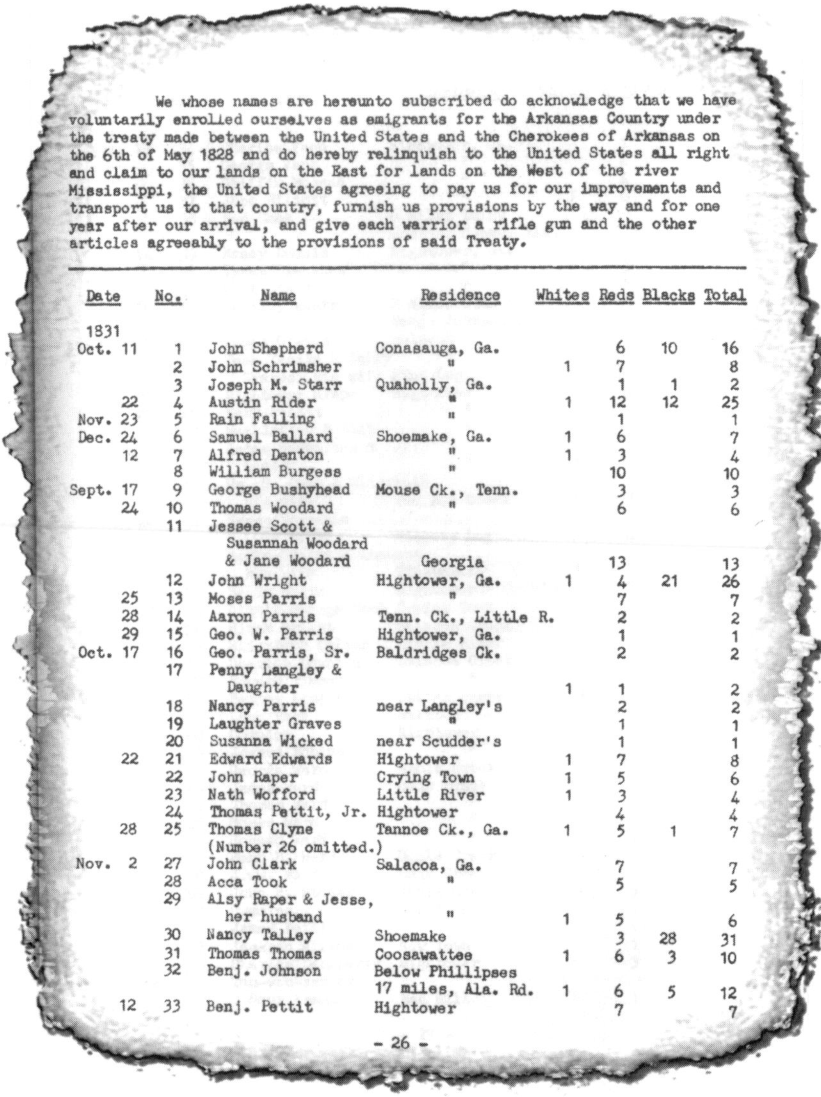

We whose names are hereunto subscribed do acknowledge that we have voluntarily enrolled ourselves as emigrants for the Arkansas Country under the treaty made between the United States and the Cherokees of Arkansas on the 6th of May 1828 and do hereby relinquish to the United States all right and claim to our lands on the East for lands on the West of the river Mississippi, the United States agreeing to pay us for our improvements and transport us to that country, furnish us provisions by the way and for one year after our arrival, and give each warrior a rifle gun and the other articles agreeably to the provisions of said Treaty.

Date	No.	Name	Residence	Whites	Reds	Blacks	Total
1831							
Oct. 11	1	John Shepherd	Conasauga, Ga.		6	10	16
	2	John Schrimsher	"	1	7		8
	3	Joseph M. Starr	Quaholly, Ga.		1	1	2
22	4	Austin Rider	"	1	12	12	25
Nov. 23	5	Rain Falling	"		1		1
Dec. 24	6	Samuel Ballard	Shoemake, Ga.	1	6		7
12	7	Alfred Denton	"	1	3		4
	8	William Burgess	"		10		10
Sept. 17	9	George Bushyhead	Mouse Ck., Tenn.		3		3
24	10	Thomas Woodard	"		6		6
	11	Jessee Scott & Susannah Woodard & Jane Woodard	Georgia		13		13
	12	John Wright	Hightower, Ga.	1	4	21	26
25	13	Moses Parris	"		7		7
28	14	Aaron Parris	Tenn. Ck., Little R.		2		2
29	15	Geo. W. Parris	Hightower, Ga.		1		1
Oct. 17	16	Geo. Parris, Sr.	Baldridges Ck.		2		2
	17	Penny Langley & Daughter		1	1		2
	18	Nancy Parris	near Langley's		2		2
	19	Laughter Graves	"		1		1
	20	Susanna Wicked	near Scudder's		1		1
22	21	Edward Edwards	Hightower	1	7		8
	22	John Raper	Crying Town	1	5		6
	23	Nath Wofford	Little River	1	3		4
	24	Thomas Pettit, Jr.	Hightower		4		4
28	25	Thomas Clyne	Tannoe Ck., Ga.	1	5	1	7
		(Number 26 omitted.)					
Nov. 2	27	John Clark	Salacoa, Ga.		7		7
	28	Acca Took	"		5		5
	29	Alsy Raper & Jesse, her husband	"	1	5		6
	30	Nancy Talley	Shoemake		3	28	31
	31	Thomas Thomas	Coosawattee	1	6	3	10
	32	Benj. Johnson	Below Phillipses 17 miles, Ala. Rd.	1	6	5	12
12	33	Benj. Pettit	Hightower		7		7

- 26 -

Sample page from printed version of Cherokee Emigration Rolls, 1817-1835. This book by Jack. D. Baker is a transcription of these rolls from National Archives microfilm and is available from most Cherokee book sources.

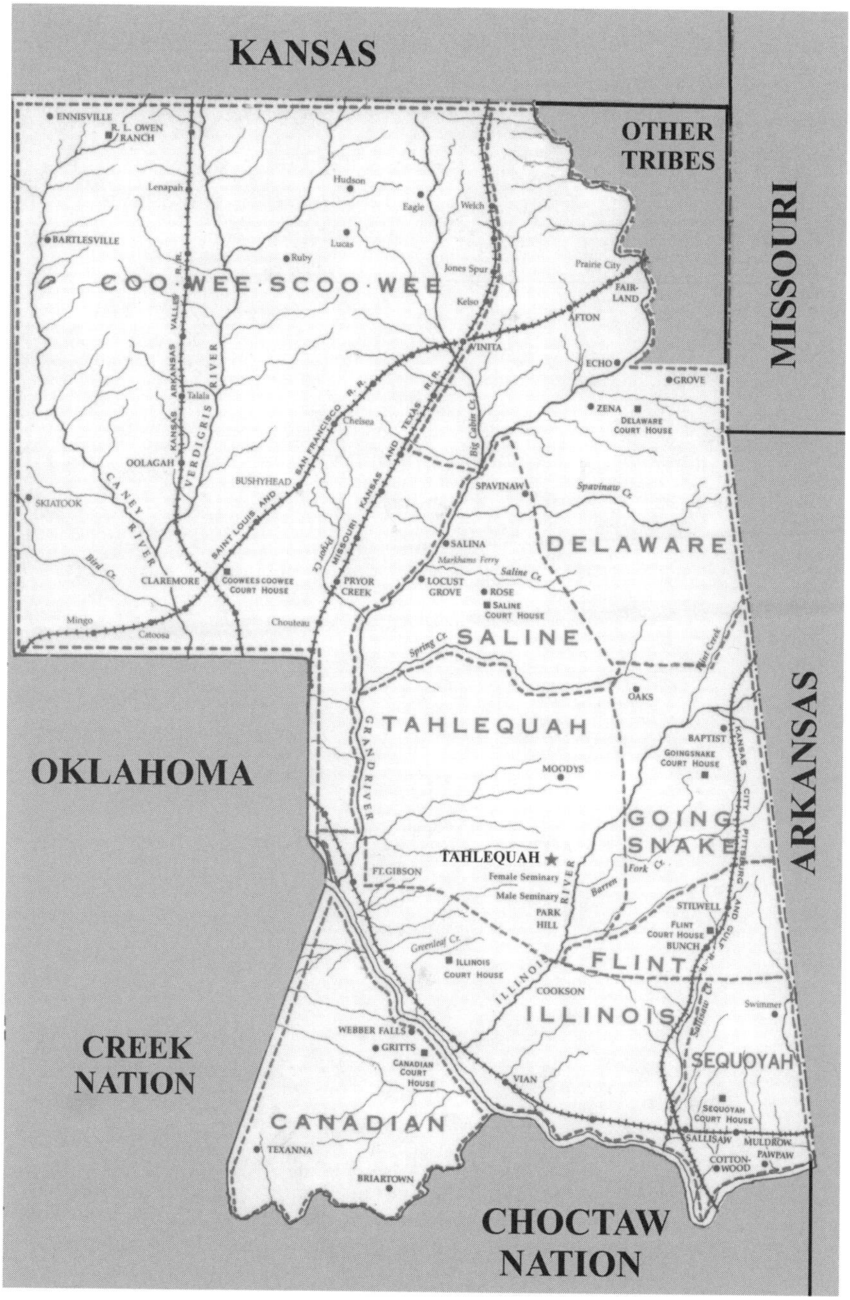

In 1828, the Cherokees ceded their treaty acquired lands in Arkansas for land in Indian Territories (later to become Oklahoma). This map depicts the Cherokee Nation territory.

were actually removed. The Commissioner of Indian Affairs in 1835 (a Major Currey), who was in charge of this census, classified as "Indian" anyone with 1/4 degree or more Indian blood.

In 1838, several hundred Cherokees in the East (the figure is thought to be much higher by some scholars) escaped into the mountains of North Carolina and some of these later became known as the Eastern Band of Cherokees. Others dispersed to various parts of the country and managed to assimilate into white communities. At about the same time, many Cherokees elected to take advantage of Article12 of the 1835 treaty which allowed those desiring to stay in the east to do so if they met certain criteria.

The Henderson Roll includes only family heads by name, but records numerous columns of data including residence by state, county and watercourse, number of persons in household by age and sex, inter-married whites, racial mix, slaves, whether persons could read English, various agricultural data, including acres cultivated and bushels harvested.

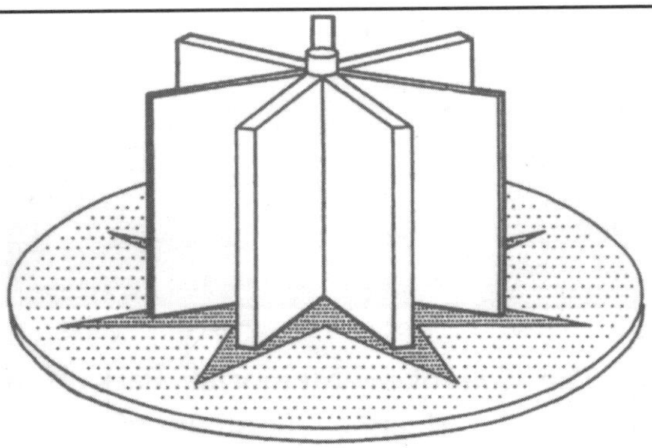

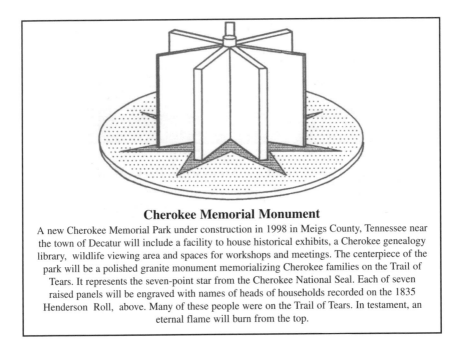

Cherokee Memorial Monument

A new Cherokee Memorial Park under construction in 1998 in Meigs County, Tennessee near the town of Decatur will include a facility to house historical exhibits, a Cherokee genealogy library, wildlife viewing area and spaces for workshops and meetings. The centerpiece of the park will be a polished granite monument memorializing Cherokee families on the Trail of Tears. It represents the seven-point star from the Cherokee National Seal. Each of seven raised panels will be engraved with names of heads of households recorded on the 1835 Henderson Roll, above. Many of these people were on the Trail of Tears. In testament, an eternal flame will burn from the top.

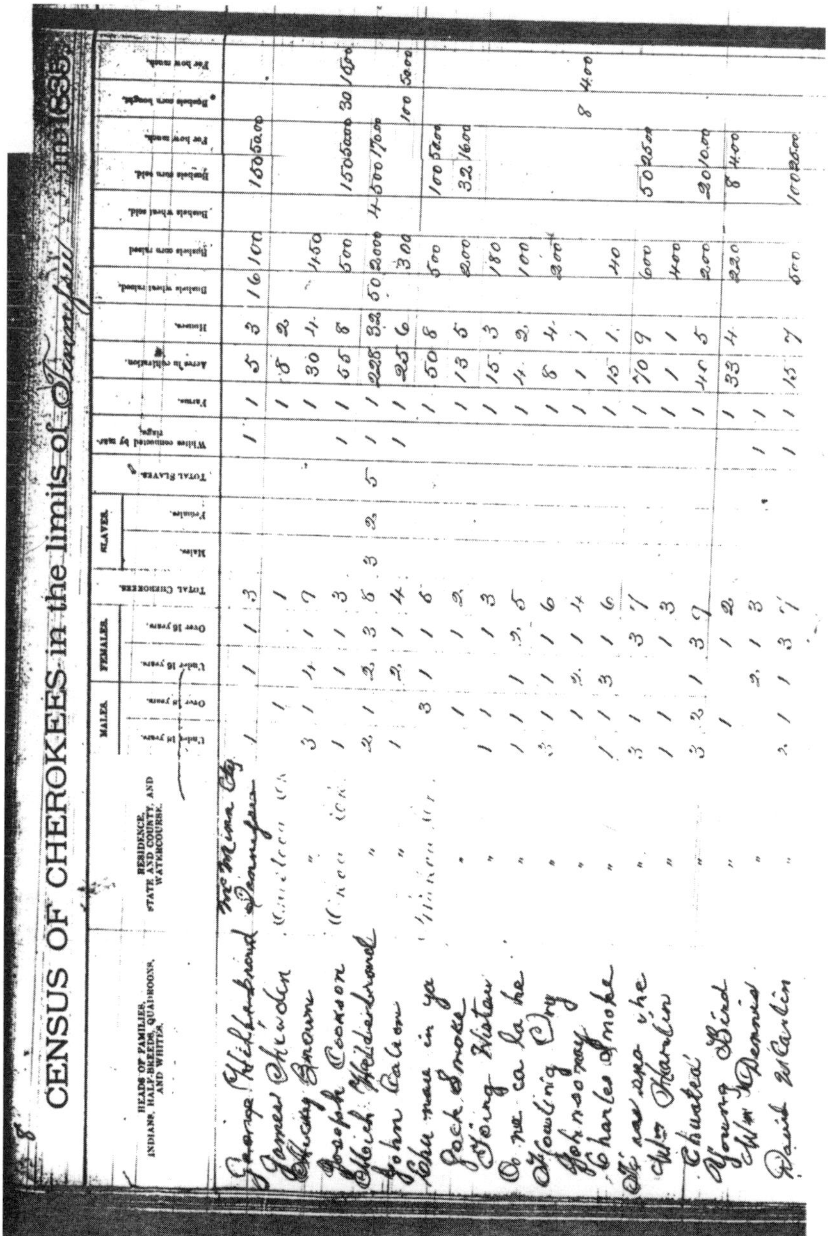

Partial Henderson Roll page (1835). Intended as a final enumeration of Eastern Cherokees to be removed to the west before they were forced to move on the Trail of Tears to Oklahoma. Many of the entries on this roll are very difficult to read.

The Mullay Roll of 1848. (#7RA-06) Listing of 1,517 Cherokees living in North Carolina after the removal of 1838. Agent John C. Mullay took this census pursuant to an act of Congress in 1848. Each eligible Cherokee was to receive $53.33 plus interest at 6% from the date of ratification of the treaty of New Echota. This roll has no index.[See sample page on page 31].

The Siler Roll of 1851. (#7RA-06) A listing of 1,700 Cherokees living in North Carolina, Tennessee, Georgia and Alabama who were entitled to a per capita payment pursuant to acts of Congress in 1850 and 1851. It is commonly agreed that many Cherokees wanted no part of the payment or any connection with white government officials and simply ignored it. [See samples on pages 32-33].

The Old Settler Roll, 1851. (M-685) lists Cherokees still living in 1851who were already residing in Oklahoma when the main body of the Cherokee arrived in the winter of 1839 (Trail of Tears).Approximately one third were Old Settlers and two thirds were new arrivals. Accordingly, a treaty in 1846 concluded that the old settlers were entitled to one-third of the removal payments authorized in the removal treaty of 1835. This roll is a listing of those receiving these per capita payments. It lists each individual by district with his/her children unless the mother was an emigrant Cherokee. In this case, the children were listed with their mother on the Drennen Roll of 1852, listed on pages 35-36. There were 44 family groups listed as non-residents. (Note: Guion Miller used this roll in compiling the 1910 record listed later). A book version entitled "Cherokee Old Settlers" by David Keith Hampton also incorporates the 1896 Old Settler Payroll listed later. Available from book sources listed later.

The Chapman Roll, 1852. (M-685) prepared by Albert Chapman is a listing of those Cherokee actually receiving payment based on the above Siler 1851 roll. In 1851 and 1852, the per capita payments were made by Chapman based on Silar's census to 2,134 individuals (This roll played an important part in the preparation of the Guion Miller

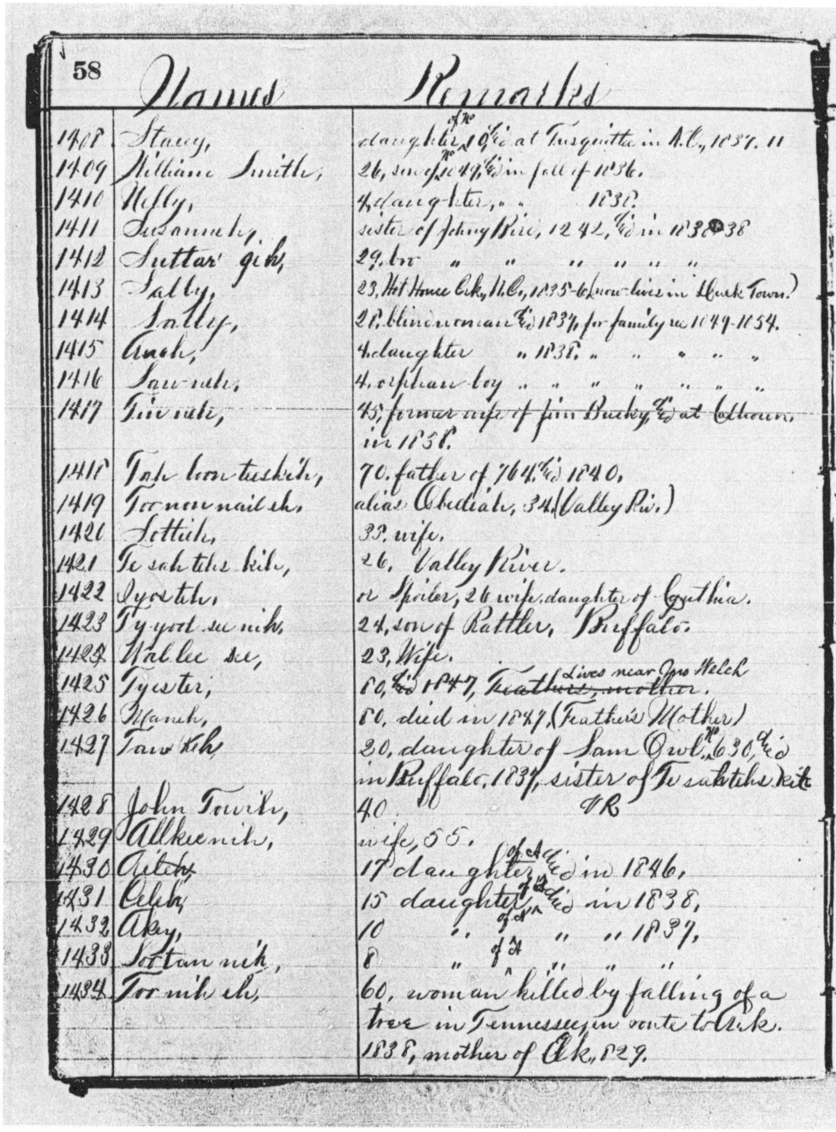

58

	Names	Remarks
1408	Stacy,	daughter of No. 10, died at Tusquittee in N.C., 1837. 11
1409	William Smith,	26, son of No. 1049, died in fall of 1836.
1410	Nelly,	4, daughter, " " 1838.
1411	Susannah,	sister of Johny Bird, 1242, died in 1838 38
1412	Suttar gih,	29, bro " " " " " "
1413	Sally,	23, Hot House Crk, N.C., 1835-6 (now lives in Buck Town)
1414	Sally,	28, blind woman died 1837 for family see 1049-1054.
1415	Anch,	4, daughter " 1838. " " " " "
1416	Saw-neh,	4, orphan boy " " " " " " "
1417	Tinneh,	45, former wife of Jim Bucky, died at Calhoun, in 1838.
1418	Tah loon tuskih,	70, father of 764, died 1840.
1419	Toonowailsh,	alias Obediah, 34 (Valley Riv.)
1420	Settih,	33, wife.
1421	Te sah tihe kih,	26, Valley River.
1422	Iyostih,	or Spider, 26 wife, daughter of Cynthia.
1423	Ty-yost se nih,	24, son of Rattler, Buffalo.
1424	Wal lee see,	23, Wife.
1425	Tyester,	60, died 1847, ~~Feathers, mother.~~ Lives near Jno Welch
1426	Mauh,	60, died in 1847, (Feather's Mother)
1427	Taw kih,	20, daughter of Sam Owl, No. 630, died in Buffalo, 1837, sister of Te sahtehe kih VR
1428	John Towih,	40.
1429	Allkeenih,	wife, 55.
1430	Aitch	17 daughter of A. died in 1846,
1431	Celia,	15 daughter of A. died in 1838,
1432	Aky,	10 " of A. " " 1837,
1433	Sortannih,	8 " of A. " " "
1434	Toonih eh,	60, woman killed by falling of a tree in Tennessee en route to Ark. 1838, mother of Ak, 829.

Sample Roll Page from Mullay Roll, 1848.

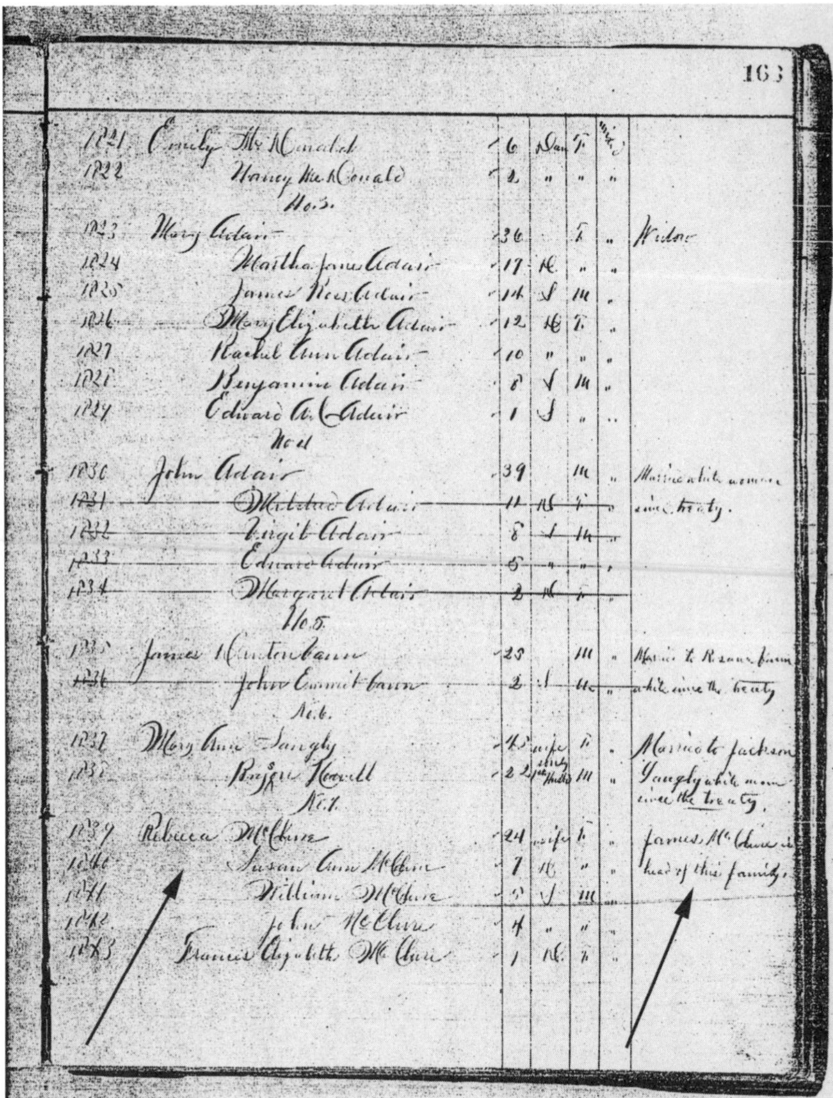

163

1821	Emily McDonald	6	Dau	F	"	
1822	Nancy McDonald	2	"	"	"	
	No. 3					
1823	Mary Adair	36		F	"	Widow
1824	Martha Jane Adair	17	D	"	"	
1825	James Rees Adair	14	S	M	"	
1826	Mary Elizabeth Adair	12	D	F	"	
1827	Rachel Ann Adair	10	"	"	"	
1828	Benjamin Adair	8	S	M	"	
1829	Edward A. Adair	1	S	"	"	
	No. 4					
1830	John Adair	39		M	"	Married white woman since treaty.
~~1831~~	~~Mildred Adair~~	~~11~~	~~D~~	~~F~~	"	
~~1832~~	~~Virgil Adair~~	~~8~~	~~S~~	~~M~~		
~~1833~~	~~Edward Adair~~	~~5~~	~~"~~	~~"~~	"	
~~1834~~	~~Margaret Adair~~	~~2~~	~~D~~	~~F~~		
	No. 5					
1835	James [illegible]	25		M	"	Married to R. [illegible] white since the treaty
~~1836~~	~~John Emmit [illegible]~~	~~2~~	~~S~~	~~M~~	"	
	No. 6					
1837	Mary Ann Langly	45	wife	F	"	Married to Jackson Langly white man since the treaty.
1838	Rogers Howell	22	step child	M	"	
	No. 7					
1839	Rebecca McClure	24	wife	F	"	James McClure is head of this family.
1840	Susan Ann McClure	7	D	"	"	
1841	William McClure	5	S	M		
1842	John McClure	4	"	"		
1843	Frances Elizabeth McClure	1	D	F	"	

Sample Page from Siler Roll, 1851.

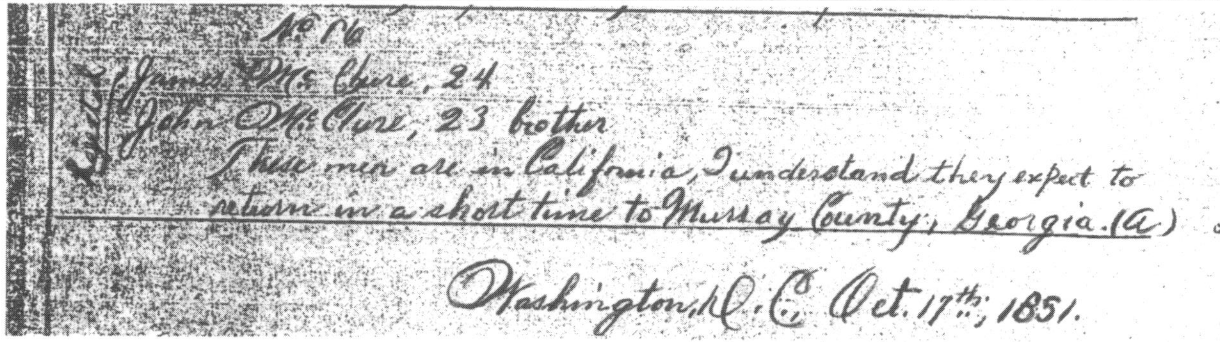

No 16

James McClure, 24

John McClure, 23 brother

These men are in California, I understand they expect to return in a short time to Murray County, Georgia. (A)

Washington D.C. Oct. 17th; 1851.

Note the entry by Siler that James McClure, age 24, and his brother, John were rejected on this roll because they were out of state in California when the roll was taken (these were gold rush days in the west). Remarks on the previous page beside Rebecca McClure indicate she is James' wife. It's important to read every note or number you see on any roll page because they often provide valuable information. As will be seen later, James McClure eventually shows up in the Cherokee Nation West (Oklahoma), but John does not. This roll entry just might be the only clue available to family researchers to indicate his likely whereabouts after he left Georgia.

Second Sample from Siler Roll, 1851.

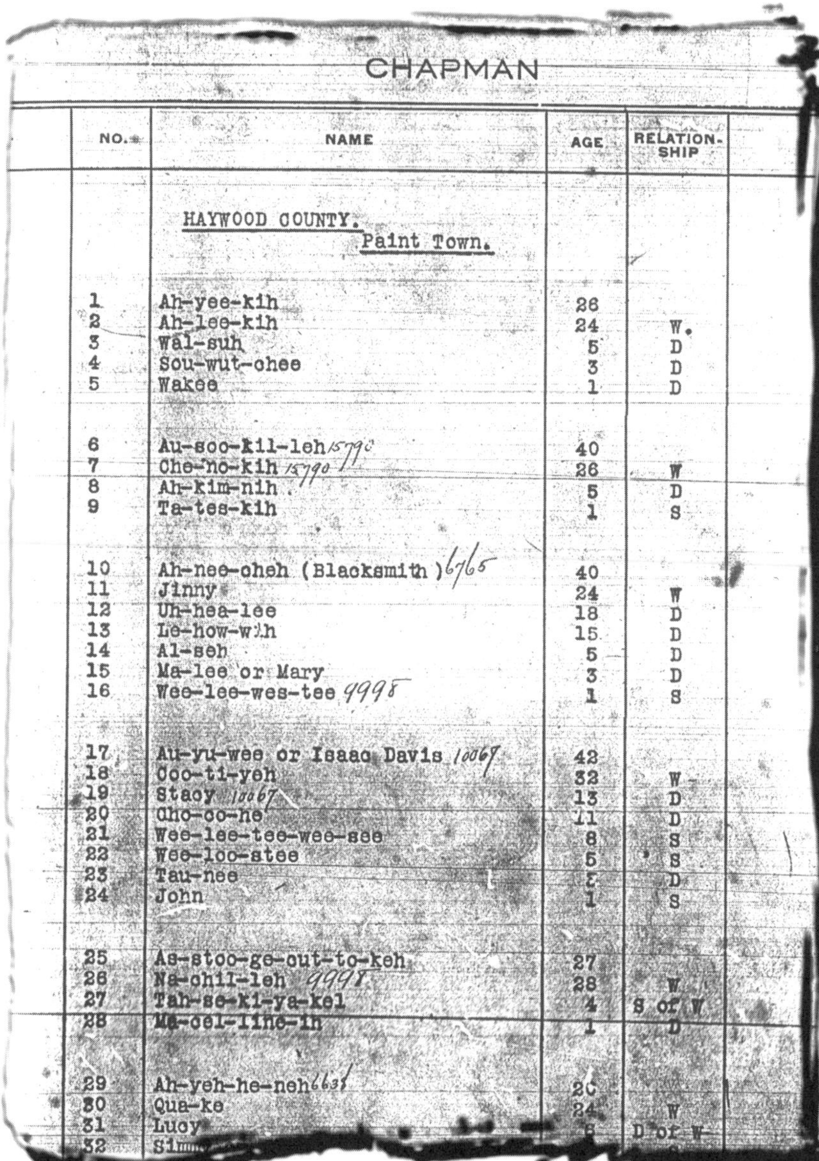

CHAPMAN

NO.	NAME	AGE	RELATIONSHIP
	HAYWOOD COUNTY. Paint Town.		
1	Ah-yee-kih	26	
2	Ah-lee-kih	24	W.
3	Wal-suh	5	D
4	Sou-wut-chee	3	D
5	Wakee	1	D
6	Au-soo-kil-leh 15790	40	
7	Che-no-kih 15790	26	W
8	Ah-kim-nih	5	D
9	Ta-tes-kih	1	S
10	Ah-nee-cheh (Blacksmith) 6765	40	
11	Jinny	24	W
12	Uh-hea-lee	18	D
13	Le-how-w?h	15	D
14	Al-seh	5	D
15	Ma-lee or Mary	3	D
16	Wee-lee-wes-tee 9998	1	S
17	Au-yu-wee or Isaac Davis 10067	42	
18	Coo-ti-yeh	32	W
19	Stacy 10067	13	D
20	Cho-co-he	11	D
21	Wee-lee-tee-wee-see	8	S
22	Wee-loo-stee	5	S
23	Tau-nee	3	D
24	John	1	S
25	As-stoo-ge-out-to-keh	27	
26	Na-chil-leh 9998	28	W
27	Tah-se-ki-ya-kel	4	S of W
28	Ma-cel-line-ih	1	D
29	Ah-yeh-he-neh 6638	20	
30	Qua-ke	24	W
31	Lucy	6	D of W
32	Sim[illegible]		

Chapman Roll Page, 1852.

roll completed in 1910. Anyone who could trace their ancestry to an individual on the Chapman Roll was included on the Miller roll) [See sample page on page 34].

Drennen Roll 1852. (M-685) prepared by John Drennen as a first Census of the "New" arrivals of 1839 to Oklahoma on the Trail of Tears. It contains the names of 14,094 individuals who received a payment of $92.83 made to those living in the west who came there as a result of the 1835 treaty. A section of it, known as the "Disputed Roll," lists 273 individuals who emigrated west before the Treaty of 1835, but returned east before the removal. [See sample page on page 36].

Federal Census 1860. (M-653 Rolls 52 & 54) contains Indian lands in Arkansas.

Tompkins Roll 1867. (#7RA-04) Required by an 1866 Treaty, this appears to be the first post civil war census of Cherokee citizens and freedmen west of the Mississippi River. Approximately 13,566 are listed. Study this roll carefully, because the method of recording was inconsistent with other rolls. Some districts listed only Indian names while others listed English names. There are also Indices of Freedmen with this roll.[See sample page on page 37].

Swetland Roll 1869. Prepared by S.H. Swetland as a listing of those Cherokee and their descendants who were listed as remaining in North Carolina by Mullay in his 1848 Census. An act of Congress in 1868 provided for a removal and subsistence payment.[Washington, D.C. Archives]

Federal Census 1880. (T-9) Check Federal Territorial Census rolls using the names and locations found in the Indian Rolls. (Note the 1880 Indian Schedules for this Federal Census were destroyed.)

Roll of Rejected Claimants, 1878-80. (#7RA-25) By case number, microfilm roll # 1 includes persons whose applications for citizenship were rejected by the Cherokee Citizenship Commission.

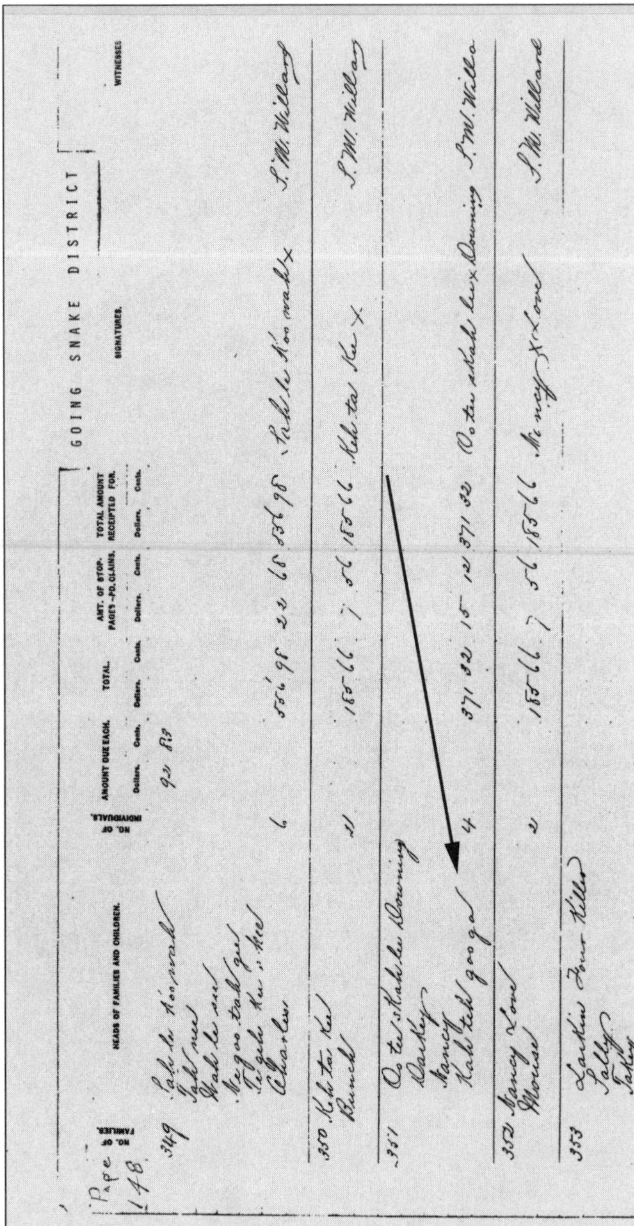

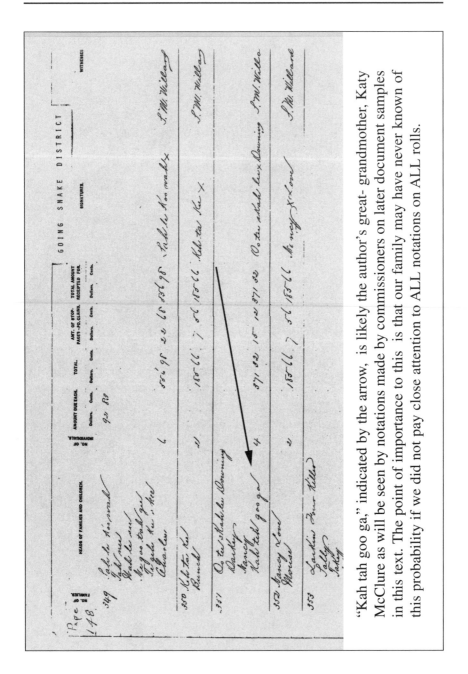

"Kah tah goo ga," indicated by the arrow, is likely the author's great- grandmother, Katy McClure as will be seen by notations made by commissioners on later document samples in this text. The point of importance to this is that our family may have never known of this probability if we did not pay close attention to ALL notations on ALL rolls.

Partial Drennen Roll Page, 1852.

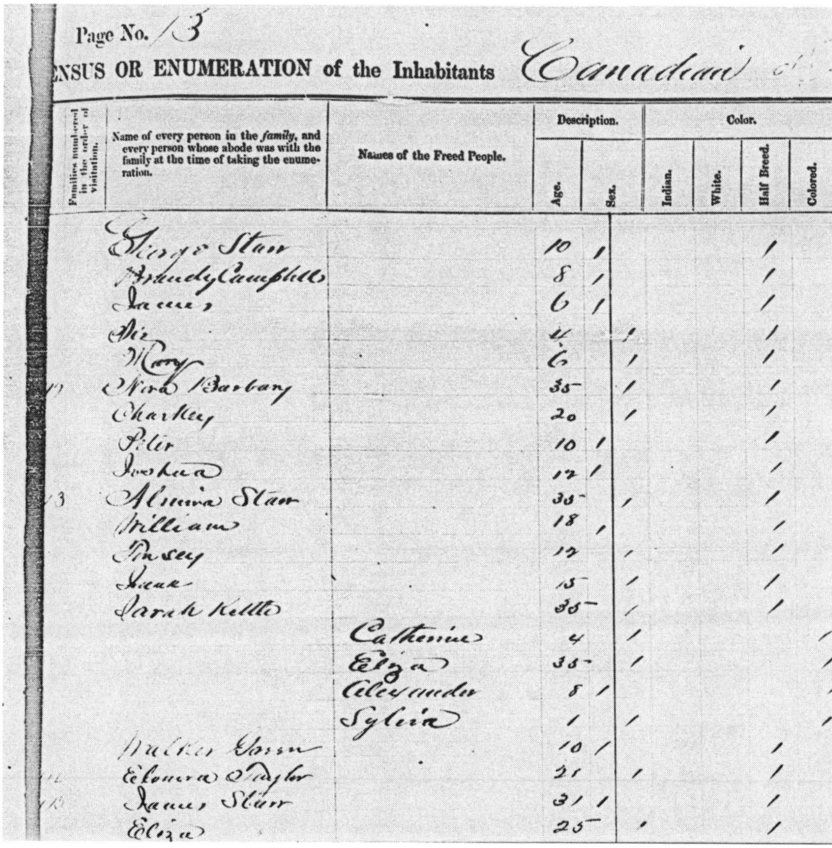

Page No. 13

[CE]NSUS OR ENUMERATION of the Inhabitants Canadian

Families numbered in the order of visitation.	Name of every person in the *family*, and every person whose abode was with the family at the time of taking the enumeration.	Names of the Freed People.	Age.	Sex.		Indian.	White.	Half Breed.	Colored.
	George Starr		10	/				/	
	Brandy Campbell		8	/				/	
	James		6	/				/	
	Nie		4		/			/	
	Mary		6		/			/	
1?	Nora Barbary		35		/			/	
	Charley		20		/			/	
	Peter		10	/				/	
	Joshua		12	/				/	
13	Almira Starr		35		/			/	
	William		18	/				/	
	Pinsey		12		/			/	
	Isaac		15		/			/	
	Sarah Kettle		35		/			/	
		Catherine	4		/				/
		Eliza	35		/				/
		Alexander	8	/					/
		Sylvia	1		/				/
	Walker Starr		10	/				/	
1?	Elenora Taylor		21		/			/	
1?	James Starr		31	/				/	
	Eliza		25		/			/	

Tompkins Roll, 1867. Partial Page.

Cherokee Census, 1880. (#7RA-07) In 1879, the Cherokee National Council authorized this census as a list of persons entitled to a per capita payment of $16.55. It is sometimes referred to as the list for "bread money" as the purpose of the payment was for the purchase of "bread stuffs." The census was arranged in 6 schedules, including Cherokee citizens, Adopted whites, Shawnees, Delawares. Freedman, Orphans, Citizenship claimants whose applications were either pending or rejected, Intruders, and Individuals living in the nation under permit. This census was later used by the Dawes Commission for verification of citizenship for purposes of land allotments.

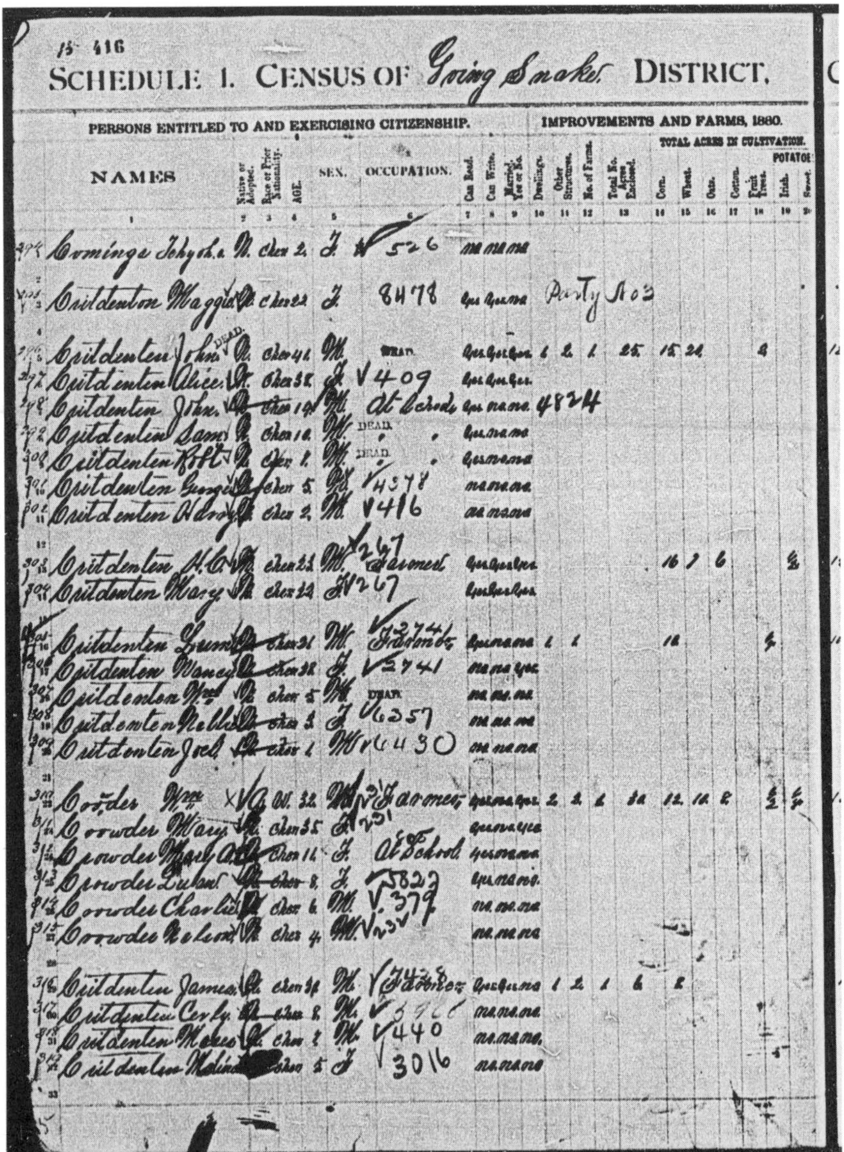

15 416

SCHEDULE 1. CENSUS OF Going Snake DISTRICT,

PERSONS ENTITLED TO AND EXERCISING CITIZENSHIP. — IMPROVEMENTS AND FARMS, 1880.

NAMES	Native or Adopted	Race or Prior Nationality	Age	Sex	Occupation	Can Read / Can Write / Married	Improvements and Farms
Cominge Johyoh.a	N.	Cher	2.	F.	526	no no no	
Critdenton Maggie	N.	Cher	22	F.	8478	yes yes no	Party No 3
Critdenten John (DEAD)	N.	Cher	41.	M.	DEAD	yes yes yes	1 2 1 25 15 21 4
Critdenten Alice	N.	Cher	35.	F.	409	yes yes yes	
Critdenten John	N.	Cher	19	M.	At School	yes no no	4824
Critdenten Sam	N.	Cher	10.	M.	DEAD	yes no no	
Critdenten Robt	N.	Cher	1.	M.	DEAD	yes no no	
Critdenten George	N.	Cher	5.	M.	4378	no no no	
Critdenten Harry	N.	Cher	2.	M.	416	no no no	
Critdenten H. C.	N.	Cher	22	M.	267 Farmer	yes yes yes	16 7 6 4
Critdenten Mary	N.	Cher	22	F.	267	yes yes yes	
Critdenten Lum	N.	Cher	31	M.	2741 Farmer	yes no no	1 1 12 4
Critdenten Nancy	N.	Cher	32	F.	2741	no no yes	
Critdenten Wm	N.	Cher	5	M.	DEAD	no no no	
Critdenten Nellie	N.	Cher	3.	F.	6357	no no no	
Critdenten Joel	N.	Cher	1	M.	6430	no no no	
Crowder Wm	A.	W.	32.	M.	251 Farmer	yes no yes	2 2 1 30 12 10 8
Crowder Mary	N.	Cher	35.	F.	251	yes no yes	
Crowder Mary A.	N.	Cher	11.	F.	At School	yes no no	
Crowder Susan	N.	Cher	8.	F.	5827	yes no no	
Crowder Charlie	N.	Cher	6.	M.	379	no no no	
Crowder Nelson	N.	Cher	4.	M.	232	no no no	
Critdenten James	N.	Cher	34	M.	7428 Farmer	yes yes no	1 2 1 6 8
Critdenten Cerly	N.	Cher	8.	M.	5966	no no no	
Critdenten Moses	N.	Cher	2	M.	440	no no no	
Critdenten Malinda		Cher	5	F.	3016	no no no	

1880 Cherokee Census - partial page.

Lipe Receipt Roll, 1880 (#7RA-33). Prepared by the Cherokee Nation treasurer, D.W. Lipe, listing persons who actually received bread payment listed above.

Commission Docket Book 1880-84 (#7RA-26). A listing by case number and session of the Cherokee citizenship committee. Includes individual names, nature of claims and decisions.

Roll of North Carolina Cherokees, 1881. (#7RA-74). A listing of North Carolina Cherokees who moved to the Cherokee Nation.

Cherokee Seminaries Register, 1881-82. (#7RA-91). Register of students and boarders at the male and female seminaries. [See sample page on page 40].

Cherokee Census, 1883 (#7RA-29). Authorized by the National Council in 1883, this list includes orphans, prisoners and "supplemental roll of citizens."

Receipt Roll, 1883 (#7RA-56 and 57). Prepared for a per capita payment of $15.50 authorized by the National Council.. The list is by enrollment number and district and includes the names of witnesses to the payment as well as the person receiving payment.

Hester Roll, 1883 (M-685) . Prepared by Joseph G. Hester as a listing of Eastern Cherokee in 1883. This Roll is an excellent source of information. Includes ancestors, Chapman Roll Number, age, English name and Indian name. Copies of the previous census were made available to Hester and he was required to account for all persons on the previous rolls by either including them on the new roll, noting their deaths on the old rolls or describing their whereabouts as unknown. This completed roll was submitted to the Secretary of Interior in1884. It contained 2,956 persons residing in North Carolina,Tennessee, Georgia, Alabama, South Carolina, Virginia, Illinois, Kansas, Colorado, Kentucky, New Jersey, and California. Those living west of the Mississippi and listed by Mr. Hester were descendants of members of the Eastern Band and had no affiliation with the Cherokee Nation in the west.

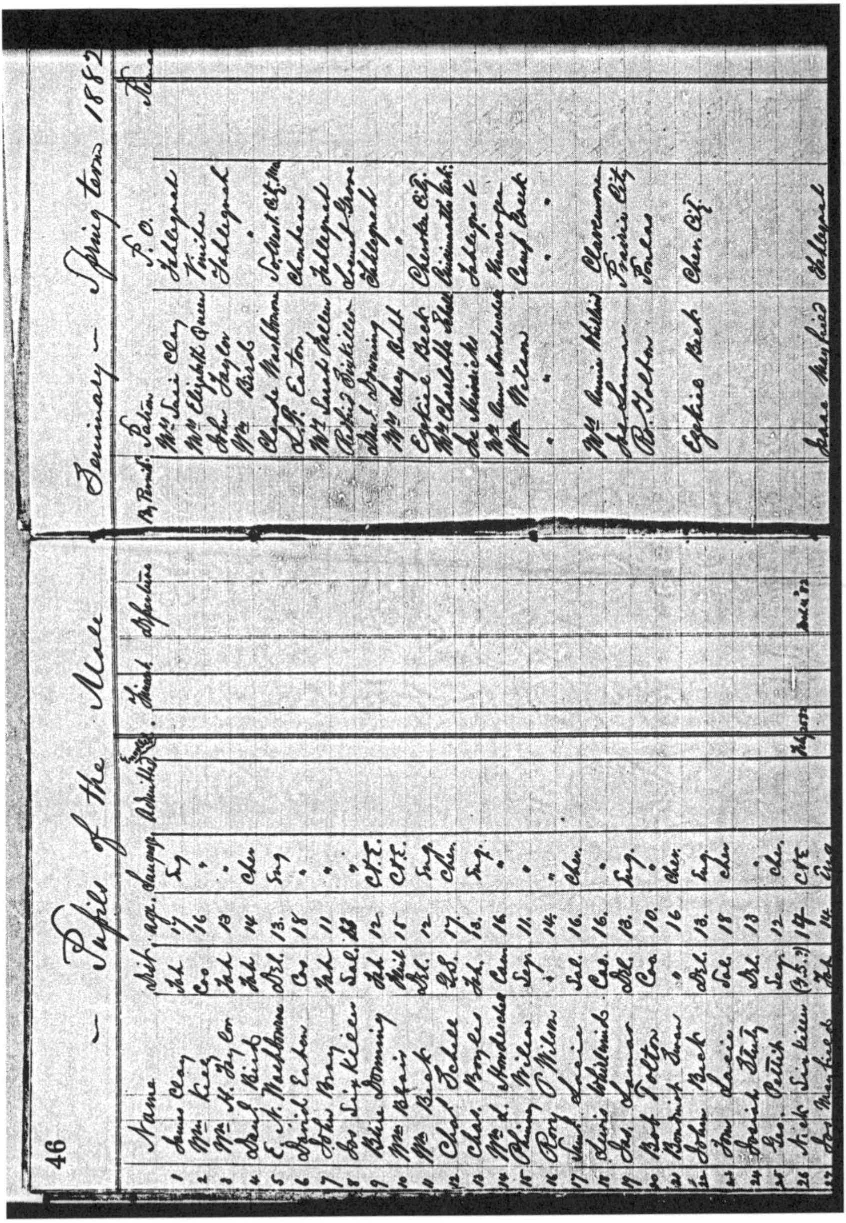

Page from Register of Students at the Male Seminary, Spring Term 1882.

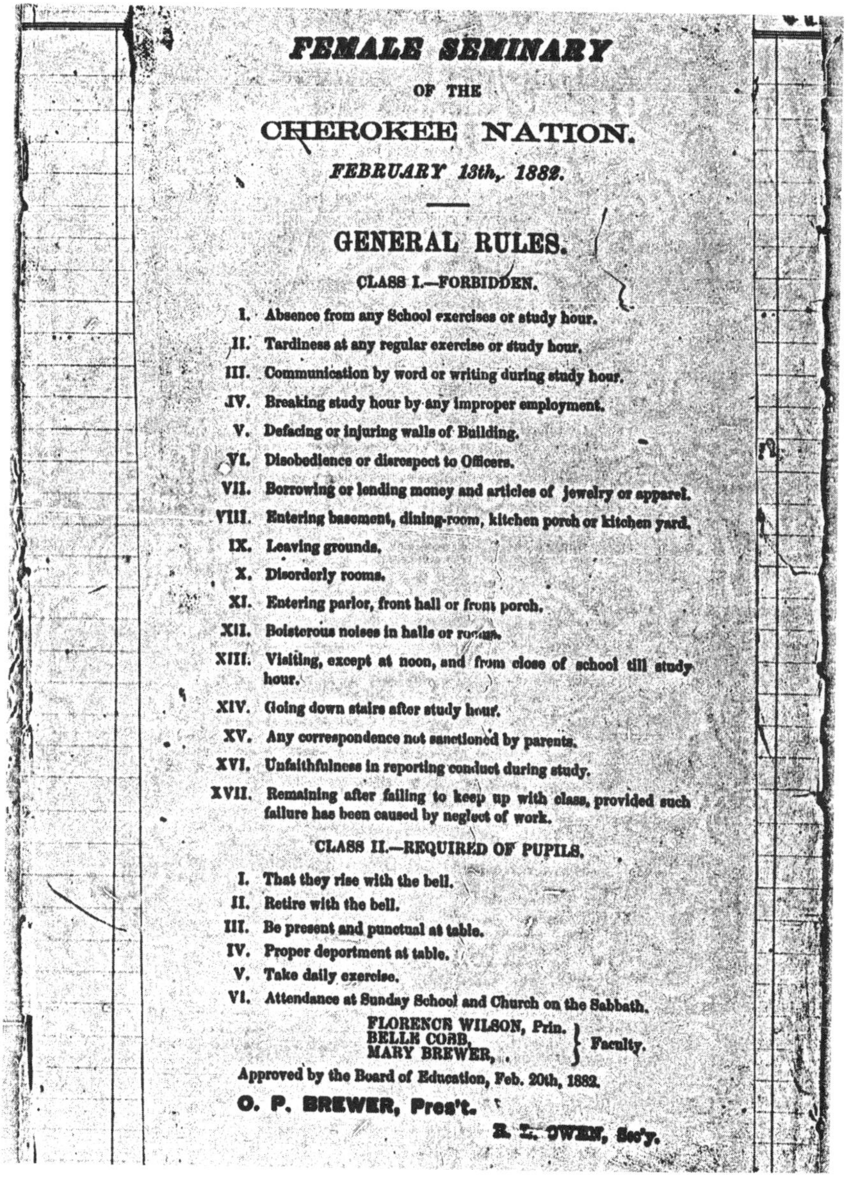

FEMALE SEMINARY

OF THE

CHEROKEE NATION.

FEBRUARY 13th, 1882.

GENERAL RULES.

CLASS I.—FORBIDDEN.

I. Absence from any School exercises or study hour.
II. Tardiness at any regular exercise or study hour.
III. Communication by word or writing during study hour.
IV. Breaking study hour by any improper employment.
V. Defacing or injuring walls of Building.
VI. Disobedience or disrespect to Officers.
VII. Borrowing or lending money and articles of jewelry or apparel.
VIII. Entering basement, dining-room, kitchen porch or kitchen yard.
IX. Leaving grounds.
X. Disorderly rooms.
XI. Entering parlor, front hall or front porch.
XII. Boisterous noises in halls or rooms.
XIII. Visiting, except at noon, and from close of school till study hour.
XIV. Going down stairs after study hour.
XV. Any correspondence not sanctioned by parents.
XVI. Unfaithfulness in reporting conduct during study.
XVII. Remaining after failing to keep up with class, provided such failure has been caused by neglect of work.

CLASS II.—REQUIRED OF PUPILS.

I. That they rise with the bell.
II. Retire with the bell.
III. Be present and punctual at table.
IV. Proper deportment at table.
V. Take daily exercise.
VI. Attendance at Sunday School and Church on the Sabbath.

FLORENCE WILSON, Prin.
BELLE COBB,
MARY BREWER, } Faculty.

Approved by the Board of Education, Feb. 20th, 1882.

O. P. BREWER, Pres't.

R. L. OWEN, Sec'y.

Posted rules of Female Seminary, 1882.

The Cherokee Female Seminary opened in May, 1851 and was destroyed by fire in April, 1887. The above three columns, now on the grounds of the Cherokee Museum and Heritage Center, Tahlequah, OK, are all that remain. 25 such columns encircled the east, south and west sides of the brick building built by Cherokee craftsmen.

Cherokee Census Roll, 1886 (#7RA-58). On July 28, 1897 an act of the Cherokee Council directed this roll be made of persons who received a per capita payment in 1886. It includes the name of the head of household as well as all members of the household, their ages and relationship.[See sample page on page 44].

Cherokee Census Roll, 1890 (#7RA-60). Created also in 1897 as a result of the council act listed immediately above. Listings are the same except it goes a step further to include whether each household member was a Cherokee, Delaware, Shawnee, White Person or Freedman.

Cherokee Receipt Roll, 1890 (#7RA-59). Listing of persons who received a per capita payment of $13.70 made by the Cherokee Nation treasurer.

Cherokee Census Roll, 1890 (#7RA-08). This census contains a wealth of information including 6 schedules of status; Indian by type, orphan, rejected claimant, intruder, etc., and 105 columns of information pertaining to each i.e., age, marriage status, whether the person could read or write, and occupation designator - agricultural manufacturing, etc. *[The physical size of each page makes it impossible to sample here, but to give some idea of the data it includes, entries for the author's great grandmother (listed then as Katie Teehee) are as follows: She was 39 years old, unmarried, able to read but unable to write; She had two dwellings and five other structures on two farms valued at $525; 42 acres were fenced and in cultivation; she owned 75 hogs, 54 cattle, 11 horses, 2 mules, 115 domestic fowl, 88 fruit trees and 7 plows. During the previous year, her farm yield included: 180 bushels of corn, 18 bushels of rye, 25 bushels of Irish potatoes and 50 bushels of sweet potatoes; 6000 lbs. of seed cotton, 4 bales of cotton and 8 tons of hay].*

Wallace Roll, 1890-93 (#7RA-51) (Freedmen Roll & Index). This roll was based on an 1883 list taken of freedmen (freed blacks) entitled to a per capita payment authorized in 1888. **It was set aside as fraudulent by the U.S. Court of Claims and was never recognized by the Cherokee National Council.**

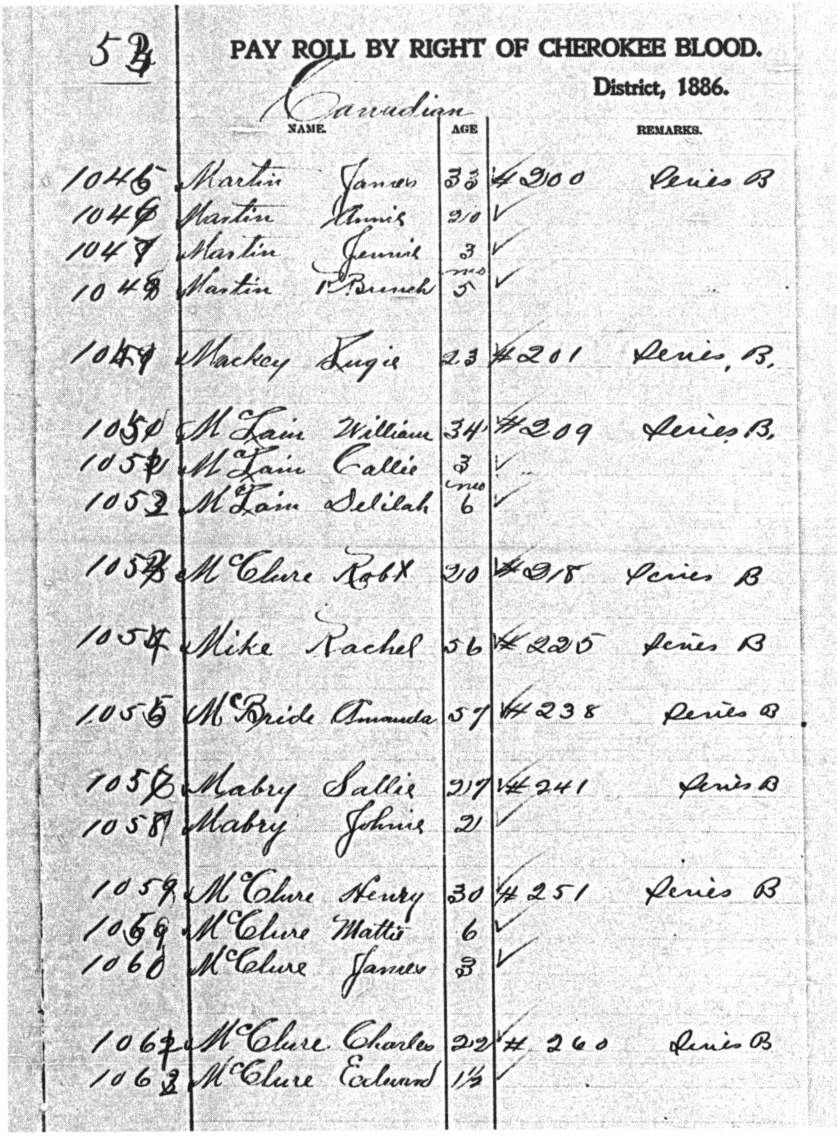

52

PAY ROLL BY RIGHT OF CHEROKEE BLOOD.

Canadian District, 1886.

	NAME.		AGE	REMARKS.	
1045	Martin	James	33	#200	Series B
1046	Martin	Annie	20	✓	
1047	Martin	Jennie	3	✓	
1048	Martin	P. Bunch	5 mo	✓	
1049	Mackey	Lugie	23	#201	Series, B.
1050	McLain	William	34	#209	Series B.
1051	McLain	Callie	3	✓	
1052	McLain	Delilah	6 mo	✓	
1053	McClure	Robt	20	#218	Series B
1054	Mike	Rachel	56	#225	Series B
1055	McBride	Amanda	57	#238	Series B
1056	Mabry	Sallie	27	#241	Series B
1057	Mabry	Johnie	21	✓	
1058	McClure	Henry	30	#251	Series B
1059	McClure	Mattie	6	✓	
1060	McClure	James	3	✓	
1061	McClure	Charles	22	# 260	Series B
1062	McClure	Edward	1½	✓	

Sample Page, Canadian District, 1886 Cherokee Census.

Cherokee Census Roll, 1893 (#7RA-54). In addition to Cherokee citizens, this list also includes intermarried whites, adopted whites and Creek Indians living in the Cherokee Nation.

Starr Roll, 1894 (#7RA-38). Prepared as a receipt roll for each person authorized to receive a per capita "strip payment" of $265.70 for the sale to the United States of over 6 1/2 million acres of Cherokee land known as the Cherokee Strip.

Cherokee Census Roll 1894. This roll was taken in 1897, but was based on an 1894 payroll.

Cherokee Census Roll, 1896 (#7RA-19). This is the first census which includes any reference to blood degree. Also includes place of birth of enrollees as well as Adopted Whites, Orphans, Asylum Inmates, Colored, Doubtful Citizens, Rejected Persons, Shawnee and Delawares.

Clifton Roll (Cherokee Freedmen), 1896 (# 7RA51-3). Prepared by commission appointed by the U.S. Dept. of the Interior, based on testimony taken from May to August, 1897. Includes freedmen and their descendants and a supplemental list of freedmen whose citizenship was rejected by the Cherokees, but approved by the commission.

Old Settler Payment Roll 1896. (T-985). The 1896 Payment Roll is based on the 1851 Old Settler Roll listed earlier and listed each payee's 1851 roll number, name, age, sex, and post office address. This roll can be an important source to determine the descendants of persons listed on the Old Settler rolls and not still living in 1896 when a per capita payment of $159.10 was paid. Their heirs could receive the payment.[See Old Settler Roll, 1851 listing for availability of printed version of this roll].[See sample page on page 47].

Shawnee - Cherokee Census and Payroll, 1896. (# 7RA-26). Contains each individual's name, roll number, age, sex, address and some remarks about relation to others on roll, deaths, and different names used on other rolls. The roll pertained to an equalization payment authorized by the Cherokee National Council on March 30, 1896.

Dawes Roll of 1898-1914 (M -1186). On March 3, 1893, the U.S. Congress established a commission to negotiate with the 5 Tribes (Cherokee, Choctaw, Creek, Chickasaw, and Seminole Nations) in Indian Territory, to abolish their tribal governments and to allot their tribal lands to individuals. The head of this commission was U.S. Senator Henry Dawes. The tribes were not in favor of this proposal and were forced to accept it after numerous efforts, including a proposal from the Indian Nations to form their own state to be called Sequoyah. All of these efforts were ignored, blocked or sabotaged by the U.S. Government.

The U.S. Congress passed the Curtis Act in June 1898 which severely limited the power of tribal governments. It gave the Dawes Commission authority to survey and supervise the allotment of lands, sell un-allotted lands, prepare and deliver deeds, and required that a new Indian roll would be created to supersede all previous rolls. This came to be known as the Dawes Rolls. The U.S. Government sent census takers into Indian Territory (Oklahoma) to interview tribal members. To be enrolled, citizens had to complete an application (or Government agents interviewed them and filled out the application), then it was decided if the person was "qualified" to be on the roll.

Camp of Dawes Enrollment Party, 1902.
Photo Courtesy Archives and Manuscripts Division, Oklahoma Historical Society.

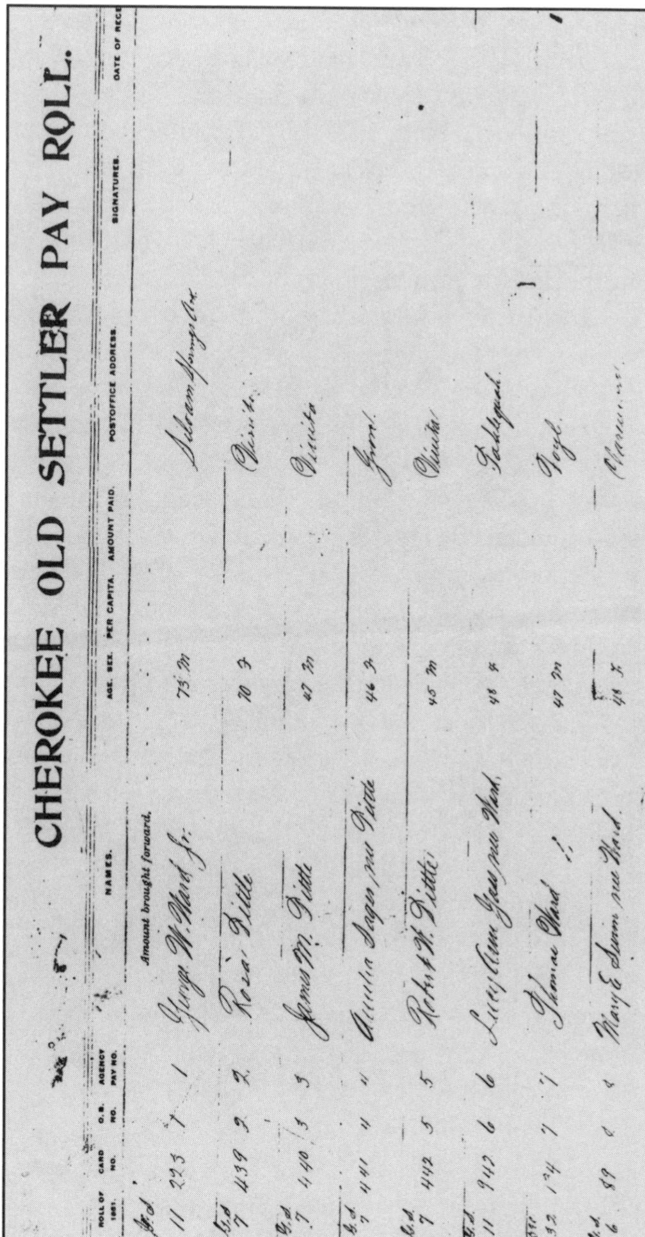

CHEROKEE OLD SETTLER PAY ROLL.

ROLL OF 1851.	CARD NO.	O.S. NO.	AGENCY PAY NO.	NAMES.	AGE.	SEX.	PER CAPITA.	AMOUNT PAID.	POSTOFFICE ADDRESS.	SIGNATURES.	DATE OF RECE
				Amount brought forward,							
S.d. 11	223	1	1	George W. Ward Sr.	73	m			Siloam Springs Ark.		
S.d. 7	439	2	2	Rosa Pettit	70	f			Vinita		
S.d. 7	440	3	3	James M. Pettit	47	m			Vinita		
S.d. 7	441	4	4	Aurelia Sager, nee Pettit	46	f			Grove		
S.d. 7	442	5	5	Robert W. Pettit	45	m			Vinita		
S.d. 11	943	6	6	Lucy Ann Gess nee Ward	48	f			Tahlequah		
32	124	7	7	Thomas Ward	47	m			Foyil		
S.d. 6	89	8	8	Mary E. Swim nee Ward	48	f			Claremore		

Partial sample page, Cherokee Old Settlers Payroll, 1896.

The Dawes commission enrolled tribal citizens under several categories: Citizens by Blood, Citizens by Marriage, New Born Citizens by Blood, Minor Citizens by Blood, Freedmen (former Indian black slaves), New Born Freedmen, and Minor Freedmen. Delaware Tribal members adopted by the Cherokee Nation were enrolled as a separate group within the Cherokee Nation records. There are also a few Mississippi Choctaw and some Chickasaw cards that refer to tribal members never finally enrolled.

A family census card contains the information provided by individual applicants from the same family group or household. The cards include notation of the action taken by the Dawes Commission such as rejected, approved, or doubtful. For each applicant, they list name, enrollment number, age, sex, degree of Indian blood, relationship to head of family, parent's names, and references to enrollment on earlier rolls (used by the commission for verification of eligibility). Some references to enrollment cards of relatives are noted, as well as notations about births, deaths, changes in marital status, and actions taken by the Commission and the Secretary of the Interior.

It is important to note that the card numbers DO NOT match the Roll numbers. There is an index to the final rolls which provides the roll number for each person. The actual applications may contain information which is not on the Census card. Researchers should examine both the Census Card and the Application (Applications are contained in Enrollment "Packets" listed below)[See Page 50 for Sample of Dawes Census Card].

The Dawes Rolls were U.S. Government tribal enrollment records which were used to enumerate all the Indians in a particular tribe. When everyone was counted, tribal land held in common was taken away, allotments were made to everybody listed on the rolls, then all that was left over was sold to white settlers, railroads, and private companies, usually at an absurd discount.

This was supposed to be a final step in the assimilation of the "Indian problem" within the United States. Many Cherokees refused to enroll and did so only after a federal court order threatened them with imprisonment. Some refused to accept land allotments, even after the enrollment, and were arbitrarily assigned parcels by the government.

Included within the available Archives documents pertaining to the

Dawes enrollment proceedings are:

Dawes Commission Enrollment Cards. 1899-1907 (M1186). Microfilm roll 1 is an index. Rolls 2-38 are Cherokee cards. (Rolls 39-93 contain cards for the other five civilized tribes).[See sample card on page 50].

Dawes Commission Enrollment Packets, 1899-1907 (M1301). Almost all of these contain records of interviews which contain more information than that on the census cards above. Some have death or marriage certificates, etc. included as supporting evidence.[See sample page on page 51. Another partial application appeared on page 13].

Final Dawes Rolls of Citizens and Freedmen, 1902-1906. (M1186). This roll continues to serve as the only basis for determining eligibility for membership in the Cherokee Nation of Oklahoma.

Record of Allotments, 1903-1914. Records of final land allotments by Dawes enrollment number including legal descriptions of the tracts and appraised values.[See sample documents on pages 52-54].

The Guion Miller Roll and Applications, 1906 (M-1104 and M-685). On July 1, 1902, the U.S. Congress gave the U.S. Court of Claims jurisdiction over any claim against the United States filed by the Cherokee Tribe, or any band thereof. Three lawsuits were brought against the U.S. Government as grievances from Treaties violation(s).

1.The Cherokee Nation v. the United States, Case # 23199
2.The Eastern & Emigrant Cherokees v. the U.S., Case # 23212
3.The Eastern Cherokee v. the U.S., Case # 23214

On May 18, 1905 the U.S. Court of Claims ruled in favor of the Eastern Cherokee and directed the Secretary of the Interior to identify persons entitled to a portion of the money appropriated by the U.S. Congress on June 30, 1906 to be used for payment of the claims. Special Agent Guion Miller, U.S. Dept. of the Interior, began this work and then was appointed by the U.S. Court of Claims as a Court Special Commissioner.

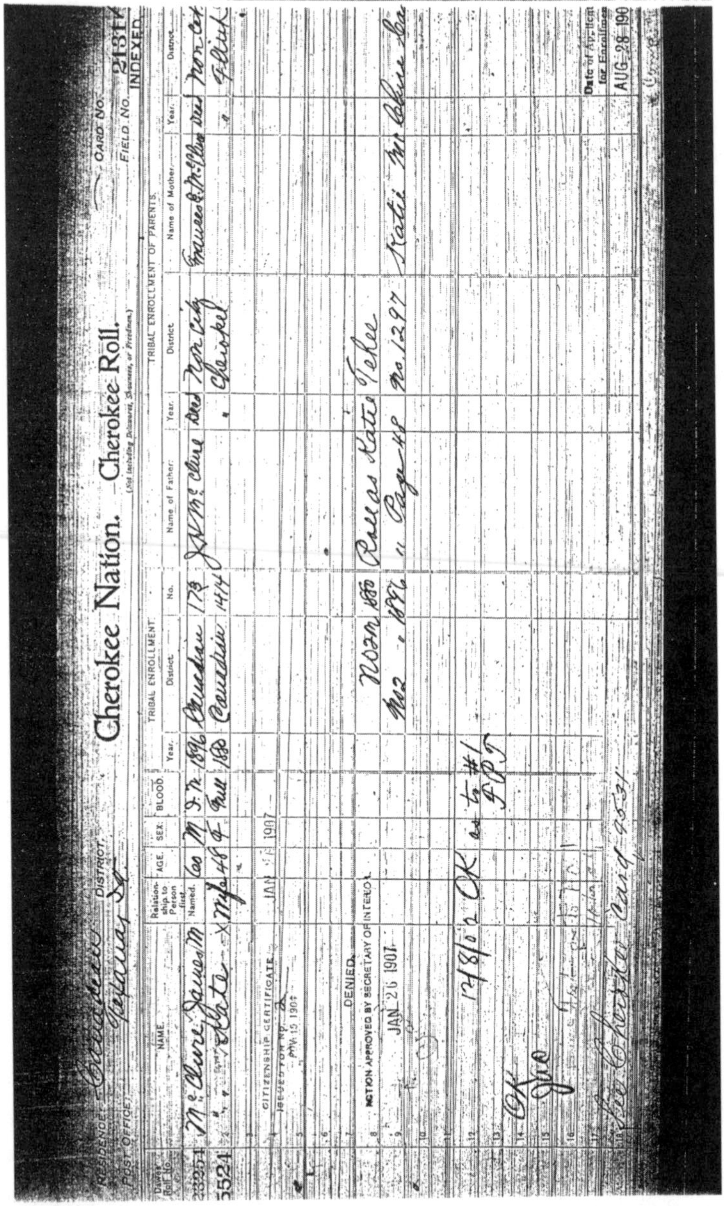

Cherokee Nation. Cherokee Roll.

RESIDENCE: DISTRICT. POST OFFICE. CARD No. FIELD No. 2131 INDEXED

Dawes' Roll No.	NAME	Relationship to Person first Named	AGE	SEX	BLOOD	Year	District	No.	Name of Father	Year	District	Name of Mother	Year	District
23254	McClure, James M		60	M	I.W.	1896	Canadian	173	J. W. McClure	dead	Non Cit	Frances McClure	dead	Non Cit
5524	" Kate	Wife	48	F	Full	1880	Canadian	1414		"	Cherokee		"	Flint

CITIZENSHIP CERTIFICATE ISSUED FOR NO. 2 MAY 15 1904

DENIED.

ACTION APPROVED BY SECRETARY OF INTERIOR JAN 26 1907

No 2 on 1880 Roll as Katie Tehee

No 2 " 1896 " Page 48 No. 1297 Katie McClure

12/8/02 OK as to #1

See Cherokee card 9531

Date of Application for Enrollment AUG 28 190

Dawes Enrollment Card. Notice stamped entries on card which reflect that citizenship for James McClure was denied (he was white); his wife Kate McClure was admitted. Handwritten notes refer to previous roll entries, "No 2 on 1880 roll as Katie Tehee," and "No. 2 on 1896 roll as Katie McClure." Another notation at the bottom reads "See Cherokee card 9531." This is the census card of another family member. All such notations should be followed up on carefully as they often can lead to important genealogical information. Numbers to the left of applicant's names (23254 and 5524) are Dawes roll numbers; the "field number" upper right is the census card number.

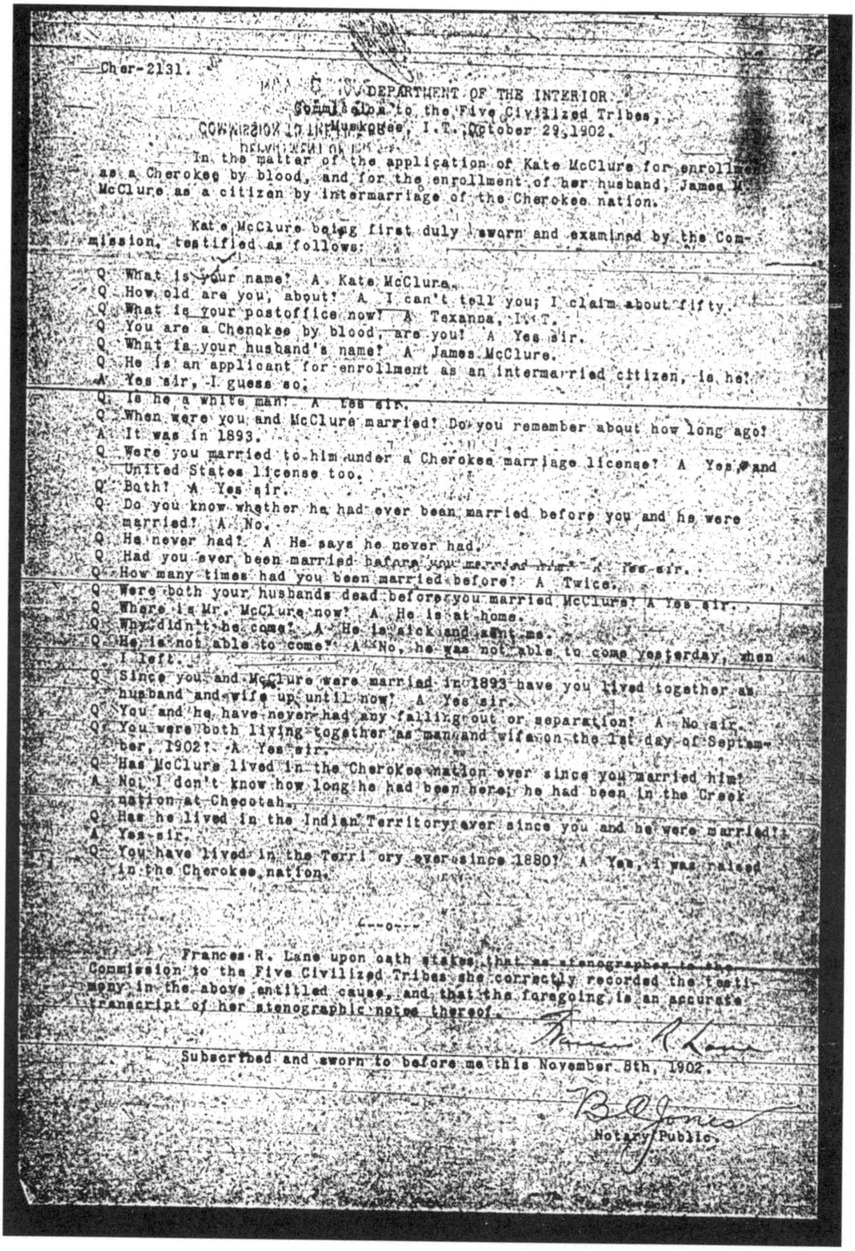

Cher-2131.

DEPARTMENT OF THE INTERIOR.
Commission to the Five Civilized Tribes,
Muskogee, I. T., October 29, 1902.

In the matter of the application of Kate McClure for enrollment as a Cherokee by blood, and for the enrollment of her husband, James M. McClure as a citizen by intermarriage of the Cherokee nation.

Kate McClure being first duly sworn and examined by the Commission, testified as follows:

Q What is your name? A Kate McClure.
Q How old are you, about? A I can't tell you; I claim about fifty.
Q What is your postoffice now? A Texanna, I. T.
Q You are a Cherokee by blood, are you? A Yes sir.
Q What is your husband's name? A James McClure.
Q He is an applicant for enrollment as an intermarried citizen, is he?
A Yes sir, I guess so.
Q Is he a white man? A Yes sir.
Q When were you and McClure married? Do you remember about how long ago?
A It was in 1893.
Q Were you married to him under a Cherokee marriage license? A Yes, and United States license too.
Q Both? A Yes sir.
Q Do you know whether he had ever been married before you and he were married? A No.
Q He never had? A He says he never had.
Q Had you ever been married before you married him? A Yes sir.
Q How many times had you been married before? A Twice.
Q Were both your husbands dead before you married McClure? A Yes sir.
Q Where is Mr. McClure now? A He is at home.
Q Why didn't he come? A He is sick and sent me.
Q He is not able to come? A No, he was not able to come yesterday, when I left.
Q Since you and McClure were married in 1893 have you lived together as husband and wife up until now? A Yes sir.
Q You and he have never had any falling out or separation? A No sir.
Q You were both living together as man and wife on the 1st day of September, 1902? A Yes sir.
Q Has McClure lived in the Cherokee nation ever since you married him?
A No, I don't know how long he had been here; he had been in the Creek nation at Checotah.
Q Has he lived in the Indian Territory ever since you and he were married?
A Yes sir.
Q You have lived in the Territory ever since 1880? A Yes, I was raised in the Cherokee nation.

---o---

Frances R. Lane upon oath states that as stenographer to the Commission to the Five Civilized Tribes she correctly recorded the testimony in the above entitled cause, and that the foregoing is an accurate transcript of her stenographic notes thereof.

Frances R Lane

Subscribed and sworn to before me this November 8th, 1902.

B C Jones
Notary Public.

Record of interview of Kate McClure by Dawes commission (included in Enrollment Packet).

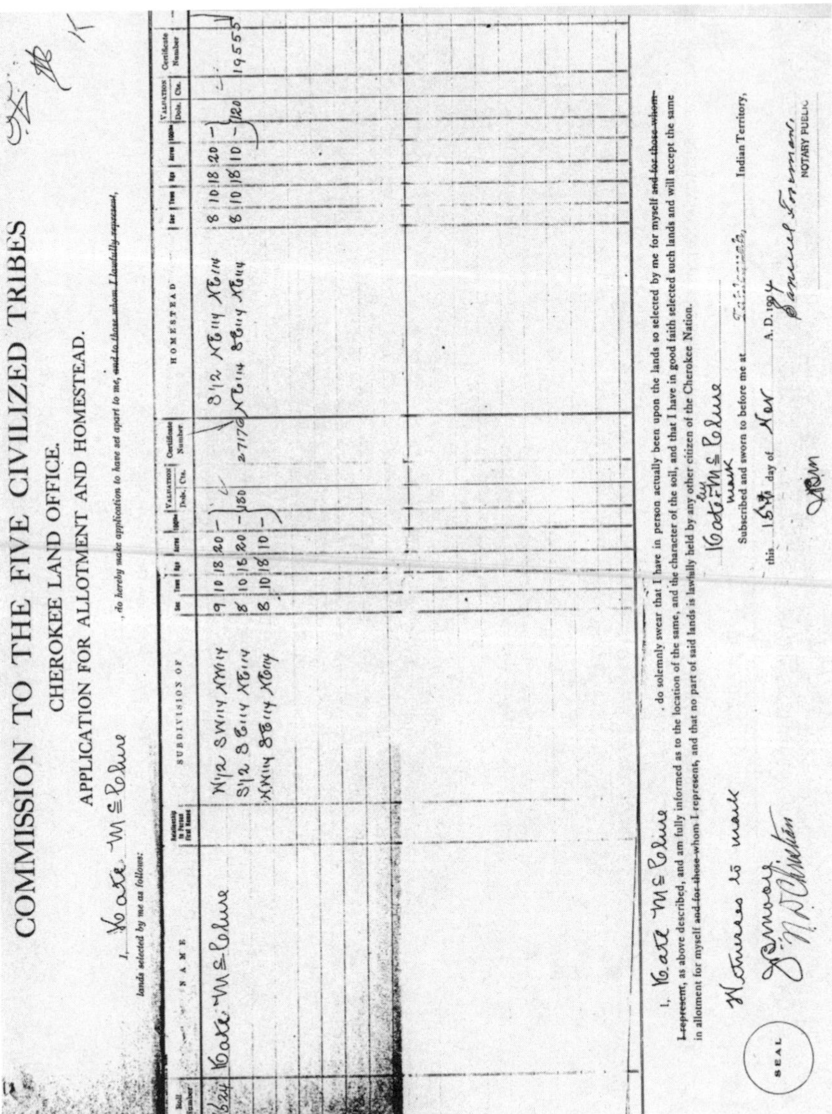

COMMISSION TO THE FIVE CIVILIZED TRIBES

CHEROKEE LAND OFFICE.

APPLICATION FOR ALLOTMENT AND HOMESTEAD.

I, Kate McClure, do hereby make application to have set apart to me, ~~and to those whom I lawfully represent,~~ lands selected by me as follows:

Roll Number	Name	Subdivision of	Sec	Twp	Rge	Acres	Valuation	Certificate Number	Homestead	Sec	Twp	Rge	Acres	Valuation	Certificate Number
3524	Kate McClure	N1/2 SW1/4 NW1/4	9	10	18	20			S1/2 NE1/4 NE1/4	8	10	18	20		
		S1/2 SE1/4 NE1/4	8	10	18	20	130	27170	NE1/4 SE1/4 NE1/4	8	10	18	10	120	19555
		NW1/4 SE1/4 NE1/4	8	10	18	10									

I, Kate McClure, do solemnly swear that I have in person actually been upon the lands so selected by me for myself ~~and for those whom I represent~~, as above described, and am fully informed as to the location of the same, and the character of the soil, and that I have in good faith selected such lands and will accept the same in allotment for myself ~~and for those whom I represent~~, and that no part of said lands is lawfully held by any other citizen of the Cherokee Nation.

Kate (her mark) McClure

Witnesses to mark

[illegible]

Subscribed and sworn to before me at Tahlequah, Indian Territory, this 15th day of Nov A.D. 1904

Samuel Foreman, NOTARY PUBLIC

SEAL

Application for Land Allotment and Homestead, 1904.

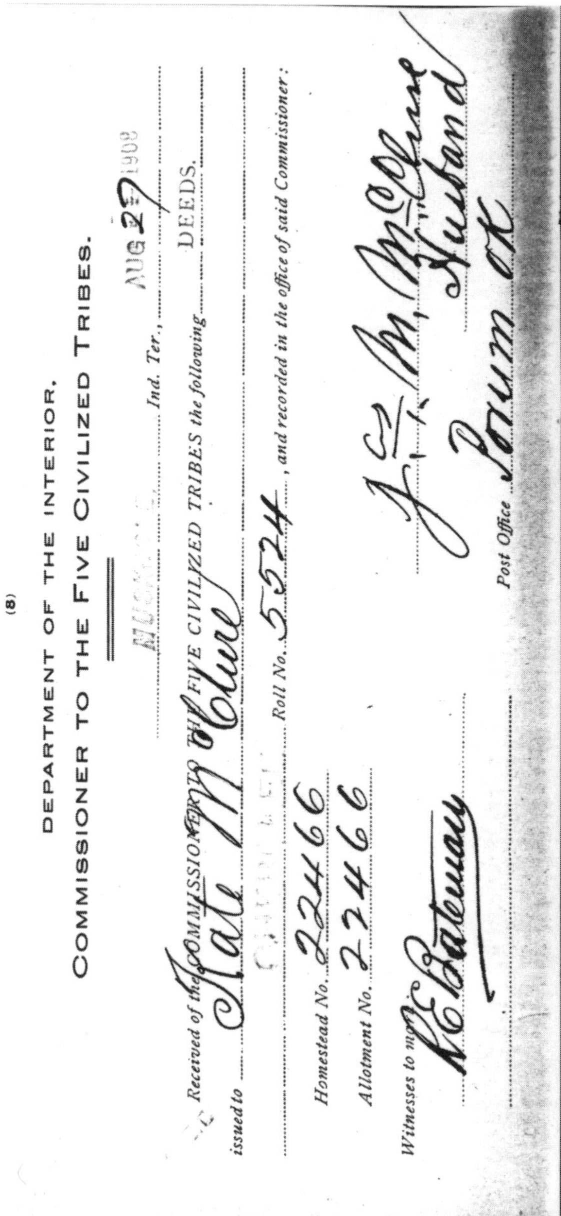
(8)

DEPARTMENT OF THE INTERIOR.

COMMISSIONER TO THE FIVE CIVILIZED TRIBES.

Ind. Ter., AUG 27 1908

Received of the COMMISSIONER TO THE FIVE CIVILIZED TRIBES the following DEEDS,

issued to Kate McClure

Roll No. 5524, and recorded in the office of said Commissioner:

Homestead No. 22466

Allotment No. 22466

Witnesses to mark:

Post Office

The first deeds to Cherokee allotments were delivered in June, 1906. Each member of the tribe received land equal in value to 110 acres of average allottable land (value of $325.60) which included a similar homestead of 40 acres. Freedmen received 40 acres.

Many full-bloods, mainly the Night-Hawk Keetoowahs, refused to make land selections so arbitrary allotments were made by the Commission. This photo was taken in 1917 at a Night-Hawk meeting near Gore, OK. Photo courtesy of Archives and Manuscripts Division, Oklahoma Historical Society.

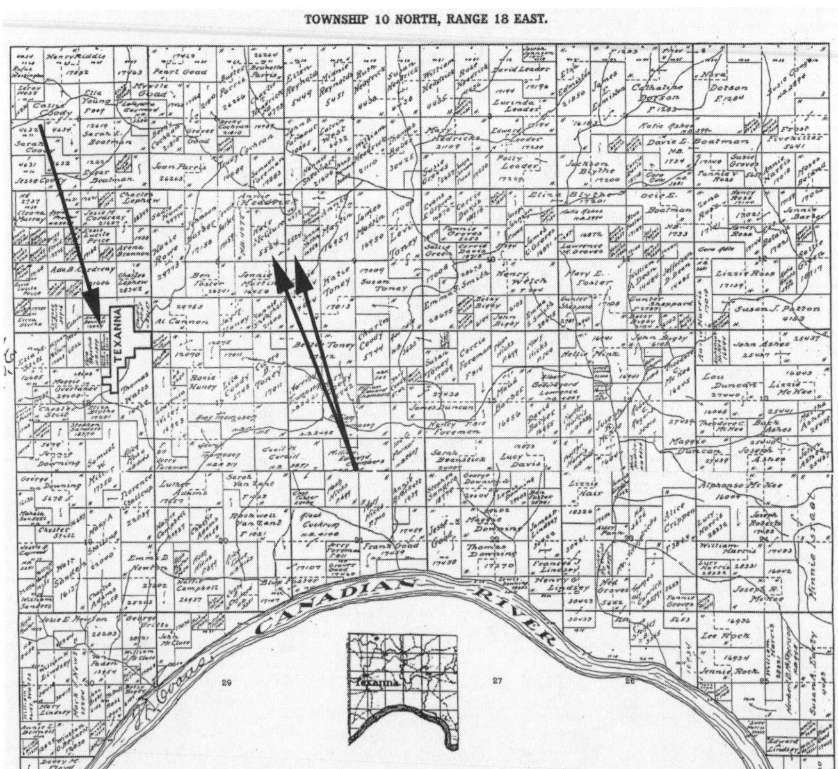

Land allotment jackets include plat maps showing allottee's name and Dawes roll number. The area shown is six square miles. Arrows above indicate three of the land parcels allotted to Kate McClure near the town of Texana, OK.

The Court decree specified that the money was to be distributed to all Eastern & Western Cherokees alive on May 28, 1906 who could establish that they were members of the Eastern Cherokee Tribe or descendants of such members. They could not be members of any other tribe. All claims had to be filed prior to August 31, 1907.

In Agent Miller's report of May 28, 1909, he listed 45,847 applications listing approximately 90,000 individual claimants. Among these 30,254 were enrolled and eligible for a share of the funds; 27,051 lived west of the Mississippi River, and another 3,203 lived east of the Mississippi River. The Roll includes information on both accepted and non-accepted applicants and the individual applications themselves contain a wealth of genealogical data. [See application samples on pages 56-59]. Miller used previous census lists and rolls of the Cherokees: the Hester, Chapman, and Drennen rolls, and other materials from 1835 to 1884, but did not include Old Settler Cherokees.

These records are part of the U.S. National Archives, Record group 75, Records of the Bureau of Indian Affairs, previously mentioned. Other records relating to this enrollment, including the applications themselves, however, are in U.S. National Archives Record Group 123.

Available in book index form, the Guion Miller Roll "Plus" by Bob Blankenship is about $30.00; Dawes Roll "Plus" by Bob Blankenship is also about $30.00. Contact your local bookstore or order direct from Cherokee Roots, P.O. Box 525, Cherokee N.C. 28719. Phone (704) 497-9709. The Blankenship family (Eastern band of Cherokees) also offers two other valuable books - Cherokee Roots, volumes I & 2 which contain name/roll number listings for most of the major rolls and a fee- based research service pertaining to census rolls.

Morrison's Indian Research, P.O. Box 41, Boaz, Alabama 35957 Phone(205)-593-7336 is another service that offers economical rolls and records searches. (Robert and Sue Morrison are members of the Cherokee Tribe of Northeast Alabama). The registration office at the Cherokee Nation in Tahlequah, OK lists the following researchers if you feel you need to hire professional help:

Mrs. Robin Mooney
P.O. Box 123
Park Hill, OK 74451

Mrs. Jerri McLemore
1120 Cottonwood CT
Pryor, OK 74361

Indian Territory Genealogical & Historical Society
C/O John Vaughn Library, NSU
Tahlequah, OK 74464

Commissioner of Indian Affairs,
Washington, D. C.

SIR:

I hereby make application for such share as may be due me of the fund appropriated by the Act of Congress approved June 30, 1906, in accordance with the decrees of the Court of Claims of May 18, 1905, and May 28, 1906, in favor of the Eastern Cherokees. The evidence of identity is herewith subjoined.

1. State full name—
   English name: Katy McClure.
   Indian name: Ga-du-u-ie.
2. Residence: Porum,
3. Town and post office: Porum,
4. County: Cherokee Nation,
5. State: Indian Territory.
6. Date and place of birth: About 1851 in Goingsnake District.
7. By what right do you claim to share? If you claim through more than one relative living in 1851, set forth each claim separately: For my own share. For my mother: Darky Buzzardflopper. My grandparents: Young Tiger and Susie Downing. My great aunts: Nellie, Lewrey, Lucy Woodard and Wutti Crittenden. My cousins: Leti and Nancy Lewrey and Jim Woodard. For my share in the estate of my deceased husband: John Tehee.
8. Are you married? Yes.
9. Name and age of wife or husband: James M. McClure, age 66 years.
10. Give names of your father and mother, and your mother's name before marriage.
    Father—English name: Not known.
    Indian name:
    Mother—English name: Darky Downing.
    Indian Name: Darky
    Maiden name: Darky Downing.
11. Where were they born?
    Father: Not known.
    Mother: In Cherokee Nation, east.
12. Where did they reside in 1851, if living at that time?
    Father: Not known.
    Mother: In Goingsnake District.
13. Date of death of your father and mother—
    Father: Not known. Mother: About 1858

6—634

Page 1 of a 3 page Guion Miller Roll Application, 1909.

14. Were they ever enrolled for annuities, land, or other benefits? If so, state when and where:
Mother on Emigrant Cherokee Pay roll of 1851 in Goingsnake District.

15. Name all your brothers and sisters, giving ages, and if not living, the date of death:

Name	Born	Died
(1) Oo-gu-yo-sti. dead.		
(2) Nellie Owen, dead.		
(3) Jim Buzzardflopper, dead.		
(4)		
(5)		
(6)		

16. State English and Indian names of your grandparents on both father's and mother's side, if possible:

Father's Side	Mother's Side
Not known.	Young Tiger and Susie Downing, nee Crittenden.

17. Where were they born? In Cherokee Nation, east.

18. Where did they reside in 1851, if living at that time?
In Cherokee Nation.

19. Give names of all their children, and residence, if living; if not living, give dates of deaths:

(1) English name: Ga-do-ni Still, dead.
Indian name: Darky Buzzardflopper, my mother, dead.
Residence: Tarnee Downing, dead.

(2) English name: George Downing, Texana, I.T.
Indian name:
Residence:

(3) English name:
Indian name:
Residence:

(4) English name:
Indian name:
Residence:

(5) English name:
Indian name:
Residence:

20. Have you ever been enrolled for annuities, land, or other benefits? If so, state when and where: On Emigrant Cherokee Pay roll of 1851 in Goingsnake District, On Cherokee Authenticated roll of 1880, and am a Cherokee Allottee.

6-624

Page 2, Guion Miller Roll Application, 1909.

21. To expedite identification, claimants should give the full English and Indian names, if possible, of their paternal and maternal ancestors back to 1835: My grandfather, Young Tiger Downing, lived in Cherokee nation, east, in 1835

REMARKS.

(Under this head the applicant may give any additional information that he believes will assist in proving his claims.)

My grandmother, Susie Downing had three sisters: Nellie Lowrey, nee Crittenden, Lucy Woodard, nee Crittenden and Wutti Crittenden. My great aunt, Nellie Lowrey, had two daughters, Liti and Noncy Lowrey, they were living in Flint District in 1851 and died without descent. My great aunt, Lucy Woodard, had one son, Jim, or "Ge-ta-qua" Woodard, who died without descent. My first Husband was George Tehee, he was living in Tahlequah District in 1851. He was the son of Charles and Jennie Tehee, and a brother of John Tehee of Tahlequah. I refer to his application, as a method of identification. I refer to the claim of my uncle, George Downing, as my interests are identical with his in the Downing family. My husband, George Tehee died Nov. 24, 1889.

NOTE.—Answers should be brief but explicit; the words "Yes," "No," "Unknown," etc., may be used in cases where appropriate. Read the questions carefully.

I solemnly swear that the foregoing statements made by me are true to the best of my knowledge and belief.

her mark
Evan Groves
J. J. Sevier

(Signature.) Katy her mark McClure

Subscribed and sworn to before me this 8 day of Jan, 1907

My commission expires June 10, 1909

Geo W Blackstone
Notary Public.

AFFIDAVIT.

(The following affidavit must be sworn to by two or more witnesses who are well acquainted with the applicant.)

Personally appeared before me J. J. Sevier and Evan Groves, who, being duly sworn, on oath depose and say that they are well acquainted with Katy McClure who makes the foregoing application and statements, and have known her for 40 years and 25 years, respectively, and know her to be the identical person she represents herself to be, and that the statements made by her are true, to the best of their knowledge and belief, and they have no interest whatever in her claim.

Witnesses to mark. | Signatures of witnesses.

J. J. Sevier
Evan Groves

Subscribed and sworn to before me this 8 day of Jan, 1907

My commission expires June 10, 1909

Geo W Blackstone
Notary Public.

NOTE.—Affidavits should be made, whenever practicable, before a notary public, clerk of the court, or before a person having a seal. If sworn to before an Indian agent or disbursing agent of the Indian service, it need not be executed before a notary, etc.

5-624

Page 3, Guion Miller Roll Application, 1909.

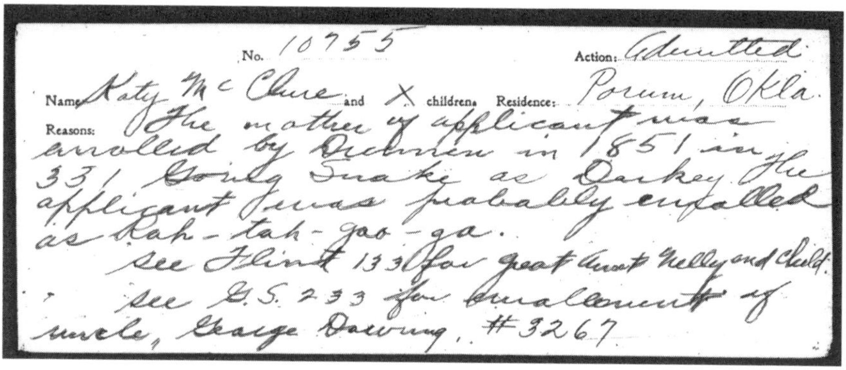

No. 10755 Action: Admitted

Name Katy McClure and X children. Residence: Porum, Okla.

Reasons: The mother of applicant was enrolled by Drennen in 1851 in 331 Going Snake as Darkey. The applicant was probably enrolled as Kah-tah-goo-ga.

See Flint 133 for great Aunt Nelly and child.

See G.S. 233 for enrollment of uncle, George Downing, #3267.

Another document from the Guion Miller Roll Applications Packet. Remember our note on page 36 (Drennen Roll sample) regarding "Kah-tah-goo-ga?" This was the record we were referring to. "Kah-tah-goo-ga" obviously was the Indian name used by Katy McClure when she was a baby. Note other important family references and roll numbers on the document above.

Cherokee Nation Tribal Complex, Tahlequah, Oklahoma, 1998.
Photo by Lee Hicks, Jr.

If you are fortunate enough to find a family member's name listed on either the Dawes or Miller rolls, be sure to order copies of the applications completed by the commission to establish their roll entrees. These contain a store of other valuable family information. Refer to the *"Quick Step Guide"* in a later chapter for assistance.

Information condensed from the Guion Miller Roll applications has also been transcribed in multiple book form by: Jordan, Jerry Wright. *Cherokee by Blood: Records of Eastern Cherokee Ancestry in the U.S. Court of Claims, 1906-1910 (9 volumes)*. To order or inquire, contact Heritage Books, 1540 East Pointer Ridge Pl, Suite 400, Bowie, MD 20716 Phone (301) 390-7709. Cost is $34 per volume (paperback).

Council Roll of Eastern Band of Cherokees, 1907. A roll of persons recommended for enrollment by the Tribal Council to Inspector Frank Churchill (below). This roll has also been called the Blythe, French and Harris roll. (Washington D.C. archives).

Churchill Roll, 1908. Prepared by Frank C. Churchill as a listing of Eastern Cherokee to "Certify" Members of the Eastern Band. Two rolls contain accepted and rejected members; both English and Indian names. (Like the Hester roll listed earlier, this census has lots of information).

Federal Census, 1900. See separate listing on page 64.

Federal Census 1910 (T-624), 1,784 rolls, Indian Schedules are at the end of the identified Enumeration District ED (Use the Federal Census Index Books for ED of County of Residence).

Federal Census 1920 (T-625), 8,585 rolls, Native American Indians may be identified as Black, Indian, Other, or white.

Baker Roll, 1924. (A-35). Taken pursuant to an act of June 4, 1924, this was supposed to be the "final Roll" of the Eastern Cherokee. The land was to be allotted and all were to become citizens. Fortunately, the Eastern Cherokee avoided the termination procedures, unlike their brothers and sisters in the Cherokee Nation West. **The Baker Roll Revised serves as the current membership basis of the Eastern**

Band of Cherokee Indians in North Carolina.[See sample page on page 62].

Register of Indians in World War I, 1917-18 (# 7RA347).

Eastern Band Cherokee Census, North Carolina, (M595-23), 1915-22.

Eastern Band Cherokee Census, North Carolina, (M595-24), 1923-29.

Eastern Band Cherokee Census, North Carolina, (M595-25), 1930-32.

Eastern Band Cherokee Census, North Carolina, (M595-26), 1933-39.[See sample page on page 63].

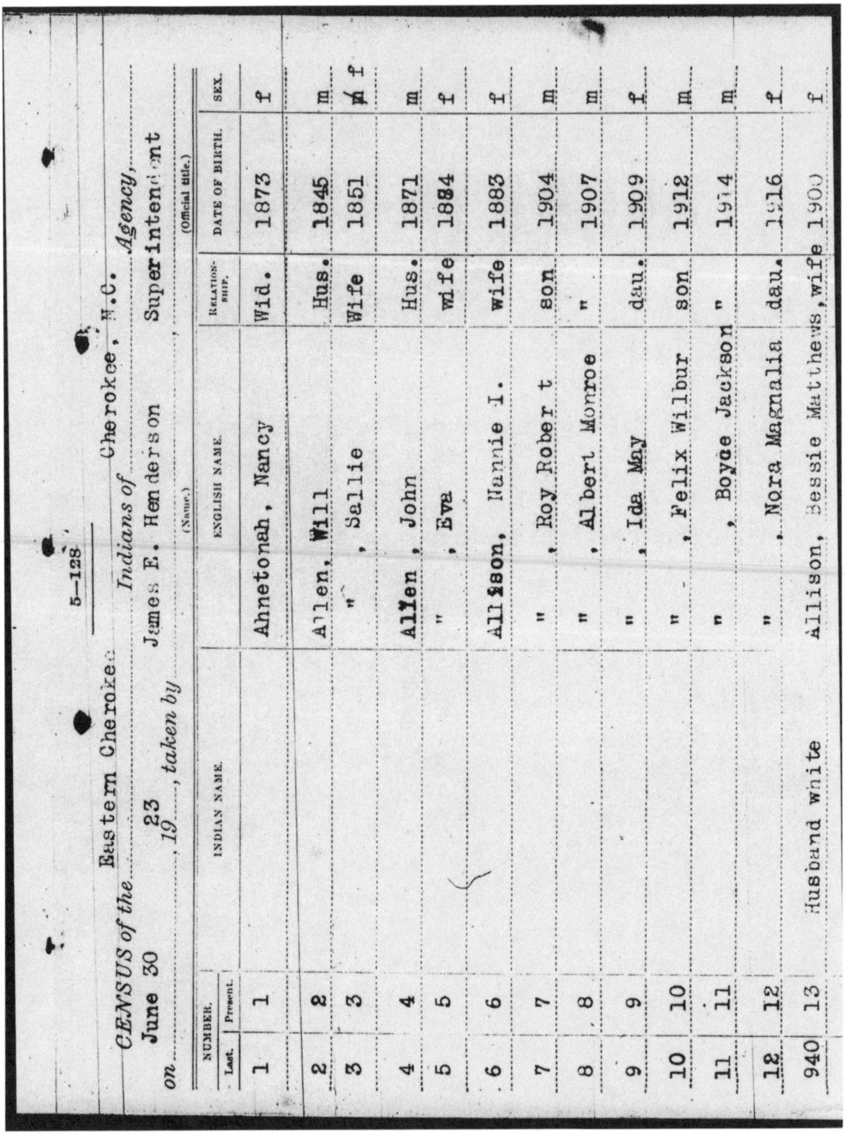

5—128

CENSUS of the Eastern Cherokee Indians of Cherokee, N.C. Agency,

on June 30, 1923, taken by James E. Henderson (Name.), Superintendent (Official title.)

Number: Last.	Number: Present.	Indian Name.	English Name.	Relationship.	Date of Birth.	Sex.
1	1		Ahnetonah, Nancy	Wid.	1873	f
2	2		Allen, Will	Hus.	1845	m
3	3		" , Sallie	Wife	1851	~~m~~ f
4	4		Allen, John	Hus.	1871	m
5	5		" , Eva	wife	1884	f
6	6		Allison, Nannie I.	wife	1883	f
7	7		" , Roy Robert	son	1904	m
8	8		" , Albert Monroe	"	1907	m
9	9		" , Ida May	dau.	1909	f
10	10		" , Felix Wilbur	son	1912	m
11	11		" , Boyce Jackson	"	1914	m
12	12		" , Nora Magnalia	dau.	1916	f
940	13	Husband white	Allison, Bessie Matthews	wife	1900	f

Baker Roll Page, Eastern Band of Cherokees, 1923.

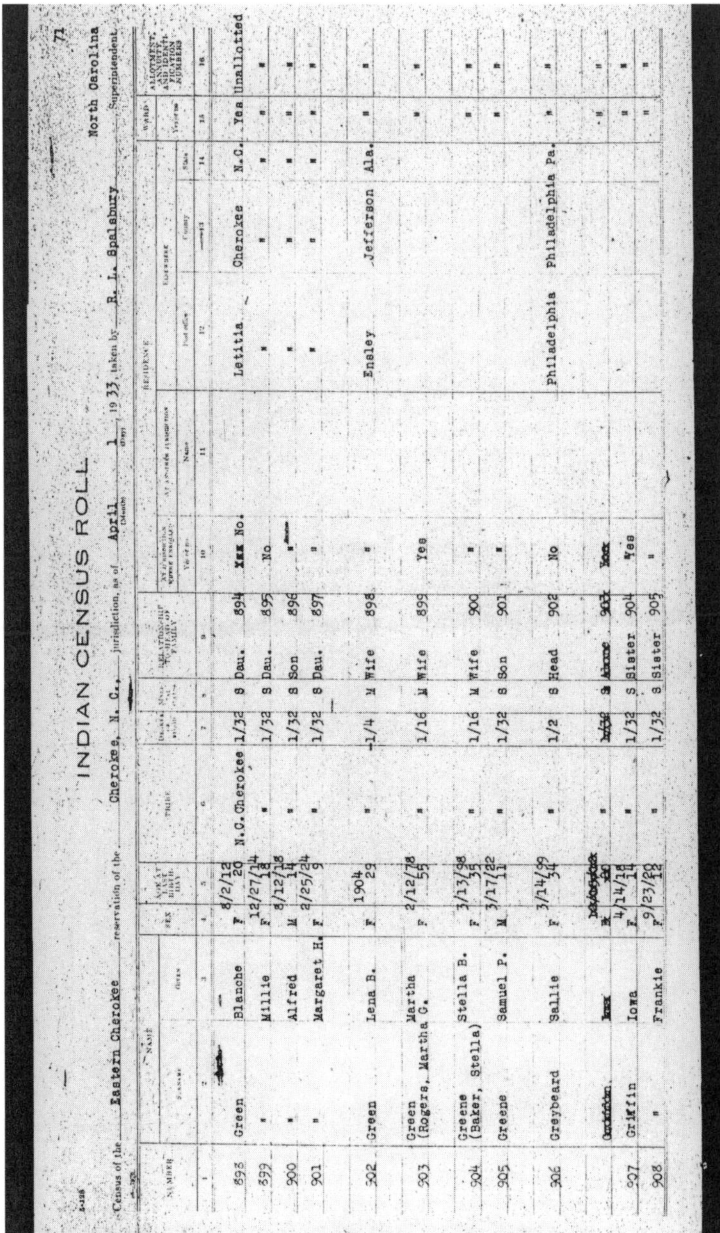

5-128 71

INDIAN CENSUS ROLL

Census of the Eastern Cherokee reservation of the Cherokee, N. C., jurisdiction, as of April 1, 1933, taken by R. L. Spalsbury, Superintendent. North Carolina

Number	Surname	Given	Sex	Age at last birthday	Tribe	Degree of blood	Marital status	Relationship to head of family		At jurisdiction where enrolled	At another jurisdiction	Post office	County	State	Ward	Allotment, annuity and identification numbers
1	2	3	4	5	6	7	8	9		10	11	12	13	14	15	16
898	Green	Blanche	F	8/2/12 20	N.C. Cherokee	1/32	S	Dau.	894	No.		Letitia	Cherokee	N.C.	Yes	Unallotted
899	"	Millie	F	12/27/14 18	"	1/32	S	Dau.	895	No		"	"	"	"	"
900	"	Alfred	M	8/12/18 14	"	1/32	S	Son	896	"		"	"	"	"	"
901	"	Margaret H.	F	2/25/24 9	"	1/32	S	Dau.	897	"		"	"	"	"	"
902	Green	Lena B.	F	1904 29	"	1/4	M	Wife	898	"		Ensley	Jefferson	Ala.	"	"
903	Green (Rogers, Martha G.)	Martha G.	F	2/12/78 55	"	1/16	M	Wife	899	Yes					"	"
904	Greene (Baker, Stella)	Stella B.	F	3/13/98 35	"	1/16	M	Wife	900	"					"	"
905	Greene	Samuel P.	M	3/17/22 11	"	1/32	S	Son	901	"					"	"
906	Greybeard	Sallie	F	3/14/99 34	"	1/2	S	Head	902	No		Philadelphia	Philadelphia	Pa.	"	"
	Griffith	[illegible]	M	[illegible]	"	1/32	S	[illegible]	903	[illegible]					"	"
907	Griffin	Iowa	F	4/14/18 14	"	1/32	S	Sister	904	Yes					"	"
908	"	Frankie	F	9/23/20 12	"	1/32	S	Sister	905	"					"	"

Roll page of Census, Eastern Band of Cherokees, 1933.

The 1900 Federal Census

This particular U.S. census, available on microfilm at many libraries, has been listed separately because it contains a vast amount of information regarding all Indian tribes including Cherokee. With the exception of Oklahoma, there is a separate section at the end of each county of each state listing it's Native American residents. In the Oklahoma section, Natives in all areas outside of the territory of the Five Civilized Tribes (Cherokee, Creek, Choctaw, Chickasaw and Seminole) are shown grouped at the end of the microfilm (microfilm number 1241344). Residents of the Five Civilized Tribes are shown at the end of the entire census after the listings for the state of Wyoming... the Cherokees are on microfilm numbers 1241843, 1241844, 1241845, and 1241846. Keep in mind that there may have been many not enrolled and residing in various states. These will be listed at the end of their county within the microfilms for their state of residence, provided they did not hide their native heritage.

The following information is included:

1. Both English and Indian names of all family members in the household.
2. Relationship of each family member to the head-of-household.
3. Age and birth dates by year and month.
4. Number of times married.
5. Length of marriage.
6. Listings for any plural spouses for each spouse in household.
7. Place of birth and parents place of birth.
8. Tribal affiliation and parent's tribe.
9. Degree of white blood, if any.
10. Number of children; number still living.
11. Indication of either fixed or moveable dwelling.
12. Property rented or owned.
13. Employed (by occupation) or "Ration Indian" (indicating federal support).
14. Length of unemployment if unemployed.
15. Ability to read, write or speak English.

Records Other Than Census Rolls

Numerous other records are available in the National Archives which include records of the Bureau of Indian Affairs, U.S. Army Mobile Units, Supreme Court, U.S. District Courts, U.S. Court of Appeals, U.S. Court of Claims, and Veterans Administration. Since the Cherokee Indians were not usually subject to state courts, their civil and criminal court records are normally found in the Federal Court records.

The Bureau of Indian Affairs records include the Indian Removal records, Land Division, Enrollment of the Eastern Cherokee, Law and Probate Division (this deals with the heirs of deceased Indian allottees), Civilization Division, Indian Civil War Claims, Statistics Division, Finance Division, and the Miscellaneous Division. Bureau of Indian Affairs Field Office records available for Cherokees include Cherokee Agency, East, located at FARC, Atlanta and Cherokee Agency, West, located at the National Archives in Washington.

In 1938, the Adjutant General's Office transferred its collection of Confederate records to the National Archives. While many of the Confederate records were destroyed before seizure by the Union Army, some records still exist. Roll 74, Compiled Records Showing Service of Military Units in Confederate Organizations contains information about the Indian organizations. Also, compiled military service records have been reproduced on microfilm by the National Archives that include service records of Confederate soldiers, Confederate States Army Casualties, and also documents pertaining to battles in Indian Territory (Also see Appendix One).

An excellent text on this subject is *"The Confederate Cherokees - John Drew's Regiment of Mounted Rifles,"* by W. Craig Gaines, Louisiana State University Press (1989). Military records for individuals who served since 1900 are housed at the Military Personnel

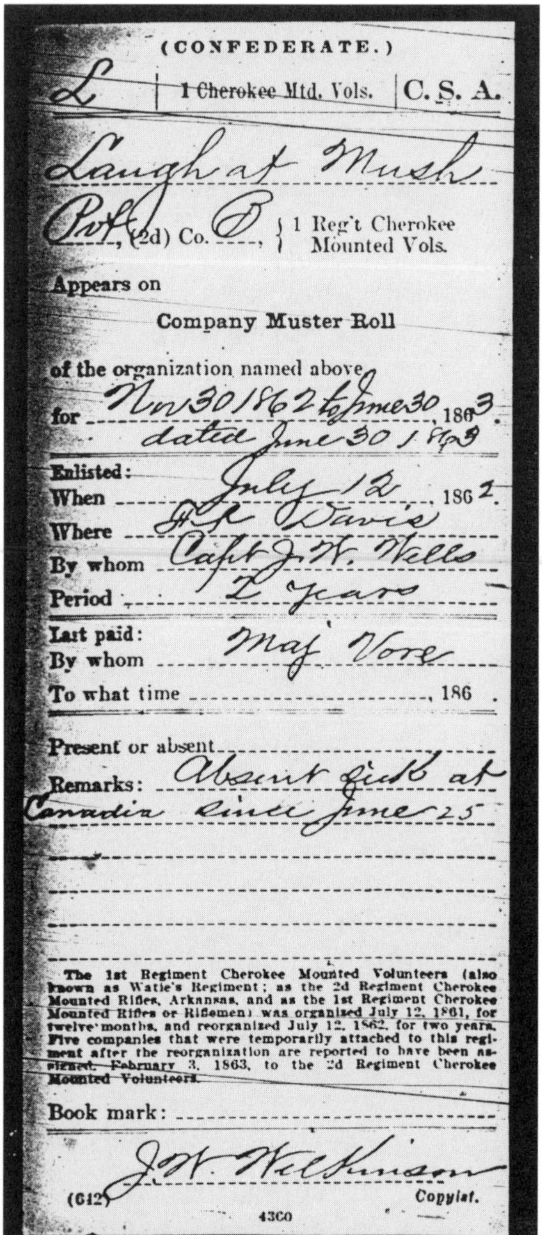

(CONFEDERATE.)

L | 1 Cherokee Mtd. Vols. | C. S. A.

Laugh at Mush

Pvt, (2d) Co. B, 1 Reg't Cherokee Mounted Vols.

Appears on

Company Muster Roll

of the organization named above,

for Nov 30 1862 to June 30, 1863.

dated June 30 1863

Enlisted:

When July 12, 1862.

Where Ft Davis

By whom Capt J. W. Wells

Period 2 years

Last paid:

By whom Maj Vore

To what time ______, 186 .

Present or absent

Remarks: Absent sick at Canadia since June 25

The 1st Regiment Cherokee Mounted Volunteers (also known as Watie's Regiment; as the 2d Regiment Cherokee Mounted Rifles, Arkansas, and as the 1st Regiment Cherokee Mounted Rifles or Riflemen) was organized July 12, 1861, for twelve months, and reorganized July 12, 1862, for two years. Five companies that were temporarily attached to this regiment after the reorganization are reported to have been assigned, February 3, 1863, to the 2d Regiment Cherokee Mounted Volunteers.

Book mark:

J. W. Wilkinson

(612) Copyist.

4360

Muster Roll Document from Cherokee
Mounted Volunteers, C.S.A.

Records Center, 9700 Page Boulevard, St. Louis, MO 63132. The American Indian Veterans Association, P.O. Box 543, Isleta, MN 87022, Phone 505-869-9284 can also be a source of information.

Recognize that many persons with some degree of Indian Blood are not mentioned in any federal records because they were not officially recognized as a tribal member or they severed their tribal-connections by moving away from the bulk of their tribe. The U. S. Bureau of Indian Affairs classifies these Cherokees as "Category four" Native Americans and states, *"information about Indian ancestry of individuals in Category four is more difficult to locate. This is primarily because the federal government has never maintained a list of all the persons of Cherokee Indian descent, indicating their tribal affiliation, degree of Indian blood or other data." They go on to say that "during the removal, a number remained in the southeast and gathered in North Carolina where they purchased land and continued to live. Others went into the Appalachian Mountains to escape being moved west and many of their descendants may still live there now."*

The Indian Archives in the Oklahoma Historical Society, Oklahoma City (See address in following *Selected Archives Section*), contain approximately 430,000 pages and 740 bound volumes relating to the Cherokee. This is the largest collection of Indian documents in the United States outside of the National Archives, and some private collections also are housed there.These include the works of several noted Indian historians as well as an excellent collection of Oklahoma newspapers. Today, the Federal Records Center provides the society a copy of any microfilm it produces that pertains to Indian records.

The OHS collection chronicles not only the official activities of the Cherokee Nation government, but day-to-day events in the lives of the Cherokee people: marriage licenses, wills and probate, cemeteries, elections, missionary and religious records, trader's permits...the list is enormous and all of it is potentially important to family researchers. The bulk covers a time span of 1858-1906, however some files provide information back to 1820. A comprehensive listing of the portions of the records that are available on microfilm - *Guide to Cherokee Indian Records Microfilm*

Collection (1996) by Sharron Standifer Ashton - is available from Ashton Books, 3812 Northwest Sterling, Norman, OK. 73072-1240.

A fully searchable Compact Disk of this collection which also includes a Dawes Roll index, catalog of all Indian material available from the National Archives and other helpful data is available from: Genref, 874 West North St., Orem, UT 84057 (Phone 801-225-3256).

Tennessee State Library and Archives in Nashville (See *Selected Archives Address Listings*) offers an excellent selection of material for Cherokee research. In addition to many of the National Archives Source microfilms listed earlier, the following references are available there:

Records of the Cherokee Agency in Tennessee, 1801-1835. NA # M208, TSLA Mf. # 52, reel 13.

Hoskins, Shirley. "Reservations." Gwy Ye: Cherokee Blood Newsletter 14 (1987): 13-23, E99.C5 C99.

TSLA Microfilm # 815 (Cherokee Collection), Reel One includes:

Surveys (Incomplete)
Spoilation Claims.
List of Persons Who Have Not Received Any Compensation for Improvements Removed, 1824.

TSLA Microfilm # 815 (Cherokee Collection), Reel Eight contains genealogy information on the following surnames: Ridge, Ross, Sequoyah (George Guess), Lovely, Meigs, Clingan, Hildebrand, Lowery, McLemore, McNair, Parks, Taylor, Vann, and Walker.

Hoskins, Shirley Coats. Cherokee Property Evaluations,1836 Chattanooga, Tennessee, 1984. E99.C5 C54.

McGhee, Lucy Kate. Cherokee and Creek Indians. Returns of Property Left in Tennessee and Georgia, 1838.E93.M32.

Martini, Don. Southeastern Indian Notebook: A Biographical and Genealogical Guide to the Five Civilized Tribes, 1685-1865. Ripley, MS: Ripley Printing Company, 1986.

Records of the Cherokee Agency in Tennessee

These records consist of two journals containing copies of letters received and sent by the Cherokee Indian Agency in Tennessee from 1822 to 1835 with occasional references dating back to 1801. Much of this data involves financial requests, disbursements and accounting, but there are also letters from and to the War Department and communications from Indian Chiefs concerning other public business. The following pages copied from the microfilm provide examples of the type of family information they contain.

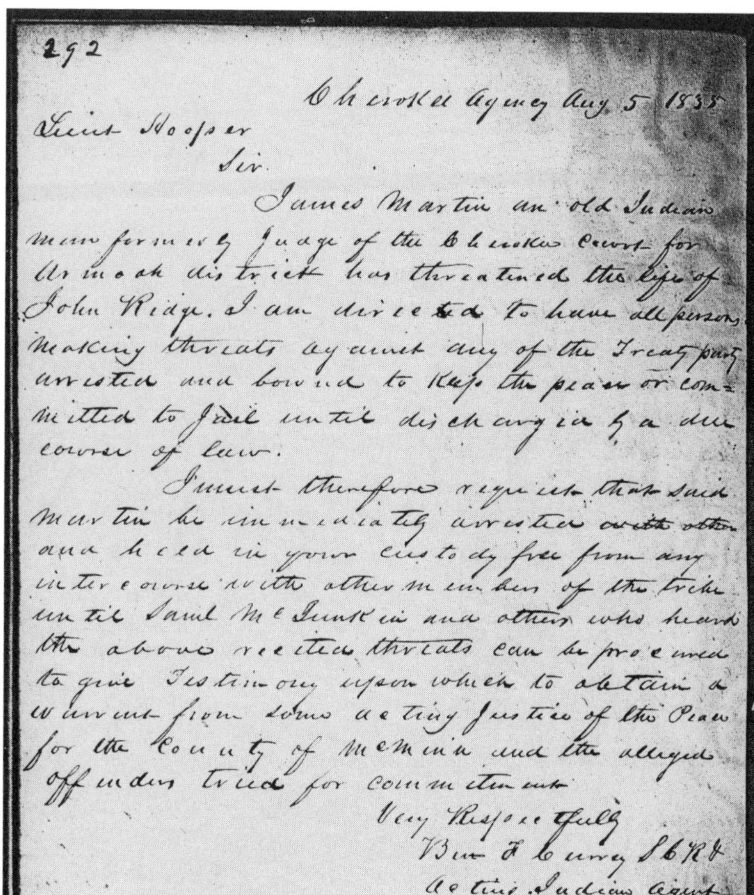

292

Cherokee Agency Aug 5 1835

Lieut Hooper

Sir.

James Martin an old Indian man formerly Judge of the Cherokee Court for Amoah district has threatened the life of John Ridge. I am directed to have all persons making threats against any of the Treaty party arrested and bound to keep the peace or committed to jail until discharged by a due course of law.

I must therefore request that said Martin be immediately arrested with other and held in your custody free from any intercourse with other members of the tribe until Saml McJunkin and others who heard the above recited threats can be procured to give Testimony upon which to obtain a warrant from some acting Justice of the Peace for the County of McMinn and the alleged offenders tried for commitment.

Very Respectfully
Ben F Currey SCR&
Acting Indian Agent

Cherokee Agency Letter Sample-1.

Sample 1 reads:

Cherokee Agency Aug. 5 1835

Lieut Hooper

Sir.

James Martin an old Indian man formerly judge of the Cherokee Court for Ar m o oh district has threatened the life of John Ridge. I am directed to have all persons making threats against any of the Treaty party arrested and bound to keep the peace or committed to jail until discharged by a discourse of law.

I must therefore request that said Martin be immediately arrested ("with other" is stricken) *and held in your custody free from any intercourse with other members of the tribe until Samuel McJunken and others who heard the above cited threats can be procured to give testimony upon which to obtain a warrant from some acting Justice of the Peace for the county of McMinn and the alleged offenders tried for commitment.*

Very Respectfully
Ben F. Curry SCRG
Acting Indian Agent

DID YOU KNOW?

On Dec. 29, 1829, the Legislature of Georgia passed an act appropriating a large part of the Cherokee Nation, incorporating it into the territory of their state. It extended the laws of Georgia over this section of the Cherokee Nation and provided that all laws, ordinances or regulations enacted by the government of the Cherokee Nation should be null and void, and made it illegal for any person to justify under any tribal laws. Mississippi and Alabama did the same. The state of Georgia further enacted that any member who sought to influence another not to emigrate to the West should be punished by imprisonment in jail or the penitentiary. It also provided **" that no Indian or descendant of an Indian residing within the Creek or Cherokee Nations of Indians shall be deemed a competent witness in any court of this state to which a white person may be a party."** Governor George Gilmer added an edict giving notice that all Cherokee lands including gold mines belonged to the state and warned Indians and anyone engaged with their consent to cease operating the mines under penalty of Georgia law. *U.S Senate Document No. 512, Vol. II, Twenty-third Congrees, first session, "Indian Removal."*

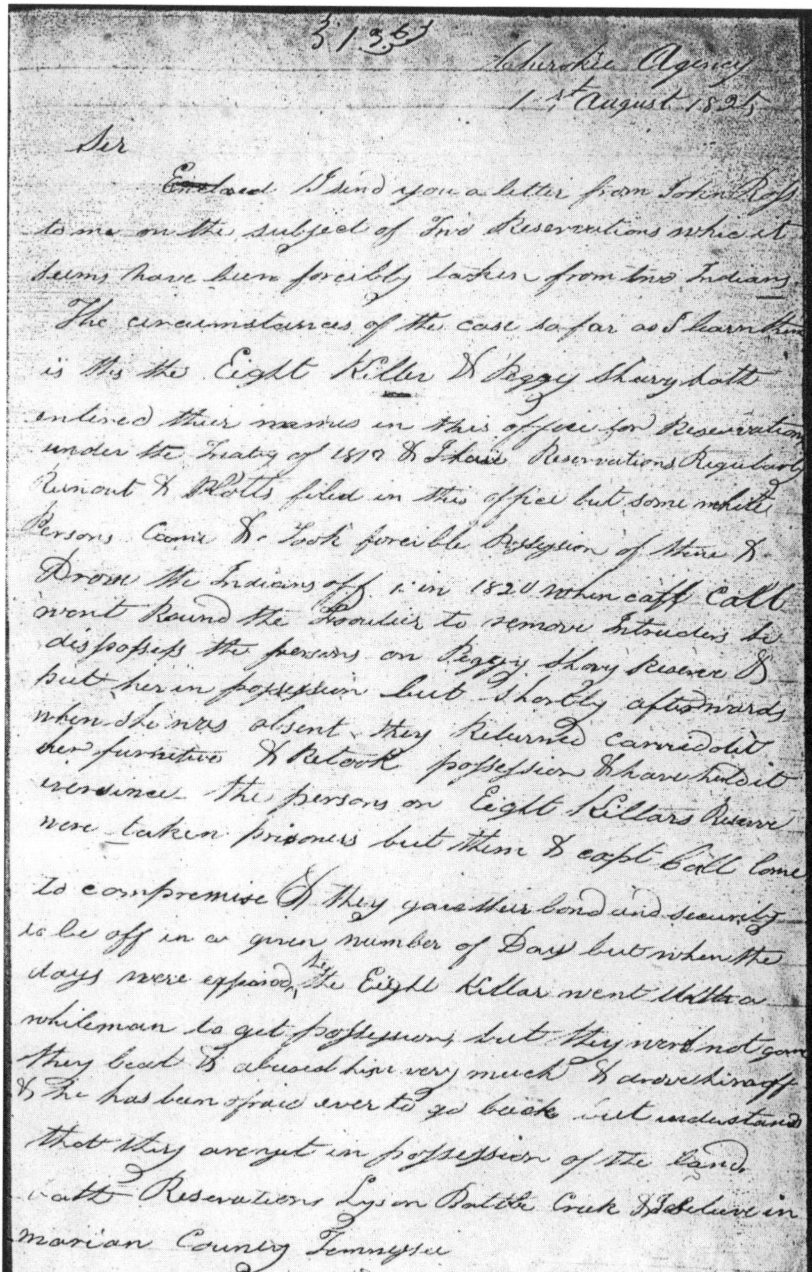

31363

Cherokee Agency
1st August 1825

Sir

Enclosed I send you a letter from John Ross to me on the subject of two Reservations which it seems have been forcibly taken from two Indians.

The circumstances of the case so far as I learn them is this the Eight Killer & Peggy Shorey both entered their names in this office for Reservations under the Treaty of 1817 & I have Reservations Regularly Resurvd & Plotts filed in this office but some white Persons came & took forcible possession of them & Drove the Indians off. in 1820 when capt Call went Round the Frontier to remove Intruders he dispossess the persons on Peggy Shorey Reserve & put her in possession but Shortly afterwards when she was absent they Returned carried out her furniture & Retook possession & have held it ever since. the persons on Eight Killers Reserve were taken prisoners but them & capt Call come to compromise & they gave their bond and security to be off in a given number of Days but when the days were expired, the Eight Killer went with a whiteman to get possession but they were not gone they beat & abused him very much & drove him off & he has been afraid ever to go back but understand that they are yet in possession of the land.

both Reservations Lys on Battle Creek & I believe in Marian County Tennessee

Cherokee Agency Letter Sample-2.

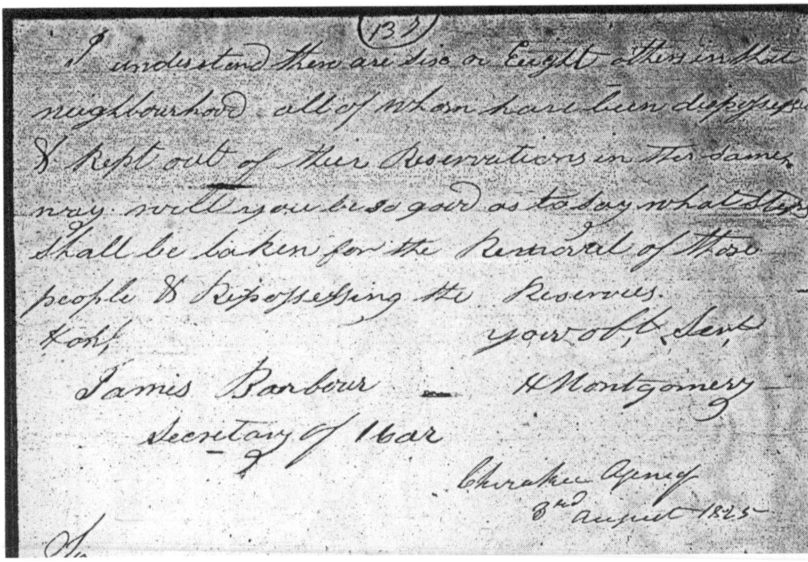

I understand there are six or Eight others in that neighbourhood all of whom have been dispossessed & kept out of their Reservations in the same way will you be so good as to say what steps shall be taken for the Removal of those people & Repossessing the Reserves.

Honl,

your obt, Servt

James Barbour — H Montgomery

Secretary of War

Cherokee Agency
3rd August 1825

Cherokee Agency Letter Sample-2, continued.

Sample 2 reads:

Cherokee Agency
1st August 1825

Sir

Enclosed I send you a letter from John Ross to me on the subject of Two Reservations which its seems have been forcibly taken from two Indians. The circumstances of the case so far as I learn them is that this Eight Killar and Peggy Shorey both entered their names in this office for reservations under the treaty of 1817 & I have reservations regularly runout and plats filed in this office but some white people came and took forcible possession of them and drove the Indians off in 1820. When Capt Call went round the (. . . . . . .) to remove intruders he dispossessed the persons on Peggy Shoreys reserve and put her in possession but shortly afterwards when she was absent, they returned carried off her furniture & retook possession & have had it ever since - the persons on Eight Killars reserve were taken prisoners but then Capt Call came to compromise & they gave their bond and security to be off in a given number of days but when the days were expired the Eight Killar went with a white man to get possession but they were not gone. They beat and abused him very much and drove him off & he has been afraid ever to go back but understands that they are yet in possession of the land. Both reservations lie on Battle Creek I believe in Marion County Tennessee. I undersand there are six or eight others in that neighborhood all of whom have been dispossessed & kept out of their reservations in the same way. Will you be so good as to say what steps shall be taken for the removal of those people and repossession by the reserves.

James Barbour
Secretary of War

Your Obt. Servant
H. Montgomery

Typical Cherokee Mountain Homes, 1835.
Smoky Mountains (l.) and Oklahoma (r.).

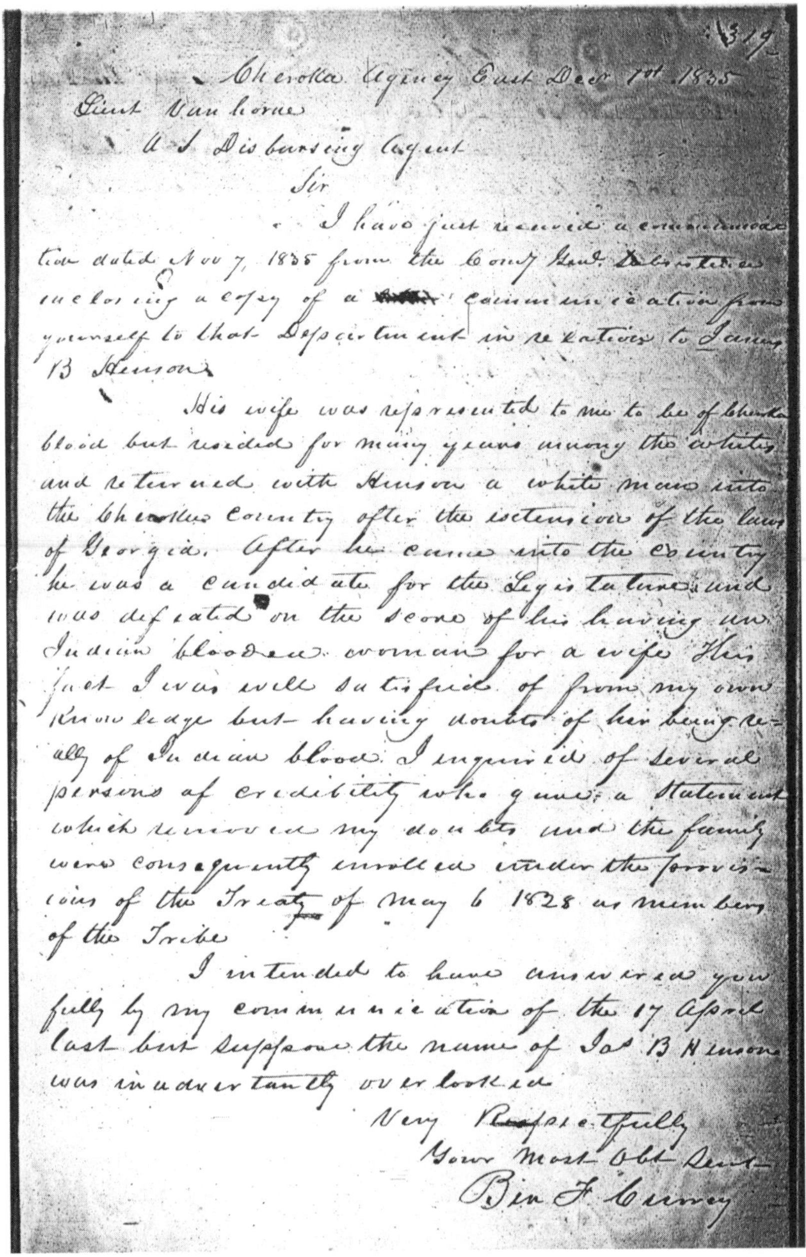

319

Cherokee Agency East Decr 1st 1835

Lieut Van horne

U. S. Disbursing Agent

Sir

I have just received a communication dated Nov 7, 1835 from the Comy Genl. Subsistence enclosing a copy of a communication from yourself to that Department in relation to James B Henson

His wife was represented to me to be of Cherokee blood but resided for many years among the whites and returned with Henson a white man into the Cherokee country after the extension of the laws of Georgia. After he came into the country he was a candidate for the Legislature and was defeated on the score of his having an Indian blooded woman for a wife. This fact I was well satisfied of from my own knowledge but having doubts of her being really of Indian blood I enquired of several persons of credibility who gave a statement which removed my doubts and the family were consequently enrolled under the provisions of the Treaty of May 6 1828 as members of the Tribe

I intended to have answered you fully by my communication of the 17 April last but suppose the name of Jas B Henson was inadvertantly overlooked

Very Respectfully

Your most Obt Servt

Ben F. Currey

Cherokee Agency Letter Sample - 3.

Sample 3 reads:

Cherokee Agency East Dec 1st .1835

Lieut Van horne
U S Disbursing Agent

Sir

I have just received a communication dated Nov 7, 1835 from the (..............) enclosing a copy of a communication from yourself to that department in relation to James B. Henson. His wife was represented to me to be of Cherokee blood but resided for many years among the whites and returned with Henson a white man into the Cherokee Country after the extension of the laws of Georgia. After he came into the country he was a candidate for the Legislature and was defeated on the score of his having an Indian blooded woman for a wife. This fact I was well satisfied of from my own knowledge but having doubts of his being really of Indian blood I inquired of several persons of credibility who gave a statement which removed my doubts and the family was consequently enrolled under the provisions of the Treaty of May 6, 1828 as members of the Tribe. I intended to have answered you fully by my communication of the 17 April last but suppose the name of James B. Henson was inadvertently overlooked.

Very Respectfully
Your Most Obt Servt-
Ben F Currey

Cherokee Citizenship Court Records

Among the most valuable records available to researchers are the microfilmed volumes containing names of persons admitted, readmitted and refused for Cherokee citizenship by the National Council and The Supreme Court after the treaty of 1866. These documents include the court dockets, and more importantly, records of testimony given in support of claims. The names and locations of family members both before and after removal often are included. (See Appendix 1 for microfilm listings).

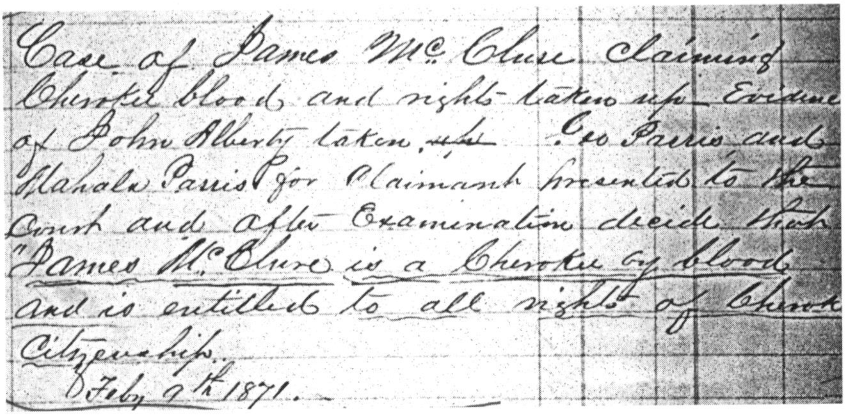

Case of James McClure claiming Cherokee blood and rights taken up Evidence of John Alberty taken, ~~also~~ Geo Parris and Mahala Parris for Claimant presented to the Court and after Examination decide that "James McClure is a Cherokee by blood and is entitled to all rights of Cherok Citizenship.
Feby 9th 1871.

Copy of Cherokee Citizenship Court docket, Feb. 9, 1871; decision in favor of James McClure for Cherokee citizenship.

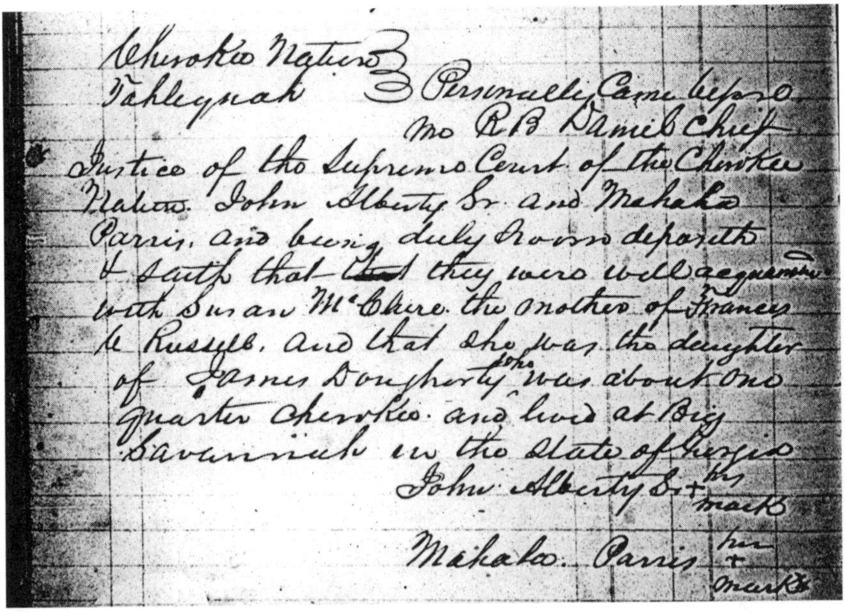

Cherokee Nation }
Tahlequah } Personally Came before me R B Daniel Chief Justice of the Supreme Court of the Cherokee Nation. John Alberty Sr. and Mahala Parris, and being duly sworn deposeth & saith that ~~they~~ they were well acquainted with Susan McClure the mother of Frances E Russell, and that she was the daughter of James Dougherty who was about one quarter Cherokee and lived at Big Savannah in the State of Georgia.

John Alberty Sr his + mark

Mahala Parris her + mark

Citizenship Court docket, Dec, 8, 1870. Testimony of witnesses attesting that Frances Russell was the daughter of Susan McClure and granddaughter of James Daugherty, a quarter-blood Cherokee who lived at Big Savannah in the state of Georgia.

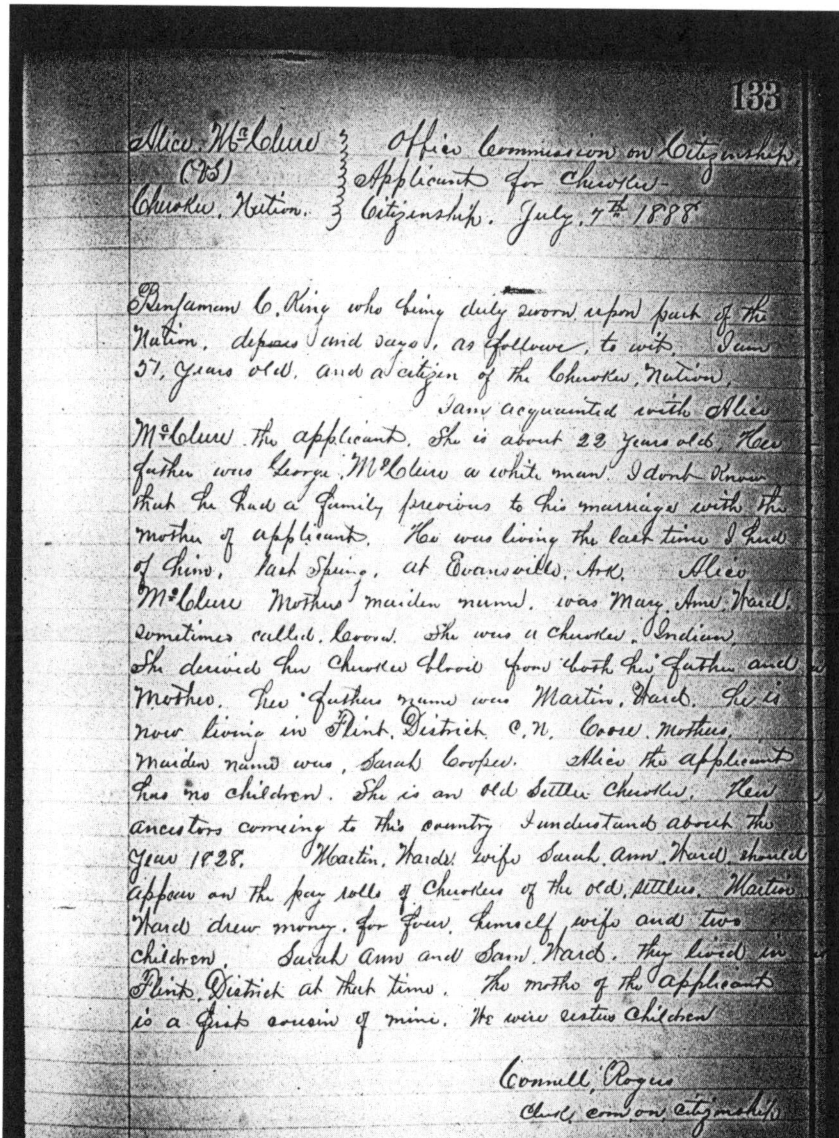

133

Alice McClure (OS) Cherokee Nation. } Office Commission on Citizenship, Applicant for Cherokee Citizenship. July 7th 1888

Benjamin C. King who being duly sworn upon part of the Nation, deposes and says, as follows, to wit. I am 37, years old, and a citizen of the Cherokee, Nation, I am acquainted with Alice McClure the applicant. She is about 22 years old. Her father was George McClure a white man. I dont know that he had a family previous to his marriage with the mother of applicant. He was living the last time I heard of him, last Spring, at Evansville, Ark. Alice McClure Mothers maiden name was Mary Ann Ward. sometimes called Coon. She was a Cherokee Indian, She derived her Cherokee blood from both her father and Mother. Her fathers name was Martin Ward. He is now living in Flint District C.N. Coon Mothers maiden name was, Sarah Cooper. Alice the applicant has no children. She is an old Settler Cherokee. Her ancestors coming to this country I understand about the year 1828. Martin Wards wife Sarah Ann Ward should appear on the pay rolls of Cherokees of the old Settlers. Martin Ward drew money for four, himself wife and two children, Sarah Ann and Sam Ward. they lived in Flint District at that time. The mother of the applicant is a first cousin of mine. We were sisters children

Connell Rogers
Clerk, com on citizenship

Citizenship Court affidavit from the clerk of the court testifying to the Indian blood of Alice McClure, 1888.

Records Relating to Intruders

One of the most critical problems faced by the Cherokee Nation in Indian Territories was non-citizen immigration which began shortly after the Civil War and continued even after land was allotted to individuals and Oklahoma became a state in 1907. Like other tribal governments, the Cherokees allowed non-Indians to live and work within its territory to provide essential services under permit systems which required the payment of taxes and other fees. But many of the immigrants were intruders who came in defiance of tribal law solely to squat on tribal lands and reap the rewards of its resources. By 1900, there were more than three times as many non-Indians as Indians. The first U.S. census of Indian Territory taken in 1890 reflected 29,166 white people and 5,127 blacks compared to 22,015 Indians living in the Cherokee Nation. This translates to an Indian population of only 39.1 percent.

By treaty, the Indians relied upon the U.S. government to protect their sovereign territory from intrusion. However, instead of enforcing the treaty agreements, the federal government challenged the Cherokee citizenship laws and refused to remove many of the persons identified as intruders by the Indians. One of the problems stemmed from an ingress of people who claimed citizenship rights by virtue of lineage to Cherokee ancestors in the east and opposition to admitting them by some Cherokee leaders claiming a right of expatriation. A Citizenship Court was established to hear such cases and although it admitted 5,000 applicants in the twenty years between 1870 and 1890, Chief Joel Bryan Mayes on February 5, 1890, transmitted a list of 5,856 names of rejected citizenship claimants who had ben declared intruders to President Benjamin Harrison. In November, 1891 in his annual address to the Cherokee National Council, Mayes stated there were in the nation "over 7,000 souls whose applications for citizenship had been denied by the citizenship court."

While there is little doubt that the majority of these applicants were recognized citizens of the United States and their only reason for seeking Cherokee citizenship was to obtain land allotments should the Cherokee country be opened for settlement, a careful review of some of the court cases also shows that the hearings often were loosely held, at best. Consequently, a number of people who were bonafide Cherokees became victims of the process. Records were few in those days and no allowance whatsoever was made for people whose ancestors had separated from their tribes or either refused or avoided the earlier enrollment processes. Proof of blood by connection to an ancestor on a previous roll was essential, and in the cases of some large families whose enrollment could ultimately result in sizable land allotments, efforts were made to discredit that. Some of my own distant maternal relatives, Hannah Flippin, et.al., fell into that category and the Cherokee authorities prosecuting her case even went so far as to accuse her and some other members of her family of fraud and bribery. Unable to provide creditable evidence of this, an insolent attempt was made to show that Hannah's grandfather John Bryant, mentioned elsewhere in this text, was not the son of his mother Lucy Bryant.

Flippin's case was unusual in that she was already a Cherokee citizen. Several years after her citizenship was granted she was summoned before the commission on citizenship "to disprove charges that she had acquired her citizenship by fraud and bribery." Not surprisingly, in 1887 the commission had written a report to Chief Dennis Bushyhead indicating "this Flippin family alone includes a total of about three hundred persons." Using the historical figure of 110 acres per person when final individual land allotments were made a few years later, the family would have stood to jointly own 33,000 acres within the Cherokee Nation! Land is power in any country. A study made of the grazing lease laws in 1889 showed that a list of twenty three Cherokees controlled (not owned) a total of 174,000 acres. The eight citizens whose names were at the top of the list each held from ten to twenty thousand acres, so it doesn't take a rocket scientist to figure a motive for the citizenship commission's actions in the case of Hannah Flippin.

Although no criminal charges were ever brought against her or any one of many accused in the proceedings (including the presiding judge and clerk of the court when she was granted her citizenship) the commission found against her. The decision was based totally on hearsay and ex parte evidence and ignored eyewitness testimony in her favor by a prominent Cherokee citizen. The court also refused to consider a report issued by Inspector C.C. Duncan, an investigator assigned by the U.S. Department of the Interior to investigate the accusations, who found no evidence of any wrongdoing. Add to this that when the decision was handed down, none of the defendants nor their attorney were even notified to be in court and it's easy to see why it sent Hannah Flippin to an early grave. Sadly, writers who use her infamous case in intruder essays or books today still skim only the surface of the public records available to them and, whether by omission or commission, report only the results, yet always insist on coloring it with insinuations of the "debauchery, bribery and corruption" that Mrs. Flippin, et al., were accused of. This unfairly leaves the impression that "debauchery, bribery and corruption" actually occurred when the records plainly show they did not.

Nevertheless, there are two sides to every issue and it is quite understandable to this writer why Cherokee leaders of the time allowed its Citizenship Court to resort to some of the extremes it did, however questionable. For almost two centuries, the Cherokee land base had continuously eroded at the hands of greedy encroachers through one fraudulent treaty after another. Even the removal of their people to the west did not halt the avarice, therefore it is not surprising that their loyalties extended primarily to those who suffered the most . . . the people and their descendants who had settled in Indian Territory at the time of the Removal and had lived there continuously ever since.

No doubt I will receive the wrath of distant maternal relatives I do not even know for making this statement, but the fact that Hannah Flippin, a person who had never lived in an Indian community in her life, was granted citizenship with all its benefits and privileges when she first migrated to Indian Territories says a lot. The endless parade of relatives that followed, especially the horde of intermarried non-Indians in the family who also filed claims, could not help but cast all of them as a predatory lot who had not paid the same dues as other citizens in the eyes of their hosts. Had I been wearing the moccasins of a court commissioner at the time, I very likely would have felt the same.

The point of importance here is that if you find an ancestor on an intruder roll, do not immediately assume they were not Cherokee. It is reasonable to expect that most of the names so recorded were actually intruders trespassing on Cherokee lands, but take the time to review the case files carefully if they exist. Yours may be an exception. Family records were few then and given the caseload confronting those handling citizenship cases, there is no question that some of the people found to be intruders were Cherokee descendants who simply could not establish their ancestry to the satisfaction of the court. Records available to you today may have not been readily accessible or even known about then. Methods of research have improved dramatically, so you may come up with proof today that your ancestor couldn't.

Contrarily, if you know that your ancestor who was always said to be of Cherokee blood definitely lived in Indian Territory, yet are unable to find them listed on regular Cherokee census rolls, you should certainly check the intruder rolls and associated records. I have met a good many people who insisted their ancestors were Cherokee yet the intruder records included unquestionable proof that they were simply non-Indians illegally residing on Indian lands. Only some of the persons declared to be intruders claimed citizenship rights.

One final note - even if you are fortunate enough to find some new information that proves an ancestor was not an intruder, forget about it changing anything in the eyes of the Cherokee Nation or the Bureau of Indian Affairs. That won't happen. In fact, this applies to any type of new information you may be able to secure even if it proves errors in the Dawes records. The Dawes rolls are referred to as the "final" rolls and they are final in every respect. Please pardon the pun, but even Jesus lacks the power to change them. Self satisfaction and possibly consideration by the officials of a state recognized tribe are the best rewards to expect here if registration is your goal.

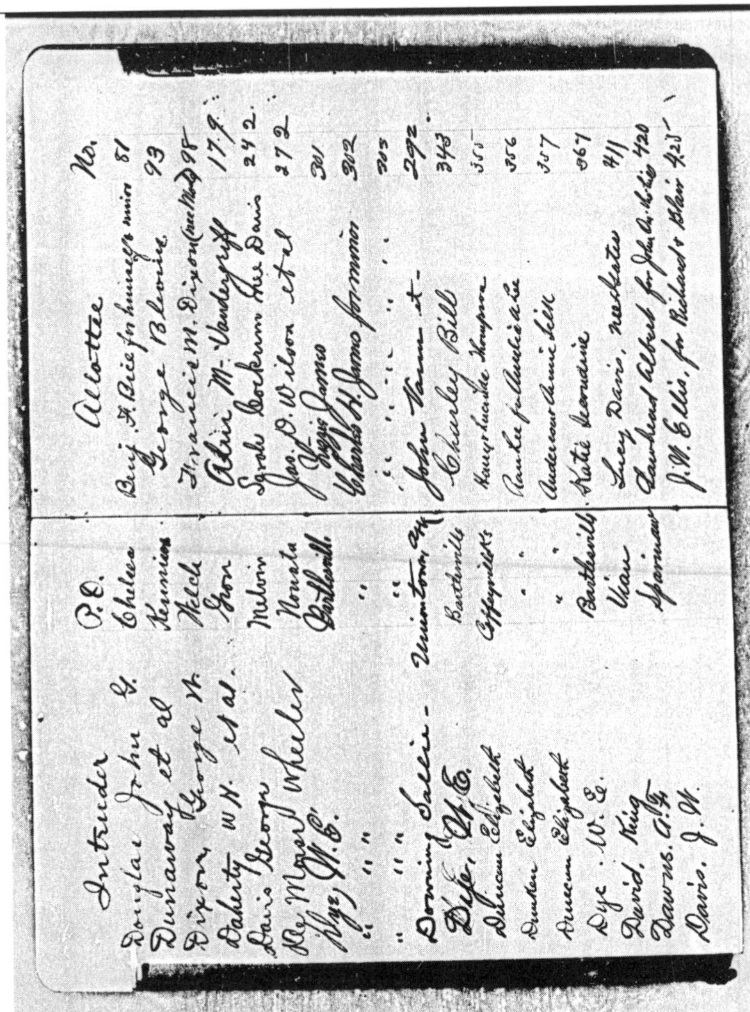

Intruder	P.O.	Allottee	No.
Douglas John G.	Chelsea	Benj. F. Rice for himself & minor	81
Dunaway et al	[illegible]	George Blevins	93
Dixon, George W.	Welch	Francis M. Dixon [illegible]	98
Daherty W.H. et al.	[illegible]	Alice M. Vandergriff	179
Davis George	Melvin	Sarah Cockrum [illegible] Davis	242
Mc Mason Wheeler	Nowata	Jas. O. Wilson et al	272
Dye, W.E.	Bartlesville	Maggie James	301
" "	"	Charles H. James for minor	302
" "	"	" "	303
Downing Sallie	Uniontown Ark	John Vann et al	292
Dye, W.E.	Bartlesville	Charley Bill	343
Duncan Elizabeth	Coffeyville	[illegible]	355
Duncan Elizabeth	"	[illegible]	356
Duncan Elizabeth	"	[illegible]	357
Dye W.E.	Bartlesville	Katie Secondine	367
David King	Vian	Lucy Davis, [illegible]	411
Dawns G.F.	[illegible]	[illegible]	420
Davis J.W.		J.W. Ellis, for Richard & Blair	425

Sample of Intruder Roll, 1909, from Microfilm 7RA53-1 which shows a person residing illegally (left column) on lands already allotted to a Cheroke citizen (right column).

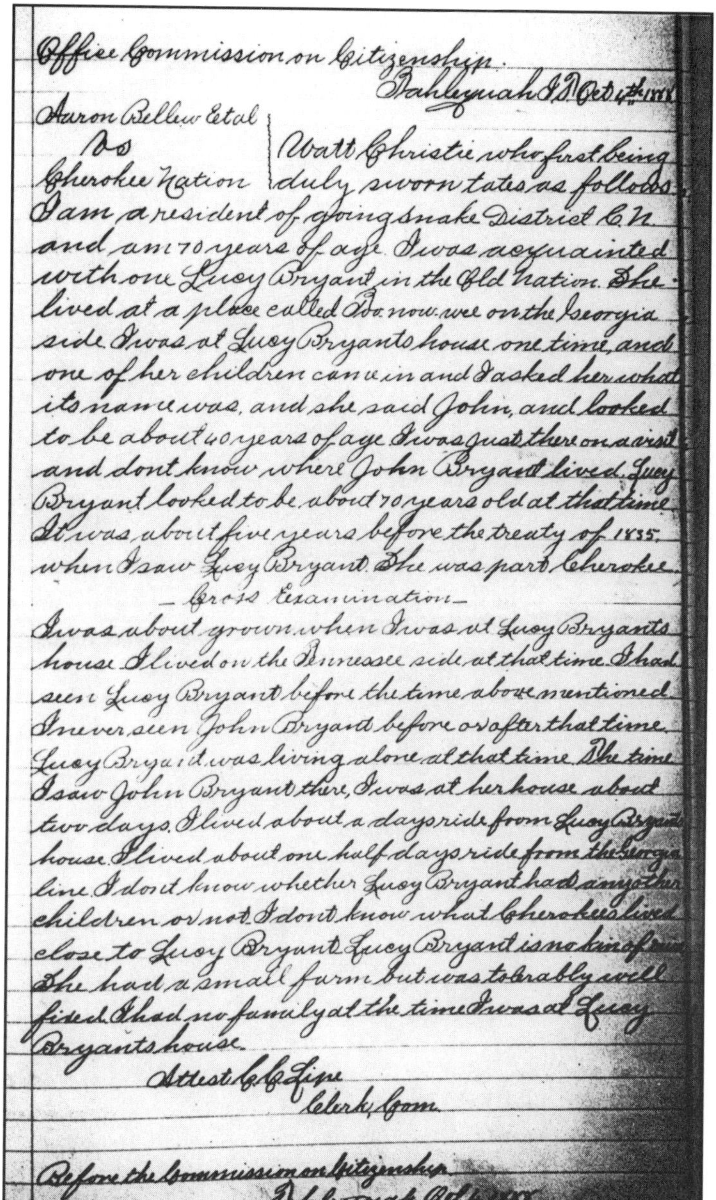

Office Commission on Citizenship.
Tahlequah I.T. Oct 4th 1888

Aaron Bellew Etal
vs
Cherokee Nation

Watt Christie who first being duly sworn tates as follows: I am a resident of going snake District C.N and am 70 years of age. I was acquainted with one Lucy Bryant in the Old Nation. She lived at a place called Ido now wee on the Georgia side. I was at Lucy Bryants house one time, and one of her children came in and I asked her what its name was, and she said John, and looked to be about 40 years of age. I was just there on a visit and dont know where John Bryant lived. Lucy Bryant looked to be about 70 years old at that time. It was about five years before the treaty of 1835 when I saw Lucy Bryant. She was part Cherokee.

— Cross Examination —

I was about grown when I was at Lucy Bryants house. I lived on the Tennessee side at that time. I had seen Lucy Bryant before the time above mentioned. I never seen John Bryant before or after that time. Lucy Bryant was living alone at that time. The time I saw John Bryant there, I was at her house about two days. I lived about a days ride from Lucy Bryants house. I lived about one half days ride from the Georgia line. I dont know whether Lucy Bryant had any other children or not. I dont know what Cherokees lived close to Lucy Bryant. Lucy Bryant is no kin of mine. She had a small farm but was tolerably well fixed. I had no family at the time I was at Lucy Bryants house.

Attest C. C. Lipe
Clerk, Com.

Before the Commission on Citizenship
Tahlequah Oct 6 1888

1888 Affidavit of Watt Christie, a prominent Cherokee citizen testifying in Hannah Flippin,et.al. intruder case that he knew Flippin's grandfather John Bryant and great - grandmother Lucy Bryant in Georgia before the Removal and that they were Cherokee.

Hannah Flippin,

Vs. Vinita, Ind. Ter., July 29, 1892.

Cherokee Nation.

Report of C. C. Duncan, U. I., in the above stated case.

Sir:--

I herewith submit the evidence in this case, together with my conclusions, for your consideration.

It was admitted by the Solicitor-General of the Cherokee Nation that Mrs. Hannah Flippin and her children, whose names appear in the record of evidence, were admitted to citizenship by a judgment of the Spiers' Commission, September Term, 1884; that the Spiers' Commission composed of Eli Spiers, John Lee, and Snake Puppy, was organized by act of Council, and had jurisdiction as to questions of citizenship.

It was claimed by the Nation that the judgment admitting Flippin was obtained by fraud, corrpution and bribery, and that the Nation through a competent tribunal had investigated passed upon it, and set aside the judgment rendered in favor of Flippin.

The National Council of the Cherokee Nation, by Act of December 8th, 1886, organized what was termed the Citizens Commission, said commission composed of A. P. Adair, D. W. Lipe, and John E. Gunter. This courtwas commonly known as the Adair Commission Court. This Act covers a good many subject-matters, but the__________Section

Page 1 - Findings of Indian Inspector C.C. Duncan, U.S. Department of the Interior, in Hannah Flippin citizenship case.

Under this section the Flippins were summoned to appear to show cause why the judgment of the Spiers court should not be set aside. At the first call, being the day they were cited to appear, the Flippins were present at court, and the Nation continued the case, setting another date for the hearing. At this time they also appeared, andthe case was again continued by the Nation. The case having been continued the court stated to Bryant, attorney for the Flippins, that he might set the time for the hearing; whereupon Bryant notified the Flippins that they might go home; that the time for the hearing had been left to him, and that he would never set the time. With this they left, and were not present, and did not know when the case was tried. But it appears, as well be seen by reference to the judgment, made a part of the record in this case, that the case was called, and a judgment rendered setting aside the decree of the Spiers court. There being no regular terms of this court it is very doubtful to my mind whether, under the circumstances this case could have been called and heard without a new summons, even though the attorney for the Flippins had been authorized by the court to set the day of the hearing.

Page 2 - Findings of Indian Inspector C.C. Duncan,
U.S. Department of the Interior, in Hannah Flippin citizenship case.

If the Adair court had jurisdiction to determine this case, it seems from the testimony submitted upon the part of the Nation there was no such proof before the Commission as would justify it in finding that the Spiers court had been bribed to render this decision in favor of Flippin. All of the testimony before the Adair court upon which they based their judgment was merely the opinion and surmises of witnesses, and all of it given after the party charged with bribery was dead. And if Associate Justice Snake Puppy did receive money to render an opinion, he received it like Lord Bacon, to render a just decision. The right of the Flippins to have the judgment as rendered was not questioned. In fact, to use the language of Jim Smith, Attorney for the Nation at the trial, "There was very little testimony in the case, but it was all to the point. That woman is a Cherokee, and I am not going to argue the case."

Taking all the testimony rendered at this ex parte trial by the Nation, if any money was paid it was to get the case to a hearing, not to decide it, and it is a fair conclusion from the evidence before the Adair court that the determination of the case had been postponed and certain officials had lead Skinner, the manager of the Flippins to believe that if they could receive money the case could be brought up; and while Skinner denies having paid any money for that purpose the evidence of the Nation goes no further than to establish that fact, and falls af far short of establishing the fact that the judgment was obtained by bribery. The Flippins had not moved to the Cherokee Nation when the judgment was rendered; they made application for citizenship with a view to moving if obtained. After they obtained

Page 3 - Findings of Indian Inspector C.C. Duncan, U.S. Department of the Interior, in Hannah Flippin citizenship case.

their judgment, and certificate of citizenship they returned to texas, disposed of their property, which seems to have been large, (especially Skinner) moved to their present homes in the Nation. Mrs. Flippin and John bought of Cherokee citizens their homes. Skinner bought $3000.00 worth of town lots in Vinita, and altogether they invested largely, and have greatly added to their holdings. Several of the family have married in the Nation; children have been born, attachments formed, and in view of all these facts, and especially the precaution and good faith with which they seemed to act in securing their citizenship, and the recognition of the same by the Cherokee Nation in the many ways as shown by the evidence, I think they should not be held to be intruders.

Respt Submitted
C C Duncan
U S Indian Inspr

Hon Secty of Interior.

Page 4 - Findings of Indian Inspector C.C. Duncan, U.S. Department of the Interior, in Hannah Flippin citizenship case.

Finding Indian Records in The U.S. Congressional Serial Set

The U.S. Congressional Serial Set is a highly valuable and readily available resource for Indian family research. While this information is easily obtained, it is not very easy to use, and so, unfortunately, it's often overlooked or disregarded by researchers. There are three things you should know before attempting to use this resource:

- Don't be intimidated by it's overwhelming size.
- In the majority of cases you will not find an "every-name" index. Most finding aids to the set are arranged by the key subject of each document.
- Indian related material contained within the Serial Set should most often be used in conjunction with other historical resource material.

The Serial Set, as it's name implies, is a vast series of documents compiled and printed for use by Congress as well as the general public. Most importantly for the Indian researcher, it contains studies requested by Congress on cemeteries, battlefields, and various investigations into the actions of the Military and the Bureau of Indian Affairs. A few tribal histories are presented by name and other tribes have brief histories included within some larger document regarding their affairs.

The records of the "early removal period" (November 30, 1831 to December 27, 1833) are contained in five volumes of the 23rd Congress, 1st Session, Senate Document No. 512. Other volumes contain reports on the conduct and results of negotiations with tribes. There are also reports on investigations of fraud in Indian affairs, reports from Indian Agents concerning the tribes under their jurisdiction, various letters from tribal officials and individual members regarding tribal or personal concerns, etc. The Serial Set also contains the original volumes of Kappler's Indian Treaties and Laws.

The most comprehensive finding aid to the Serial Set is the U.S. Serial Set Indexes published by the Congressional Information

Service, Inc., (C.S.I.) which is not a government agency. This index (available in most major public and university libraries) will help the researcher find material published as part of the Serial Set between 1789 and 1969. Remember that these indexes are general finding aids, and are not "every-name" indexes.

The C.S.I. indexes are contained in thirty-six volumes which are broken down into twelve parts by date, as follows:

Part I	1789-1857
Part II	1857-1879
Part III	1879-1889
Part IV	1889-1897
Part V	1897-1903
Part VI	1903-1909
Part VII	1909-1915
Part VIII	1915-1925
Part IX	1925-1934
Part X	1935-1946
Part XI	1947-1958
Part XII	1959-1969

Each part (or time period) is contained within three volumes as follows:

Subject Index A-K
Subject Index L-Z
Finding Aids

There is a user friendly table of contents, and you should take the time to familiarize yourself with the "User's Guide," "User Instructions" and the "Finding Lists." Indian researchers should look under the name of the specific tribe in question, however, sometimes tribes will be indexed by a name with which you are not familiar. Be sure to check for entries by the state or territory where the tribe was located. You might look under the name of a fort in the area or any other subject which could contain information on Indian or Indian-white relations. Always refer to the "Index of Subjects and Keywords" in each volume for additional clues as to where you might look for information.

Private publishers have reprinted various volumes and items from the Serial Set over the years. The Genealogical Publishing Company, for example, has reprinted several volumes from the Serial Set which will be of particular interest to Indian as well as Civil War researchers. Kappler's Treaties have been reprinted by a number of private publishers, and has been arranged by tribes in an indexed edition by Krauss and HISTREE. Krauss and HISTREE has also reprinted "Some Private Claims," Senate Document 512, 23rd Congress, 2nd Session (Indian Removal documents) with an every-name index. (HISTREE: The Journal of American Indian Family Research, P.O. Box 5982, Yuma, AZ 85366-5982).

The Serial Set includes another invaluable group of documents known as the "American State Papers". The items of greatest interest to Indian researchers are as follows:

Class II, Indian Affairs, 1789-1827
Class V, Military Affairs
Class VII, Post Office
Class VIII, Public Lands
Class IX, Claims

Class VIII (Public Lands) has been reprinted by the Southern Historical Press with a complete every-name index. It is often a good idea to use the Class VIII materials in combination with the Territorial Papers from the territory where the subject peoples either were or are currently located. Many, if not most, major genealogical collections will include "Grassroots of America" which is a computerized index to the American State Papers Land Grants and Claims (GenTex Corp., Salt Lake, 1972).

There are two specialized indexes that could be of benefit to you as you search the Serial Set. Stephen L. Johnson's Guide to American Indian Documents in the Congressional Serial Set, 1871-1899 (New York: Clearwater Publishing Co., 1977) contains a detailed cross-index as well as references to some other congressional materials which are not included in the Serial Set. You should also refer to the Biographical and Historical Index of American Indians and Persons Involved in Indian Affairs (United States

Department of Interior, Boston: G.K. Hall, 1966) which is an every-name index to the materials.

The annual reports of the Department of the Interior and the Bureau of Indian Affairs should not be overlooked, as they may provide information that you are looking for, or at least clues as to where your answers may be found. Tracking down family history in these documents is just like solving any other mystery. First you must find some clues and then you have to follow them. In this regard, remember that the government is a large and cumbersome machine that moves at it's own sometimes irritatingly slow pace. Just because an event occurred or was noted by Congress in a particular year does not mean that it was resolved or completely reviewed all at once. On the contrary, it is not unusual for issues to drag on for decades. Just keep searching for clues and hoping that one will lead you to another. The Serial Set is an invaluable source of such clues and you should definitely take the time to investigate it.

Former home of the Rev. Samuel Worcester, American Board Missionary to the Cherokees from 1827 to 1835 was the only building still standing at New Echota when citizens of Calhoun, Ga. began restoring it in the 1950s.
Photo courtesy of Georgia Dept. of Natural Resources.

Addresses for Selected Archives:

National Archives
7th and Pennsylvania Ave.
Washington, DC. 20408
Telephone: 205-501-5402

National Archives
Alaska Region
654 West Third Avenue
Anchorage, AK 99501
Telephone: 907-271-2441

National Archives
Central Plains Region
2312 East Bannister Road
Kansas City, MO 64131
Telephone: 816-926-6272

National Archives
Great Lakes Region
7358 South Pulaski Road
Chicago, IL 60629
Telephone: 312-581-7816

National Archives
Mid Atlantic Region
9th and Market Streets,
Room 1350
Philadelphia, PA 19107
Telephone: 215-597-3000

National Archives
New England Region
380 Trapelo Road
Waltham, MA 02154
Telephone: 617-647-8100

National Archives
Northeast Region
201 Varick Street
New York, NY 10014
Telephone: 212-337-1300

National Archives Pacific
Northwest Region
6125 Sand Point Way, NE
Seattle, WA 98115
Telephone: 206-526-6507

National Archives
Pacific Sierra Region
1000 Commodore Drive
San Bruno, CA 94066
Telephone: 415-876-9009

National Archives Pacific
Southwest Region
24000 Avila Road
Laguna Niquel, CA 92656
Telephone: 714-643-4241

National Archives
Rocky Mountain Region
Building 48-Denver
Federal Center
Denver, CO 80255-0307
Telephone: 303-236-0817

National Archives
Southeast Region
1557 St. Joseph Avenue
East Point, GA 30344
Telephone: 404-763-7477

National Archives
Southwest Region
501 West Felix Street
Fort Worth, TX 76115
Telephone: 817-334-5525

Alabama (Mobile Public
Library) History and
Genealogy Division
701 Government Street
Mobile, AL 36602
Telephone: 205-434-7093

Arkansas State University
Museum Library and Archives
P.O. Box 490 State University
Jonesboro, AR 72467
Telephone: 501-972-2074

Georgia State Archives
330 Capitol Avenue, S.E.
Atlanta, GA 30334
Telephone: 404-656-2358

New Echota Historic
Site Library
1211 Chatsworth Hwy
Calhoun, Ga. 30701
Telephone: 404-629-8151

Kentucky Historical
Society Library
300 Broadway
Frankfort, KY 40602
Telephone: 502-564-3016

Mississippi Dept of Archives
and History
P.O.Box 571
Jackson, MS 39205-0571
Telephone: 601-359-6876

Museum of the Cherokee
Indian Library
P.O. Box 770-A, U.S.Hwy 441
North
Cherokee, NC 28719
Telephone: 704-497-3481

Native American Resource
Center Library
Pembroke State University
College Road
Pembroke, NC 28372
Telephone: 919-521-4214

North Carolina State Library
Genealogy & Archives Branch
109 East Jones St.
Raleigh, NC 27601-2807
Telephone: 919-733-7222

Schiele Museum Reference
Library
P.O. Box 953, 1500 East
Garrison Blvd.
Gastonia, NC 28053-0953
Telephone: 704-866-6900

Oklahoma Historical Society
2100 N. Lincoln Blvd.
Oklahoma City, OK 73105
Telephone: 405-521-2491

Thomas Gilcrease Institute
1400 Gilcrease Museum Rd.
Tulsa, OK 74127
Telephone: 918-582-3122

Cherokee National Historical Society
P.O. Box 515
Tahlequah, OK 74465
Telephone: 918-456-6007

Schusterman-Benson Library
3333 E. 32nd Place
Tulsa, OK 74135
Telephone: 918-746-5024

Muskogee Public Library
801 W. Okmulgee
Muskogee, OK 74401
Telephone: 918-682-6657

Talbot Library and Museum
P.O. Box 349
Colcord, OK 74338-0349
Telephone: 918-326-4532

Tsa-la-gi Library
124 E. Choctaw
Tahlequah, OK 74465

South Carolina Dept of Archives and History
P.O.Box 11669, 1430 Senate St.
Columbia, SC 29211-1669
Telephone: 803-734-8596

Tennessee State Archives and Library
403 7th Avenue North
Nashville, TN 37219
Telephone: 615- 741-2764

Red Clay State Historical Park Library
Route 6, Box 733
Cleveland, TN 37311
Telephone: 615-472-2626

Amon Carter Museum
Photographic Archives
3501 Camp Bowie Boulevard
Ft. Worth, TX 76107-2631
Telephone: 817-738-1933

Virginia State Library & Archives
11th Street at Capitol Square
Richmond, VA 23219-3491
Telephone: 804-786-2306

The Church of Jesus Christ of Latter-Day Saints (LDS- Mormon), Family History Center, 35 North Temple St., Salt Lake City, Utah 84150 has the largest depository of genealogical records in the world with branches in most areas. To find a branch near you call: **1-800-346-6044.**

Quick-Step Guide for Checking Cherokee Rolls and Acquiring Microfilm or Copies of Available Roll Documents

Checking Cherokee rolls (and other pertinent archive documents) for the names of ancestors is much easier than many seem to think. Use this handy guide to recap what has been covered and then follow these easy steps:

(1) Write down the full names and birth and death dates of each ancestor you believe to be of Cherokee blood. Be sure to include any variation of the spelling(s) of surnames.
(2) Referring to the official roll names listed earlier in this book, make a list of those taken during your ancestor's life. Begin with your most recent ancestor and the latest roll their name could have appeared on. Then work backwards in time searching for older ancestors on older rolls.
(3) Next, check in your local library for one of the following:

(a) microfilm index or film of the roll(s) of interest, or
(b) a printed (book) of these roll(s).

If they do not have either of these, ask them to make an acquisition by purchase, interlibrary loan, or rental from the National Archives or American Genealogical Lending Library (Heritage Quest). Occasionally, especially in smaller libraries, the staff will not be familiar with Indian-related records. Use this book to show them precisely what you need and how to acquire it. If the rolls shown as available on microfilm include an index for the particular roll, obtain that first to check it for family names.
(4) Alternatively, you can acquire the materials directly. Rolls that are available for purchase in book form are so noted with the earlier roll descriptions. These can be ordered from Cherokee booksellers shown on page 147-148.

Keep in mind that this first step is only to review the rolls to determine if your ancestor's name is listed. If you find a name that matches, DO NOT immediately assume it is your ancestor. It could merely be someone with the same name! This is one of the most common mistakes made. **Finding a name on a roll that appears to be correct is only the first step!**

The next step is to determine if a roll name is actually your ancestor and this requires obtaining the documentation that supported the roll entry. For rolls that required applications by the enrollee, the names of parents and grandparents, spouses, children, places of residence, etc. were usually required. Unfortunately, some of the older rolls contain no information except names and roll number. The descriptions of primary roll listings earlier in this chapter explain what information each roll contains and if supporting documentation is available. Of all the rolls, the **Dawes Roll, Guion Miller Roll** and **Baker Roll** record jackets contain the most information of genealogical value.

(5) The National Archives CAN NOT conduct searches for you, however they can provide copies of all available documents that support any individual Cherokee roll entry by mail once you have verified a name and roll number on any roll. This includes anything from a single copy of the roll page that a name appears on to complete roll packets as, for examples, from the final Dawes roll or Guion Miller roll. Review the National Archives roll listings/identifiers below to find the roll of interest. A $10 fee covers up to 20 pages of available documents for any one name on any one roll, i.e. if you request documents for two names, the fee is $20 or if you request documents from three different rolls for the same name, the fee is $30, etc. If you need the page(s) to be certified, there is an additional charge of $10. Following is an index of Cherokee rolls available from the National Archives. If the identifier begins with "7RA", direct your request to: National Archives, SW Region, P.O. Box 6216, Fort Worth, Texas 76115-0216. If the identifier begins with anything other than 7RA (M, T, A, etc.), direct your request to: General Reference Branch (NNRG), National Archives and Records Administration, 7th and Pennsylvania Ave NW., Washington, DC 20408. Make your check payable to "The National Archives Trust Fund" and be sure to include the name(s) and roll number(s) you are requesting.

Time Period	Microfilm #	Roll Identification
1817-1819	A21	Register of Cherokee Who Wished to Remain in the East.
1817-1838	A23	Cherokee Emigration and Muster Rolls.
1835	T496	Index to Henderson Roll and Henderson Roll.
1848	7RA06	Mullay Roll of Eastern Cherokee.
1851	M685 (roll 12)	Index to Siler Roll.
1851	7RA06	Siler Roll of Eastern Cherokee.
1852	M685 (roll 12)	Chapman Roll of Eastern Cherokee.
1852	M685 (roll 12)	Index to Drennen Roll.
1852	7RA01	Drennen Roll, "Emigrant Cherokee."
1867	A29	Powell Roll.
1867	7RA04	Tompkins Roll.
1867-1897	7RA51 (rolls 1-2)	Freedmen Rolls and Indexes. Includes Wallace Roll (1890).
1878-1889	7RA25 (rolls 1-4)	Citizenship Commission List of Claimants & Dockets.
1880	7RA07 (rolls 1-4)	Cherokee Census and Index, Schedules 1-6.
1880	7RA33 (rolls 1-2)	Lipe Payment Receipt Roll.
1881	7RA74 (roll 1)	Roll of North Carolina Cherokees who Removed to the Cherokee Nation West.
1881-1882	7RA91	Register-Cherokee Students.
1883	7RA29 (rolls 1-2)	Cherokee Census.
1883	7RA57 (rolls 1-3)	Receipt Roll for 1883 Census above.

Time Period	Microfilm #	Roll Identification
1886	7RA58 (rolls 1-2)	Cherokee Census.
1887-1889	7RA71 (roll 1)	Cherokee Citizenship (List of persons rejected).
1890	7RA08 (rolls 1-6)	Cherokee Census Schedules 1-6. (No Index).
1890	7RA59 (rolls 1-2)	Receipt Roll for 1890 Census above.
1893	7RA54 (rolls 1-2)	Cherokee Census
1893	7RA55 (roll 1)	Census of Intruders.
1894	7RA38 (rolls 1-5)	Starr Roll (Payments for sale of *Cherokee Strip*).
1896	T985	Index to Old Settlers Payment Roll.
1896	7RA34	Old Settlers Payment Roll.
1896	7RA19	Cherokee Census.
1896	7RA71	Index to Above Census NOT Including Freedmen.
1896	M1650 (rolls 21-54)	Applications.
1896	7RA70 (rolls 1-2)	Citizenship Cases, Index and Dockets.
1897	7RA51 (roll 2)	Freedman Payment Rolls and Index.
1897	7RA60 (rolls 1-3)	Copy of 1890 Cherokee Payroll.
1898-1914	M1186 (roll 1)	Index to Final Dawes Roll.
1898-1914	M1186 (rolls 2-38)	Enrollment Cards, Dawes Roll.
1898-1914	M1301 (rolls 174-399)	Applications of Enrollment, Dawes Roll.
1898-1939	M595 (rolls 22-26)	Census (North Carolina Cherokee).
1899-1905	7RA18 (roll 1)	Dawes Commission Townsite Plats.
1900-1907	7RA30 (rolls 3-9)	Lease Royalty Records.

Time Period	Microfilm #	Roll Identification
1901-1909	7RA53 (rolls 1-5)	Index and Dockets of Intruder Cases.
1907	7RA24 (roll 1)	Index to Rejected Applicants.
1908-1910	M685 (rolls 1-12)	Guion Miller Roll Index.
1906-1909	M-1104 (rolls 1-348)	Applications;U.S. Court of Claims (Guion Miller Roll).
1910	7RA80 (roll 1)	Payment to Intermarried Whites.
1910	7RA82 (rolls 1-4)	Cherokee Equalization Payroll (Includes Index).
1912	7RA81 (rolls 1-3)	Payroll and Index.
1917-1918	7RA347	Register of Indians in World War I.
1926-31	A35	Baker Roll of Eastern Cherokees in North Carolina.
Not dated	7RA51 (roll 2)	List of "Colored Persons" on the Clifton Rolls not on the 1880 Rolls.
Not dated	7RA297 (roll 1)	Index to Orders for Removal of Enrollment Restrictions.

[Note: If the Microfilm you want to obtain select printed page copies from does not appear above, check the AGLL listings in Appendix One, as explained below. If it appears there, telephone the National Archives, give them the microfilm number and ask if it is possible to obtain photocopies from that microfilm by mail].

(6) **An option is to obtain the microfilm containing the required documents either directly (by rental or purchase) or through your library.** Appendix One in the back of this book lists all of the microfilm pertaining to the Cherokee people (census rolls and other records) stocked by the American Genealogical Lending Library (Heritage Quest) and how to obtain it by purchase or rental. Some Cherokee rolls are contained on a single roll of microfilm; others require hundreds of rolls of film. If acquired directly from AGLL, you will need to bring

the microfilm to your local library to view or make paper copies of the entries. Note that for the Dawes roll, the roll number of the individual taken from the census roll index (M-1186, Roll -1) will lead to their census card found on M1186, Rolls, 2-93, and this contains a census card number. Enrollment jackets found in M-1301 are found by using this census number, not the roll number. For the Guion Miller rolls M-1104 and M-685, the roll number of the microfilm needed will be determined by the Miller application number - not the individual roll number. Be careful to watch for notations written by the census takers on these old documents that often refer to roll numbers of kin, court citations, etc. Following up on these could lead to other valuable family data.

For older rolls in which no confirming documentation exists to support the roll entry, search for supplementary data in records other than rolls. Hopefully, something can be found here to help verify this as your ancestor, not just an instance of name similarity. Numerous examples of what records to search and where to find them are listed throughout this book. Many of these also are available on microfilm, i.e., Cherokee Citizenship Court Records, Cherokee Agency Records of Tennessee, Spoilation Claims, Military Records, Marriage records, etc.

Dawes Enrollment Commission on the way to camp
in full-blood country, 1899. (Oklahoma Historical Society Photo)

Legends of Black Dutch

When researching Cherokee ancestry, oral traditions of Indian families occasionally being called "Black Dutch" instead of American Indian is one of the most common phenomenons encountered. This has been a subject of investigation and debate since I can remember and, as best I can determine, there is no authoritative finding as to its beginning.

Throughout the five southeastern "civilized tribes" especially, many descendants of Indians claim their ancestors called themselves Black Dutch to avoid being recognized as Native American, thus avoiding removal to the west. When I was teenager in the 1950s, I remember meeting two copper skinned families living in what is now the TVA Land Between the Lakes Recreation Area near Cadiz, Kentucky who were quick to proclaim they were NOT Indians, but of Black Dutch origin. Strangely enough, the oldest members could often be heard conversing among themselves in fluent Cherokee and when queried about their origins, would simply smile and say their ancestors came from East Tennessee before the Civil War. Their surname was "Knight," but the grandfather of the group was called *Suh-no-ee;* to me, no small coincidence as *Sv -no - i* in Tsalagi translates to "night" in English.

A passage displayed in the Oakville Mounds Park and Museum in Moulton, Alabama states:

"Before the Indian Removal Act of 1830, many of Lawrence County's Cherokee people were already mixed with white settlers and stayed in the country of the Warrior Mountains. They denied their ancestry and basically lived much of their lives in fear of being sent west. Full bloods claimed to be Black Irish or Black Dutch, thus denying their rightful Indian blood. After being fully assimilated into the general population years later, these Irish-Cherokee mixed blood descendants began reclaiming their Indian heritage in the land of the Warrior Mountains, Lawrence County, Alabama. During the 1900 U.S. Census, only 78 people claimed Indian heritage. In 1990, more than 2,000 individuals claimed Indian descent. Today, more than 4,000

citizens are proud to claim their Indian heritage and are members of the Echota Cherokee Tribe." (The Echota Tribe is one of 3 State recognized Cherokee tribes in Alabama).

During my festival travels, I often have the pleasure to see Mr. John Farmer of Fort Oglethorpe, Georgia, an elderly gentleman whose features would prevent the denial of Indian blood even if he desired. Mr. Farmer relates that when he was growing up, he was always told that his family was Black Dutch, yet his grandmother, who was from the mountains of North Carolina, always spoke and prayed in the Cherokee language. It was much later in life when his mother finally admitted their blood was actually a mixture of Welsh and Cherokee and his own research proved the lineage.

According to the Library of Congress, the term Black Dutch refers to Sephardic Jews, a people who lived in Spain during the Middle Ages but later migrated to the Lowlands, Belgium and the Netherlands due to the Spanish Inquisitions. One theory for the origin of the term suggests that during a Dutch revolt against the Spanish monarchy in the late 1500s, Spain, lacking sufficient troops, recruited neighboring Portuguese soldiers into regiments throughout their domain. A new race was created in the southern part of Holland during the next six decades and the mixed blood, dark-skinned children were referred to as "Black Dutch." A large number of these people may have been among the first settlers brought by way of the West Indies to North America by the Spanish.

Another thesis implies the Black Dutch were simply early German immigrants from the Black Forest area along the Swiss border of Germany whose name "Duetsch" (meaning German in their language) was simply corrupted to "Dutch" by English speakers not familiar with the term. It is said that the Melungeon people also were often referred to as Black Dutch. The mysterious and originally dark-featured people, native for over 200 years to the Appalachian mountains of East Tennessee, Kentucky, Southwestern Virginia and Western, North Carolina are often considered characters of mere mountain folk tales. But they are a very real people discovered by John Sevier's expedition in 1774 whose history seems to be lost. Among many suppositions, one of the most popular is that they were dark skinned Portuguese, mentioned above, who possibly intermarried early with Eastern Woodland Indians.

Still another possibility involves blacks and mulattos brought in early from South Africa. A regulation of 1760 passed in the Dutch Cape Colony (now western South Africa) required slaves moving between town and country to carry passes signed by their owners authorizing their travel. When the British obtained the Cape Colony from the Dutch in 1814, this pass system existed for both blacks and mixed bloods with darker features. Some of the slaves and mulatto immigrants of that era to North America were no doubt in possession of these passes issued by Dutch authorities, so it would have been natural for anyone seeing the documents to assume their blood mixture was "Black-Dutch."

In the Winter, 1997 issue of *Appalachian Quarterly* published by the Wise County, Virginia Historical Society, Darlene Wilson suggests that Black Dutch may have been only a polite euphemism used to cloak inter-unions among various light-dark races that were subjected to the hardened attitudes toward mixed ancestry people beginning in the early 1800s. I tend to agree. Many of the southern states passed harsh measures to control the lives of these so-called second class citizens or even banish them from white communities. Virginia was one of the most strict; ironically at a time when two of her favorite sons, Thomas Jefferson and Patrick Henry, were actually suggesting marriage between natives and colonists. Henry even presented a plan to the Virginia General Assembly to give a cow and fifty acres of land to any white who married an Indian!

Obviously, there are many conflicting opinions about who the Black Dutch really were or where the term started, but it is evident that people of many mixtures have used the phrase loosely throughout various periods to hide their true ethnic origins and for a variety of reasons. Native Americans fleeing U. S. Government removal efforts likely made it work in their favor, at least to some degree, when they assimilated into less-prejudiced white communities.

If your oral family traditions include strong inferences to Black Dutch, consider it a cue to concentrate your search more in white records than Indian records and hope to find hints of Indian blood therein. In years of research by my family members, none have ever seen the term "Black Dutch" recorded in any official Government Indian document. If you should discover one, please let us know.

The Tammany Society Myth

Almost every month, I receive communications from people in various parts of the country who are positive their ancestors were Indian, usually Cherokee, because they have discovered old family certificates which plainly show their relative was a *"red man."* Their name is shown with an Indian title such as *"Chief"* and the documents make references to their *"reservation, wigwam number and hunting grounds."*

Unfortunately, the exact opposite is usually true, as these papers indicate membership in an old patriotic/political organization known as the Tammany Society. It was also referred to as the Columbian Order or Tammany Hall. Tammany was founded in New York City in 1789 by William Mooney, a former Revolutionary War soldier and prominent anti-Federalist. It was originally a nationwide group with widespread interest among those devoted to preserving democratic institutions and opposing the aristocratic theories of Alexander Hamilton, James Madison and George Washington. In 1798 under control of Aaron Burr, the society helped elect Thomas Jefferson as president, Its national character was short-lived, although remnants of the Society continued mostly in the New York city municipal arena as late as 1961.

The misconceptions occur because Tammany was named after a 17th century Delaware Indian chief known for his wisdom. The society was originally organized into 13 "tribes," one in each of the 13 states and its officers were accorded American Indian titles such as *sachem and sagamore*. Individual members were called *red men;* their state of residence *reservations,* and town or locality *hunting grounds*. Meeting places were referred to as *wigwams,* and all of the paperwork relating to membership included Indian terms and designs with a look of American Indian officialdom.

Lending even more to the certainty that this organization actually had nothing whatever to do with Indians except borrowed symbolism is the fact that, in 1836, Martin Van Buren was the "grand sachem" of Tammany when he was elected president of the United States succeeding Andrew Jackson. Van Buren was a staunch supporter of Jackson whose record as anti-Indian is well chronicled.

GREAT COUNCIL OF THE UNITED STATES.

No. 7

SUSPENSION CARD

Wigwam of Ocone Tribe, No 46

Hunting Grounds of La Follette Reservation of Tenn

THIS CERTIFIES THAT [redacted] is a Red Man: (NAME IN FULL)
that he became a member of this Tribe on the 21 Sun, Plant Moon, G.S.D. 423
by adoption (ADOPTION OR BY CARD), that he is a member of the Chief (INSERT HIGHEST RANK ATTAINED) Degree; and that he was suspended from this Tribe for non-payment of dues on the 6 Sun, Buck Moon, G.S.D. 424

THIS SUSPENSION CARD has been issued by this Tribe to preserve his identity with the Order and is our invitation to him to apply for reinstatement.

This brother may make application for reinstatement in the Order to any Tribe, by presenting this Card, with the form of application on the reverse side hereof properly filled out, accompanied by the reinstatement fee of *5 fathoms and in addition thereto the fee required for the deposit of a Dismissal Certificate in the Tribe to which he makes application.

In Witness Whereof we have hereunto affixed our signatures and the seal of our Tribe this 6 Sun, Buck Moon, G.S.D. 424

(Seal)

J. a. Carr
SACHEM

Harry Conn
CHIEF OF RECORDS

*The sum to be inserted is the reinstatement fee of Tribe issuing the Card, which sum shall not exceed the amount of one Great Sun's dues.

Suspension Card from the Tammany Society issued because a member's dues were not up to date. (Member name has been deleted).

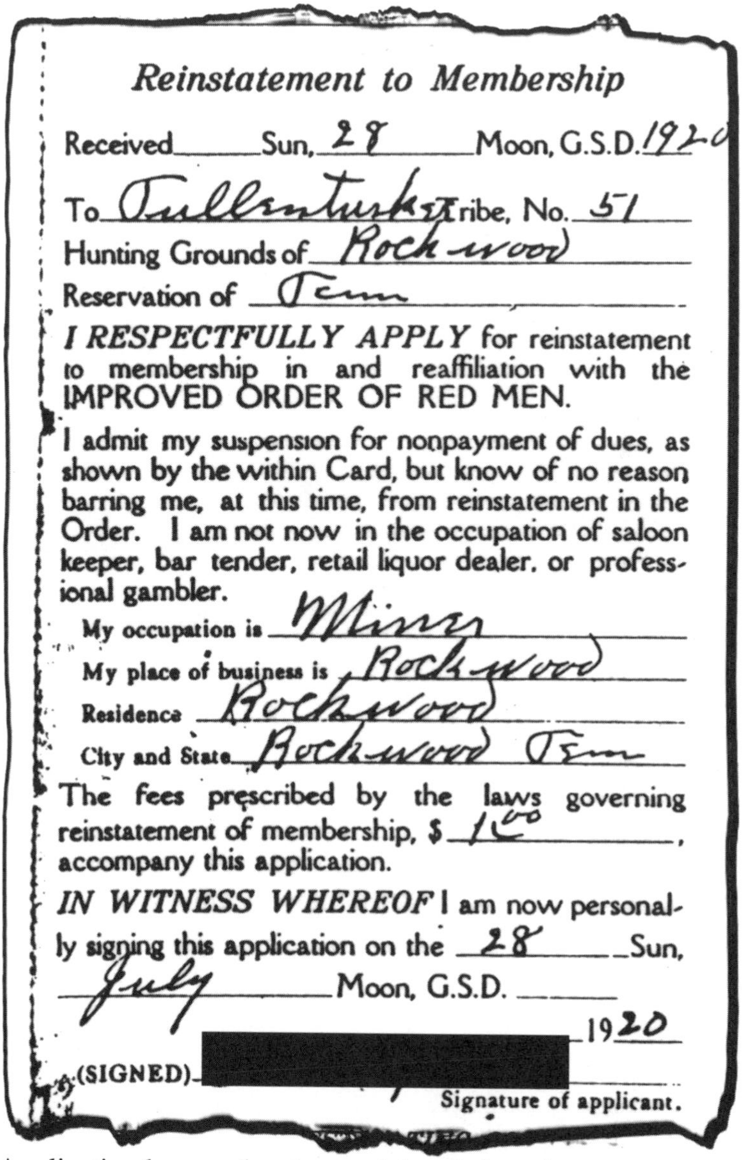

Reinstatement to Membership

Received______Sun, 28 ______Moon, G.S.D. 1920

To Tullentusk Tribe, No. 51

Hunting Grounds of Rockwood

Reservation of Tenn

I RESPECTFULLY APPLY for reinstatement to membership in and reaffiliation with the IMPROVED ORDER OF RED MEN.

I admit my suspension for nonpayment of dues, as shown by the within Card, but know of no reason barring me, at this time, from reinstatement in the Order. I am not now in the occupation of saloon keeper, bar tender, retail liquor dealer, or professional gambler.

My occupation is Miner

My place of business is Rockwood

Residence Rockwood

City and State Rockwood Tenn

The fees prescribed by the laws governing reinstatement of membership, $ 1.00, accompany this application.

IN WITNESS WHEREOF I am now personally signing this application on the 28 Sun, July Moon, G.S.D. 1920

(SIGNED) [redacted]

Signature of applicant.

Application by member (name deleted) for reinstatement to "Improved Order of Red Men," also known as the Tammany Society or Tammany Hall.

Research Notes for Adopted Cherokees

For persons of Cherokee descent who know they are adopted, tracing biological family roots can sometimes be quite a challenge. Legally, birth records are usually sealed until the adoptee is eighteen years of age. After that, in most states, adoptees have legal access to biological family records.

It is always best to try to discuss adoption particulars with adoptive parents first. Attempt to get any information available about tribal affiliation of birth parents and/or their other relatives and the state or region in which you were born. If this information is not available or difficult to obtain, it's a good idea to sign up on adoption registers and not just those associated with Native Americans. Here are some suggestions:

American Indian Adoption Resources Exchange
Council of Three Rivers American Indian Center
200 Charles St.
Pittsburgh, PA 15238
Phone 412-782-4457

Adopted and Searching Adoptee
Birth Parent Reunion Registry
401 E.74th St.
New York, NY 10021
Phone 212-988-0110

Adoptees and Birth Parents in Search
P.O. Box 5551
West Columbia, SC 29171
Phone 803-796-4508

Adoptees Together
Route 1, Box 30-B-5, Climax, N.C. 27233

National Adoption Information Clearinghouse
11426 Rockville Pike
Rockville, MD 20852

I highly recommend the following two texts which go to the heart of the adoption issue and offer helpful information for Native American adoptees in particular:

Kingsolver, Barbara. ***Pigs in Heaven.*** New York: Harper-Collins, 1989. (This loving book deals with the complexities involved between a mother and her adopted Cherokee daughter and their experiences with the Cherokee Nation of Oklahoma).

Nash, Renea D. ***Coping as a Biracial/Biethnic Teen.*** New York: Rosen Publishing Group, 1995. (Examines some of the dilemmas and special issues involved for teenagers of mixed blood who are attempting to develop their ethnic identity).

In some cases, you can find a living relative by requesting a copy of his or her social security application. This is considered classified information, but the administration can decide whether or not they think release of the information is warranted. Request and complete form SSA-L997. **Social Security Administration, Office of Central Records Operations, Baltimore, MD 21201.**

Over the years I have had a number of friends who were adopted with no idea of who their birth parents are. Naturally, this is a sensitive issue and it is quite normal to be curious about it. Patience and persistence will often pay off, however, so whatever you do, don't ever give up! My good friend, Meg Scraper Howland (Walks Alone) of Oceanside, California has spent years searching for her biological roots. She still hasn't discovered who her birth parents were, but through painstaking work, she has recently gained enrollment in the Cherokee Nation of Oklahoma. Bravo to this very special lady and cherished Cherokee sister!

Pre-Colonial and Colonial Era Intermarriages

by Brent Cox (Yanusdi), M.A.

As you have already seen, there are several approaches to tracing Cherokee ancestry. This section focuses primarily on precolonial/colonial era intermarriages between Cherokees and British or French. Most references only offer information on Cherokees of the 19th and 20th centuries. While this is important, the majority of us descend from intermarriages that occurred in the 18th century. Thus, many of these kinships came from British or French traders intermarrying with Cherokees.

Through 1776, South Carolina controlled the Cherokee trade, and most of our mixed ancestors were connected to this region. Virginia also supplied a few traders to the Cherokees, and Georgia and North Carolina still fewer. Thus, to locate your ancestors, whether from Georgia, North Carolina, South Carolina, or Virginia, most records of note are related to the South Carolina Indian trade. To begin your search for this era before "rolls" existed, I recommend that you do a surname survey in:

William L. McDowell, Jr. ed. The Colonial Records of South Carolina: Documents relating to Indian Affairs.2 Vols. Columbia: South Carolina Department of Archives and History, 1992. This set, including one other volume, can be purchased from: South Carolina Dept. of Archives & History, P.O. Box 11669, 1430 Senate St., Columbia, S.C. 29211, Phone: 803-734-8590.

If you intend to do a thorough study of your ancestors who may have intermarried with the Cherokees, this 3 volume set is indispensable. It is the most thorough record of British/Cherokee trade available. Now, here are some other important tips to keep in mind:

1. Always be aware that spellings of names are not always the same

in historical records.

a. English/French surnames vary according to region. EX: Bryant, Briant, Brian, de Bruyant.

b. All Cherokee names are phonetic spellings of either French or British pronunciation. EX: Chota (the Cherokee capitol), French=Sautee, English=Chota, Cherokee= It-sati (Eet-saw-tee). Personal names also vary according to dialect or region.

c. The Cherokees had three dialects, and names vary accordingly. EX: YellowBird (a common name), Lower dialect=Cheesquatarone, Upper dialect=Cheesquatalone.

2. Do not assume the origin of your Cherokee blood, nor the degree of blood contained. Family tradition tells us that all our grandmothers were full blood Cherokees, yet by 1900, there were very few full blood Cherokees in existence.

a. The surname you started with may lead you to another surname. More than likely, your search will end with a significant trader.

b. Do not assume anything, but be prepared to find conflicting information.

3. Search the regions around the Cherokee nation, and be aware of the fluctuating borders of both the Cherokees and the frontier.

a. There were four settlement groups in the Cherokee Nation. OVERHILLS- East Tennessee on the Little Tennessee River. VALLEY- Lower east Tennessee, southwestern North Carolina, and north Georgia. LOWER- western South Carolina, and northeastern Georgia. MIDDLE- western North Carolina.

b. All regions around these areas are possible locations to find your ancestor. The Cherokee people were mobile, and moved from place to place within/without the Cherokee Nation.

c. Check all colonial, state and local histories, frontier histories, Indian trade records. Here are some suggestions:

Colonial Records to Search:

Allan D. Chandler, ed. THE COLONIAL RECORDS OF THE STATE OF GEORGIA, Atlanta: Charles P. Boyd Printer, 1914.

Walter Clark, ed. THE STATE RECORDS OF NORTH CAROLINA, New York: AMS Press, 1968.

Kenneth G. Davies, ed. DOCUMENTS OF THE AMERICAN REVOLUTION, 1770-1783, Dublin: Irish University Press, 1976.

Wilmer L. Hall, ed. EXECUTIVE JOURNALS OF THE COUNCIL OF COLONIAL VIRGINIA, Richmond: Commonwealth of Virginia, 1945.

William P. Palmer, ed. VIRGINIA STATE PAPERS AND OTHER MANUSCRIPTS, 1652- 1781, New York: Kraus Reprint Co. 1968.

William L. Saunders, ed. THE COLONIAL RECORDS OF NORTH CAROLINA, New York: AMS Press, 1968.

David Ramsey, THE HISTORY OF SOUTH CAROLINA, Charleston: David Longworth, 1809.

For Western North Carolina

John Preston Arthur, A HISTORY OF WATAUGA COUNTY, NORTH CAROLINA, Johnson City: The Overmountain Press, 1992.

For Southwestern Virginia

Lewis Preston Summers, HISTORY OF WASHINGTON COUNTY, VIRGINIA, Johnson City: The Overmountain Press, 1989.

For North Georgia

Don L. Shadburn, UNHALLOWED INTRUSION: A HISTORY OF CHEROKEE FAMILIES IN FORSYTH COUNTY, GA. Cumming, GA.: Don Shadburn, P.O. Box 762, Cumming, Ga. 30130.

For Tennessee

There are several suggestions for this region that also give information on the frontiers and much of early Tennessee:

John Haywood, THE CIVIL AND POLITICAL HISTORY OF TENNESSEE, Knoxville: The Tenase Company, 1969.

J.G.M. Ramsey, THE ANNALS OF TENNESSEE, Knoxville: East Tennessee Historical Society, 1967.

Albigence Waldo Putnam, THE HISTORY OF MIDDLE TENNESSEE: OR LIFE AND TIMES OF GENERAL JAMES ROBERTSON, New York: Arno Press, 1971.

Samuel Cole Williams, EARLY TRAVELS IN THE TENNESSEE COUNTRY, Johnson City: The Watauga Press, 1928.

________. WILLIAM TATHAM: WATAUGAN, Johnson City: The Watauga Press, 1947.

________. DAWN OF TENNESSEE VALLEY AND TENNESSEE HISTORY, Johnson City: The Watauga Press, 1937.

________. HISTORY OF THE LOST STATE OF FRANKLIN, Johnson City: The Overmountain Press, 1993.

________. TENNESSEE DURING THE AMERICAN

REVOLUTIONARY WAR, Knoxville: Univ. of Tenn. Press, 1974.

4. Do not restrict your search, but record anything you find on your surname. Your ancestor may be using both an Indian name and an English/French name. Indian names are often evocative of nature or personality traits.

5. The Cherokee clans were based on a matrilineal system (traced thru the mother's line).
   a. In the 1750s, this system began to change due to intermarriage with European Americans.
   b. While Cherokees kept traditional matrilineal oral records, mixed Cherokees often used both patrilineal and matrilineal notations.
   c. Many Cherokee traders also had two families: a Cherokee family, and another located in South Carolina or Virginia.

6. Do not stop searching because your ancestor disappears off the records - there were no written records within the Cherokee Nation during this period.
   a. You must rely on European-American records to locate your ancestor.
   b. Do not always accept everything at face value, and be totally objective.
   c. When your ancestor (surnames) can not be found on traditional records, this is usually a good sign that they may be found within the Cherokee Nation.
   d. Remember that most Upper Creek traders had Cherokee wives.

7. When you ask your older relatives and those connected to the suspected line where they think your Cherokee ancestry came from, recognize that anything they tell you may help, even if it appears as simple trivia. Remember that you were the one chosen to carry this lineage forward and it is your duty to do so. Make genealogi-

cal connections and queries to get help from others. Try to enlist the help of all your relatives with the same surname.

8. Understand Cherokee traditions and attempt to recognize traits that exist in your current family. Your ancestors want to be remembered, so let them assist you in your work. Be aware of dreams and visions that might guide you. This may sound ridiculous, but believe me, within the Cherokee culture, it is a fact that is well known and respected. Even animals may offer clues to lead you to your kin.

Let your heart lead you as well. Native American people traditionally have "feelings" that lead us to where we want to go. Others often do not understand this phenomenon, but it is true, nonetheless. Above all, be aware that you must depend on more than traditional genealogical methods to reach the destination you seek. Cherokee genealogy, as well as all Native genealogy, is not traditional.

9. Search all abstracts, journals, and memoirs available on Cherokee families. Read the JOURNAL OF CHEROKEE STUDIES, 16 volumes available at some libraries or for sale by CHEROKEE PUBLICATIONS, Cherokee, North Carolina. This series contains many genealogical abstracts and articles about prominent Cherokees that you will not see elsewhere. Because it was advantageous for early traders to marry prominent Cherokees, most did so, so be aware that you could be kin to any of the prominent chieftains (head men). Also, be aware that one Cherokee may possess many titles or names i.e., Ostenaco can be found as Mankiller, Ootacite, Tacite, or Outacite. All four of these terms are the same word.

10. Every text that you search includes a bibliography. Make sure to search the bibliographies for other sources that might help you. Granted, this can be very time consuming, but I urge you to search every available text.

DEPOSITION OF JOHN BRYANT

[37] May 4, 1751

Memorandom [*sic*]

That John Byant personally came before me and made Oath (being duely sworn) that he was in Timossy, a lower Town of the Cherokee Nation, when he was informed of Mr. Maxwell's making his Escape from Kewoche, with several white Men in his Company. Considerably before Day, he says he was credibly informed of the Affair as follows, viz.: Mr. Beamer sent one of his Men to Hioree for Corn, who going to Kewoche aforesaid was stop't by an Indian Fellow of that Town who, when he knew where the said white Man was going, told him not to proceed, for there was four white Men killed, naming them to the said white Man, viz., Daniel Murphey, Barnard Hughs, Charles G____ and Thomas Langley, and further told him that Mr. Maxwell was gone off before Day with several white Men in his Company, and that there was no white Man left where he was going. The said Indian Fellow kept the said white Man at Kewoche that Night, and sent him off the next Morning, telling him to go whome [*sic*] and tell the white People not to stir for they should not be hurt. The Day following, the head Men of three Towns, viz., Tymossey, Chewee and Ustostee, had a Meeting and proposed the Day following to have another, intending to have Mr. Beamer to hear their Talks, and also to write to the beloved Men (as they said) Below. But the Night proceeding, Mr. Beamer came to Tymossey, wherein was this John Byant aforesaid and three more white Men. Mr. Beamer, as he went by, sent in Jas. Baldridge about an Hour before Day, warning thim to make what Haste he could and follow him. Mr. Beamer, being known to be [thoroughly] acquainted with Indian Affairs, and Humours, put them to a great Surprize and caused them forthwith to hurry off, as fast as possible.

Further the said John Bryant saith not.

Sworn this 4th Day of May, 1751 before me.

JAS. FRANCIS

Old Colonial Records like this excerpt from the South Carolina Indian Affairs Documents (1750-52) can offer clues to your ancestor's occupation, movements and location.

To Find Other Groups Among the Cherokee:

Prevost, Toni Jollay. The Delaware & Shawnee Admitted to Cherokee Citizenship and the Related Wyandotte & Moravian Delaware. Bowie, MD (1540-E Pointer Ridge Place, 20716): Heritage Books, 1993. ISBN 1556137613. [130] p. Not indexed.

Stevenson, Noel C. Genealogical Evidence: A Guide to the Standard of Proof Relating to Pedigrees, Ancestry, Heirship, and Family History. Rev. ed. Laguna Hills, CA (P.O. Box 2837, 92654): Aegean Park Press, 1989. ISBN 089412160X; 0894121596 (pbk.). [239] p. Indexed.

Walton-Raji, Angela Y. Black Indian Genealogy Research : African American Ancestors Among the Five Civilized Tribes. Bowie, MD (1540-E Pointer Ridge Place, 20716): Heritage Books, Inc., 1993. ISBN 1556138563.

Eakle, Arlene; and Cerny, Johni. The Source: A Guidebook of American Genealogy. Salt Lake City, UT: Ancestry Publishing Co., 1984. LC 84-70206; ISBN 0916489000. 786 p. Indexed.

Also see Delaware and Shawnee -Cherokee microfilm listings in Appendix One.

DID YOU KNOW?

In the 1820s the Cherokees passed two laws for the crime of rape. Because this was a crime unknown in Cherokee history, it was presumed necessary to protect Cherokee women from white men living in or passing through their nation.

Read, Read, Read and Follow the Clues!

Finding your ancestor's name on a federal roll can be elating, but don't stop there. Be sure to check for other documents that may be available in the National Archives and elsewhere. For some people, there is a multitude of documents to be found, for others, nothing.

The importance of reading everything you can get your hands on regarding Cherokee history cannot be over emphasized. This research can take you many places and more deeply into your own unique origins. Equally important, when you are least expecting it, a new clue can leap from the pages, begging for further investigation. I've had this happen many times and often the payoff was very rewarding.

Written records on my Cherokee Grandmother Lucy Bryant are very meager, but that is not necessarily true with everyone's ancestors. To illustrate just a few examples of what you can find and the importance of letting one clue lead you to another, let's use one of the other reservee's names on the same 1817 Reservation Roll that my grandmother's name appears on. Three names below Lucy Bryant's you will notice the name "Bryant Ward."

The roll itself establishes that in 1817, this individual lived on a 640-acre reserve in Georgia designated as "Chatahouchee." To attempt to find out more about this individual, what would be the next step?

My recommendation is to begin by checking for his name in the index of Emmett Starr's "History of the Cherokee Indians." This book is one of the primary resources to use for tracing Cherokee ancestry, but don't expect all surnames to be in it. The index shows no Bryant Ward, but it does show several pages containing information on a name spelled Bryan Ward (no "t" on Bryant). A review of these quickly indicates that all are relatives, but one of them, listed on Starr's page 382, is definitely the subject of our search.

It shows "Bryan" Ward as the son of one John Ward and Catherine McDaniel and brother to James, George, Samuel Charles, Elizabeth, Susie, and Nannie Ward; also that his wife's name was Temperance Stansel. Looking back at our roll on page 20, you will note the names of all his brothers listed in the section near his name and that of my grandmothers: James, George, Samuel, and Charles. The Star book indicates that Bryant's sister Susie married a William England, and sister Elizabeth married Elijah Sutton. These names also appear on other pages of that same reservation roll all but his sister Nannie are accounted for. The name listed as "Caty Ward, a widow," listed immediately above my grandmother's name, is Bryant Ward's mother as confirmed by Starr's book. Under close scrutiny, (not visible in our printed example) it can be seen that the black area in the column to the far right of the role page on the same line as Caty Ward contains a barely visible entry, "Proxy of William England." This, of course, would be her son-in-law, married to Susie.

What else is to be learned here about Bryant (Bryan) Ward from Starr's History? For one thing, it reveals that he fathered at least five children who reached adulthood, because it includes their names and the names of their spouses. Page 468 explains that his mother Catherine (Caty) was of 1/2 Cherokee blood and that she had married John Ward, the son of a white, English trader named Bryan Ward whose first wife had died (Ward's second wife was Nancy Ward, a full blood of the Wolf Clan also known as the Ghi-ga-u or famous Beloved Woman of the Cherokee).

A search of records in the Tennessee State Archives turns up a small booklet entitled "*Springplace: Moravian Mission and The Ward Family Of the Cherokee Nation by Muriel H. Wright*." There, we learn that the mother of our Bryant Ward, Caty McDaniel Ward, was the daughter of a Scottish trader named McDaniel and his full-blood Cherokee wife named "Granny Hopper," thus we can deduce that Bryant Ward is 1/4 Cherokee.

So, what happened to Bryant Ward after 1817? Did he remain on the Chattahoochee until the time of the Removal and suffer the

Trail of Tears? The Cherokee Emigration rolls of 1817-1835 were the next census rolls to be recorded, so to determine his movements, we should check that roll. Sure enough, it contains an entry as roll number 175 and reveals that on March 13, 1832, Bryant Ward of "Little River," Georgia enrolled himself and 6 family members for emigration to the Arkansas Country. A section of the same roll which includes a list of Cherokees who did actually emigrate west of the Mississippi shows that a total of 6 family members, including one male under 50 years of age, one under 25 and one under 10, plus one female under 50 and 2 under 10 arrived in the west on May 16, 1834. They had been removed "in wagons and steamboats by Lt. J.W. Harris" of the U.S. Army. Now we have a second name (Harris) that we'll want to keep an eye out for as we read.

A quick scan of surnames within the indexes of several texts dealing with the Removal turns up listings for both Lt. J.W. Harris and Bryant Ward. One very well known book is "Indian Removal" by noted author Grant Foreman, and we'll use it here to illustrate, because it not only includes interesting genealogical data about Bryant Ward, but it also offers other important references where we can go to learn more about the Removal period.

Most people associate the grief and pathos associated with the Removal of the Five Civilized Tribes to the West with only the *forced* removal period culminating in the Trail of Tears, itself, which occurred in 1838-39. But history records it differently. The cruel and unnecessary suffering of the emigrants extended well before then to when many Cherokees were voluntarily removing their families to the West. The moral responsibility for the lives and comfort of the men, women and children who were the helpless objects of their racially motivated decrees was of no importance whatsoever to a totally insensitive U.S. President, Congress and Administration.

Consider the words of Lt. Harris, a new West Point graduate of the class of1825, recorded in a journal he kept during the trip west when he was assigned to escort a number of Cherokee families (including Bryant Ward's) who were voluntarily emigrating:

"My blood chills even as I write, at the remembrance of the scenes I have gone through today. In the cluster of cedars upon the bluff which looks down upon the Creek and river, and near a few tall chimneys- the wreck of a once comfortable tenement, the destroyer had been most busily at work. Three large families of the poor class are there encamped, and I have passed much of the day with them, and have devoted the larger portion of my cares to their sufferers- but in vain were my efforts; the hand of death was upon them. At one time I saw stretched around me and within a few feet of each other, eight of these afflicted creatures dead or dying. Yet no loud lamentations went up from the bereaved ones here. They were of the true Indian blood; they looked upon the departed ones with a manly sorrow and silently digged graves for their dead and as quietly they laid them out in their narrow beds . . . There is a dignity in their grief which is sublime; and which, poor and destitute, ignorant and unbefriended as they were, made me respect them.

The dead on the sixteenth were "Alex M'Toy, D. Ross child, Bolingers ditto, Richardson's wife, T. Wilson's child, **William England,** *Brewer's child, one of Wm Vann's and three Black Foxes children; all of whom with the exception of Alex M'Toy have been decently buried and his coffin will be in readiness in a few minutes."*

Seven more died on the seventeenth and the same number the next day. Nearly all those afflicted with cholera were either suffering, or just recovering, from measles. The unusual confinement on the boats and privations to which they were not accustomed debilitated a large number of adults, who particularly were revolted by the daily diet of only saltpork which they were not in the habit of eating. Articles of diet such as coffee and sugar that they were accustomed to use in their homes were denied them unless they had money with which to buy them.

Five died on the nineteenth. One of **Bryant Ward's children died May 1** *and another the next day. Bob Shelton's child died and was buried on the third."* [From an unpublished journal in the archives of the Office of Indian Affairs, dated May 9, 1834.]

The party in which Bryant Ward's family emigrated included 457 people. By the time Harris left his charges at Dwight Mission in

Indian Territories on May 16, 1834, there had been 81 deaths. Of these, 45 were children under ten years of age. Of the members in this party who reached their new "home" alive, nearly one-half died before the end of the year.

The knowledge that Bryant Ward emigrated to the west makes it likely that there will be other documents in spoilations claims, because these people were promised they would be paid for any "improvements" they lost as a result of leaving the east. A timely request to the National Archives brought back the following records that offer more insights into this Ward family and their journey west:

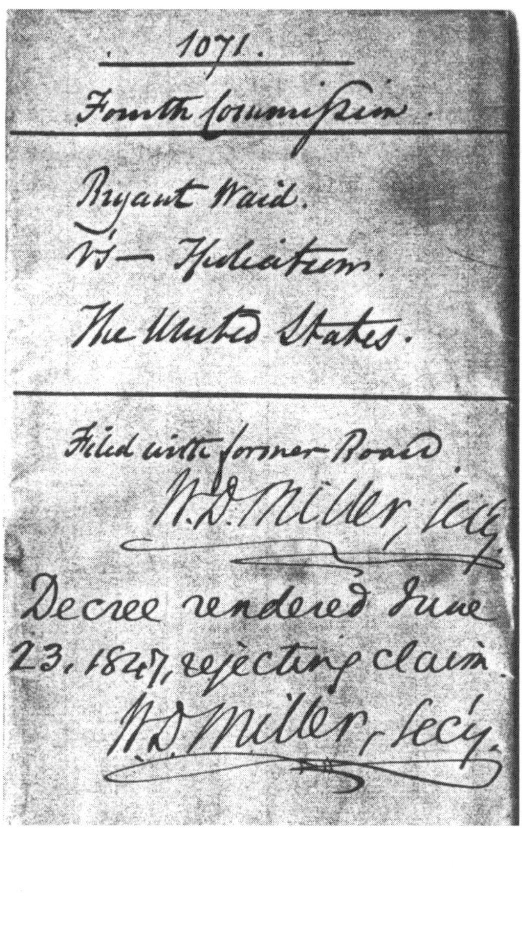
1071.
Fourth Commission.
Bryant Ward.
vs— [illegible]
The United States.
Filed with former Board.
W. D. Miller, Secy.
Decree rendered June 23, 1847, rejecting claim.
W. D. Miller, Secy.

I Bryant Ward, the within named Claimant appeared before the Commissioners and makes the following Statement.

That he is the head of a Cherokee family, Married in the Old Nation within the limits of Georgia in the year of 1818— I am a Native Cherokee and removed to this Country in the year of 1834, in a detachment under charge of Lieut Harris We were brought up the Arkansas river on the Steamboat Thomas Yateman— and ran aground at the mouth of the Cadron, some distance above Little Rock— The agent then put us on shore at that place— and furnished some teams to bring up the party of about 700 in number The wagons could not bring near all our things and they were left on the Shore— all the articles charged for in the within account were left by this Claimant and he never received them nor was paid for them afterwards The agent promised that the things should be brought up but it was never done.

I live on Grand river about one hundred miles above Fort Gibson, in the Cherokee Nation— Bryant Ward

Commissioners Office, Fort Gibson March 1st 1848
The above named Bryant Ward appeared before me and made the above Statement.

John T. Mason

Mrs Ruth McCoy, a Cherokee woman and Betsy Smith appeared before the Commissioners and testifies as follows.

That they emigrated to this Country from the Old Nation in the same party with Bryant Ward— The detachment was brought out under Charge of Lieut Harris and came up the Arkansas

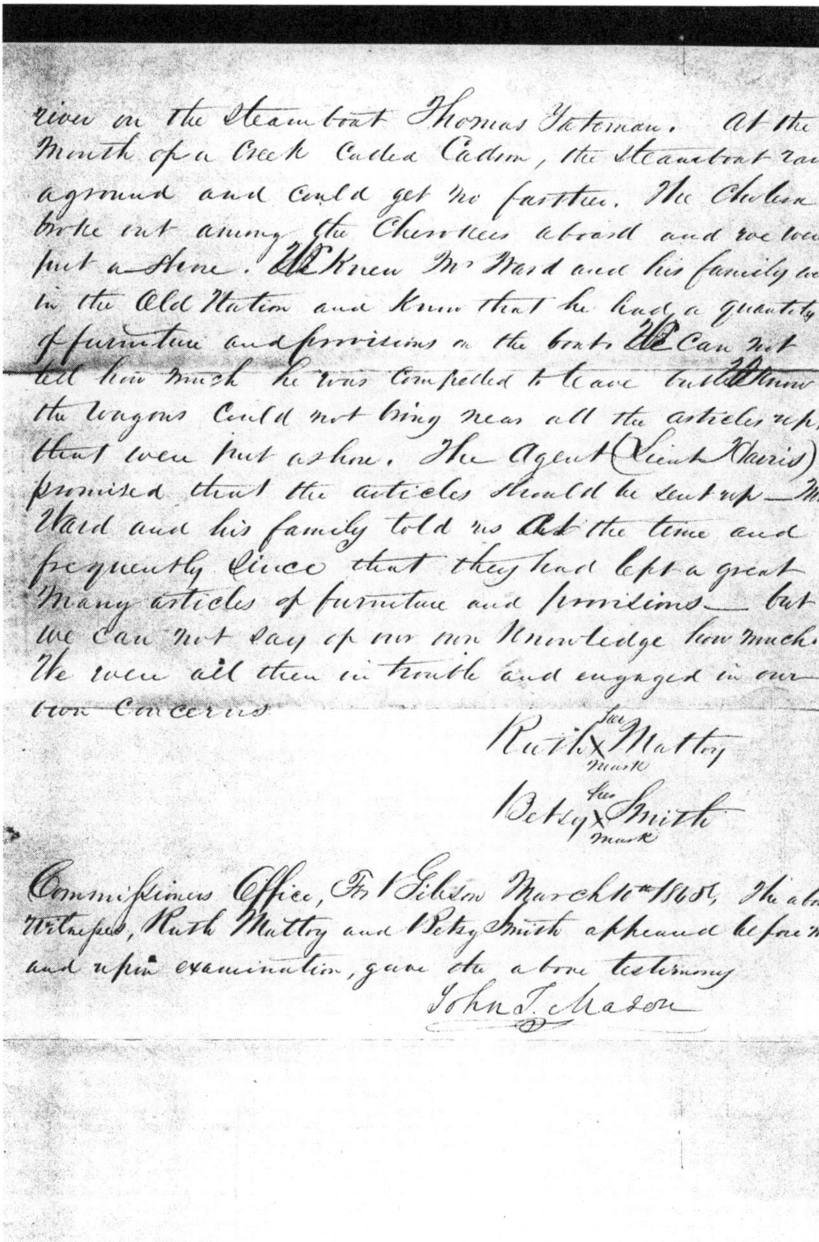

river on the Steamboat Thomas Yateman. At the
Mouth of a Creek Called Cadron, the Steamboat ran
aground and Could get no farther. The Cholera
broke out among the Cherokees aboard and we were
put a Shore. We Knew Mr Ward and his family well
in the Old Nation and Know that he had a quantity
of furniture and provisions on the boat. We Can not
tell how much he was Compelled to leave but we know
the wagons Could not bring near all the articles up,
that were put ashore. The Agent (Lieut Harris)
promised that the articles should be sent up — Mr
Ward and his family told us at the time and
frequently Since that they had left a great
Many articles of furniture and provisions — but
we Can not say of our own Knowledge how much.
We were all then in trouble and engaged in our
own Concerns

Ruth her X mark Mattoy

Betsy her X mark Smith

Commissioners Office, Fort Gibson March 10th 1845, The above
Witnesses, Ruth Mattoy and Betsy Smith appeared before me
and upon examination, gave the above testimony

John T. Mason

Ward Document continued from previous page.

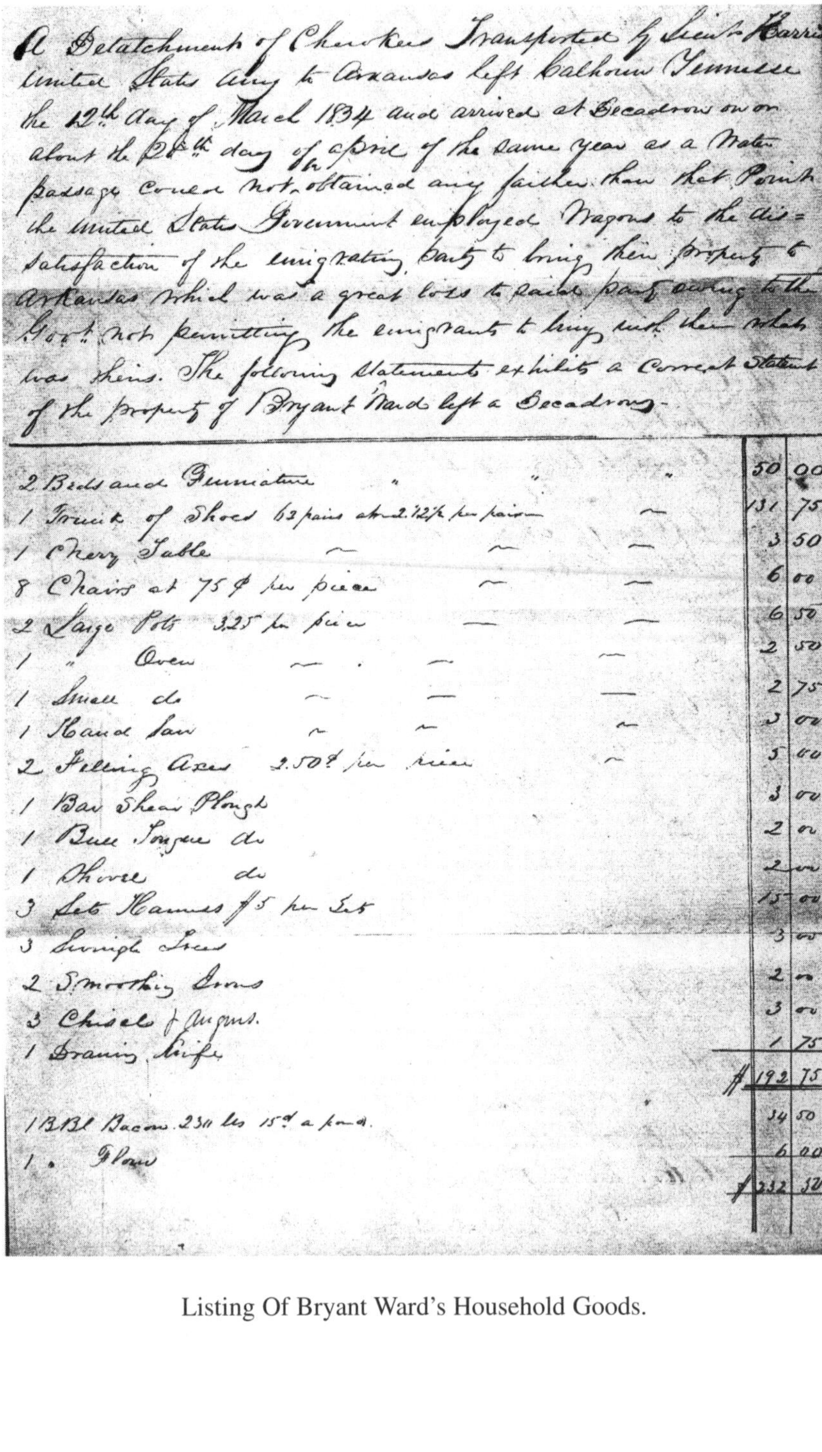

A Detatchment of Cherokee Transported by Lieut. Harris United States Army to Arkansas left Calhoun Tennessee the 12th day of March 1834 and arrived at Decadron on or about the 28th day of April of the same year as a Water passage could not obtained any farther than that Point the United States Government employed Wagons to the dis= satisfaction of the emigrating Party to bring their property to Arkansas which was a great loss to said party owing to the Govt. not permitting the emigrants to bring with them what was theirs. The following Statement exhibits a Correct Statement of the property of Bryant Ward left a Decadron-

2 Beds and Furniture	50	00
1 Trunk of Shoes 63 pairs at 2.12½ per pair	131	75
1 Cherry Table	3	50
8 Chairs at 75¢ per piece	6	00
2 Large Pots 3.25 per piece	6	50
1 " Oven	2	50
1 Small do	2	75
1 Hand Saw	3	00
2 Felling Axes 2.50¢ per piece	5	00
1 Bar Shear Plough	3	00
1 Bull Tongue do	2	00
1 Shovel do	2	00
3 Sets Harness $5 per Set	15	00
3 Single Trees	3	00
2 Smoothing Irons	2	00
3 Chisels & Augurs.	3	00
1 Drawing Knife	1	75
	$192	75
1 BBl Bacon 230 lbs 15¢ a pound.	34	50
1 . Flour	6	00
	$232	50

Listing Of Bryant Ward's Household Goods.

These records reflect that Bryant Ward appeared before the Commissioners and stated: "I am a Native Cherokee and removed to this country in the year of 1834, in a detachment under charge of Lieut. Harris. We were brought up the Arkansas River on the Steamboat Thomas Yeatman and ran aground at the mouth of the Cadron, some distance above Little Rock - The agent (referring to Lt. Harris) there put us on shore at that place- and furnished some teams to bring up the party of about 700 in number. The wagons could not bring near all our things and they were left on the shore - all the articles charged for in the written account were left by this claimant and he never received them nor was paid for them afterwards. The agent promised that the things should be brought up but it was never done. I live in Grand River about one hundred miles above Fort Gibson, in the Cherokee Nation."

/s/ Bryant Ward.

Commissions Office Fort Gibson, March 14, 1845

The above named Bryant Ward appeared before me and made the above statement.

/s/ John Tichason.

Attached to the statement is the government's decision -two years later in 1847- denying the claim! Also attached is an individual listing of household goods which apparently represents everything the family owned, showing a total value of $232.50 and the statements of two Cherokee women, Ruth Mattoy and Betsy Smith testifying in Ward's behalf.

There are numerous other documents to be had which pertain to Mr. Ward such as a will filed in Franklin County Georgia in 1815 before he removed west and records of his death, burial and later reburial due to the construction of a dam that would have inundated the graveyard, just to mention two. All of these records can provide additional clues to the history of his family and, equally important, other surnames.

Remember - one lead almost always leads to several others, and just how much you can find out about the family you are researching depends largely on how much time and effort you are willing to invest. If your relative does not appear on any Cherokee roll to give you a beginning foundation, plan on spending a lot of time reading the conventional books relating to Cherokee culture and history mentioned throughout this text and mulling over dusty old record books in secluded county courthouses. Fall back on conventional genealogy methods (the same as you would for non-Indian ancestors), roll up your sleeves and go to work.

Don't discount anything; land deeds, bills of sale, court actions, marital records, death records, and voter registrations sometimes contain information important to your search. Pay particular attention to any locally produced old family histories in your local library and church records in the area where your ancestor lived at any time. All repositories have some of these and they often contain information that you will never find anywhere else... great-great-great's maiden names, etc., and that ever-so-slight, never-again-recorded mention that they were of Indian blood!

IN REPLY REFER TO:
REAL PROP. MGMT.
Reports & Control

UNITED STATES
DEPARTMENT OF THE INTERIOR
BUREAU OF INDIAN AFFAIRS
MUSKOGEE AREA OFFICE
MUSKOGEE, OKLAHOMA 74401

MAY 27 1969

Mr. Paul Belew
P. O. Box 673
Woodward, Oklahoma 73801

Dear Mr. Belew:

It appears that Aaron Belew is the son of Mary, sometimes called Polly Bryant, a Cherokee woman by blood with whom Samuel Belew, the father of said Aaron Belew intermarried, the said Mary being a daughter of John Bryant who was a Cherokee Indian by blood as his brother-in-law, John Spencer, and James F. Randolph, who, in that year, came from Warren County, Middle Tennessee, to the Western District. They brought an ax, a hand-saw and an auger, with which tools they constructed the first house in the county on the Little North Fork of the Forked Deer River, about eight miles east of Trenton. Having done this, they retraced their steps to Warren County, and in the spring of the following year returned with their families. During the same year Luke Biggs located about four miles northwest of the present site of Trenton, —— Hughbanks (John Eubanks) settled at a point about six miles west of Dyer. At about the same time, probably in the spring of that year, Colonel David Crockett came from Lawrence County, Tennessee, and located a short distance northeast of Rutherford. In the fall, John Bergin, his brother-in-law, came and with him brought Crockett's family. L. K. Tinkle and H. McWhirter, also brothers-in-law of Colonel Crockett, came soon after, and settled in the same vicinity. Others who settled in the neighborhood of where Rutherford now is were Henry, Jacob, Humphrey and Bryant Flowers, and the Edmundsons: Robert, Allen, Michael and William. A settlement in the vicinity of Yorkville was begun very early by William Holmes, who located two miles south of that place. He was followed by the Reeds—Samuel, James, William, Robert, and Hugh—Benjamin Tyson, Benjamin S. White and John W. Needham. John B. Hogg and Thomas Gibson located on the present site of Trenton. David P. Hamilton, in 1822, began a settlement about two miles east of Humboldt. His early neighbors were Davidson Waddell, William P. Seat, George Gentry, W. G. B. Killingsworth and Alexander G. Hamilton. (In the early thirties Samuel Cole, Thomas Walker and brothers, and others moved from North Carolina into the same community. The village of South Gibson, established by Wm. P. Williams and carried forward by his brothers, Wilson and Thomas J., was the center of this neighborhood).[3] The first settler in the vicinity of Bradford was Richard Smith who, with others, subsequently joined the Mormons at Nauvoo, Ill. The settlement in the vicinity of Lynn Point was made by Robert Puckett, Hiram Partee, Samuel, William, Robert and James Baker, Peter Meyers, Dr. Joseph Dean, Joseph Dibrell, "Rutherford" David Crockett and "Little" David Crockett. The early settlers of Skullbone were William Goodman, William Stone, James Andrews, John Bryant and several sons, Patterson Crockett and John R. Tedford (Thedford?)."[4]

In 1821 when Carroll, Henderson and Madison Counties were established, there was an insufficient number of settlers to establish Gibson County. For this reason the future county was made a ward of Carroll

Partial Page from Gibson County, Past and Present (Indian Country and the Western Wilds) by Frederick Culp and Mrs. Robert Ross. This locally produced West Tennessee County History mentions the author's sixth generation great-grandfather John Bryant

Go-Back Christie and his son Amos, Cherokee chair makers at their saw mill, 1937. They gathered all their materials from neighboring woods.
Photo courtesy Archives and Manuscript Div., Oklahoma Historical Society.

Renovated Murrell Home just outside Tahlequah, Oklahoma, c.1844, was one of the few Cherokee homes not burned during the Civil War.

Recommended Texts for Researching Cherokee Indian Ancestry

The recommended texts listed herein include some Indian history references because they often mention Cherokees by name. If you plan to borrow materials through inter-library Loan, advise your librarian that some of these may be special collections materials available only at the University of Oklahoma Libraries and University of Tulsa Libraries. Many of these books are still in print and available for purchase. A list of Cherokee bookstores appears at the end of this chapter.

General Guides and Bibliography

Cherokee Roots / Bob Blankenship. 2nd ed. (Cherokee, NC : Author, 1992, 2 v.). Contents: v. 1. Eastern Cherokee rolls (includes 1817 Reservation Rolls, 1817-1835 Emigration Roll, 1835 Henderson Roll, 1848 Mullay Roll, 1851 Siler Roll, 1852 Chapman Roll, 1869 Swetland Roll, 1883 Hester Roll, 1908 Churchill Roll, 1909 Guion Miller East, 1924 Baker Roll, Enrollment procedures of Eastern Band v. 2. 1851 Old Settler Roll, 1852 Drennen Roll by family name, 1898-1914 combination Dawes and Guion Miller Rolls, Enrollment procedures of the Cherokee Nation.

Records of the Cherokee Indian Agency in Tennessee 1801-1835/Marybelle W. Chase (Tulsa, OK). Lists and Registers transcribed from National Archives BIA records).

The Cherokees: A Critical Bibliography. / Raymond D. Fogelson. (Bloomington, Published for the Newberry Library by Indiana University Press, 1978. Series: Bibliographical series (Newberry

Library. Center for the History of the American Indian).

The Five Civilized Tribes: a bibliography / Mary Huffman. (Oklahoma City, OK: Library Resources Division, Oklahoma Historical Society, 1991).

Guide to the Historical Records of Oklahoma / Bradford Koplowitz.(Bowie, M: Heritage Books, 1990).

Oklahoma history: a bibliography / Mary Huffman, Brian Basore.(Oklahoma City, OK: Library Resources Division, Oklahoma Historical Society, 1991).

Our Native Americans and Their Records of Genealogical Value / E. Kay Kirkham. (Logan, Utah: Everton Publishers, 1980-1984.LC 81-128028; 2 v.). Contents: v. 1. Federal Government records, Oklahoma Historical Society records, Genealogical Society of Utah listings v. 2. [without special title] [Using this book with the National Archives catalog on American Indians will provide citations for most major sources of records.

Recommended Genealogy Texts

American Indian Research/Dorothy Tincup Mauldin. (Order from author: 8745 E. 9th St., Tulsa, OK 74112-4185. Phone 918-835-4118).

Cherokee Planters in Georgia 1832-1838 Vol. 2/ Don L. Shadburn. (Cumming, GA: Author, rev. 1996, LC 89-51794)[Note: Available from author: P.O. Box 3121. Cumming, GA 30128].

Genealogy of "Old & New Cherokee Indian Families" / by George Morrison Bell, Sr. 1st ed. (Bartlesville, OK : Author, 1972, LC 78-189676).

History of the Cherokee Indians and Their Legends and Folk Lore

/Emmett Starr. (Oklahoma City, OK : The Warden Co, 1921; reprinted by: New York : Kraus, 1969).
Indian Blood Volumes I and II / by Richard Pangburn (Louisville, Ky: Butler Books 1996) ISBN 1-884532-05-5. These can be ordered directly from the author: 404 Greer Rd., Bardstown, Ky 40004.

Old Cherokee Families : Old Families and Their Genealogy, reprinted from History of the Cherokee Indians and their legends and folk lore / Emmet Starr ; with a comprehensive index compiled by J.J. Hill. (Norman, OK : University of Oklahoma Foundation, 1968. Emmet Starr's original edition was published in 1921).

Cherokee Connections: An Introduction to Genealogical Sources pertaining to Cherokee Ancestors/Myra Vanderpool Gormerly. (Tacoma, WA (207 S. 119th St., 98444): Family Historian Books, 1995. ISBN 1886952553. Phone 800-535-0118.

Cherokee Ancestry Resource Guide/ by Frankie Sue Gilliam.(Muskogee, OK:Twin Territories,1997). Order from Twin Territories Publishing and Fine Arts, P.O. Box 1426, Muskogee, OK 74402-1426. Phone 918-775-4814.

Exploring Your Cherokee Ancestors: A Basic Genealogical Research Guide/by Thomas Mooney (Cherokee Historical Society 1990). Order from the author at 440 State St., Tahlequah, OK 74464. Phone 918-456-2704.

Censuses, Rolls, Claims, Newspapers, Journals, and Indexes

1842 Cherokee claims: Saline District / Marybelle W. Chase. (Tulsa, OK: Author, 1988). [Note-see next listing].

1842 Cherokee claims: Tahlequah District / Marybelle W. Chase. (Tulsa,OK: Author 1989). [Researchers should note that the author has compiled booklets for several other districts. These were handwritten reports of claims filed by individuals for loss of property not included in valuations before the removal. Most will show residence in the east before removal. Transcribed from originals in The Tennessee State Library, Nashville, TN].

1880 and 1890 census, Canadian District, Cherokee Nation, Indian Territory. / transcribed by Sharon Standifer Ashton. (Oklahoma City, OK: Oklahoma Genealogical Society, 1978. Series: Special publication (Oklahoma Genealogical Society), no. 5).

Cherokee Advocate [microform]. Vol. 1, no. 1 (Sept. 26, 1844) - (March 3, 1906). Tahlequah, Cherokee Nation, s.n. Weekly. In English and Cherokee (in Cherokee syllabary). Issued with: Cherokee messenger (Aug. 1844 - May 1846); Cherokee almanac (1840, 1847, 1855, 1860); Choctaw Baptist hymn book; Choctaw intelligencer (Oct. 15, 1851). Contents: Reel 1. May 1, 1845 - June 27, 1877 Reel 2. July 4, 1877-June 29, 1883 Reel 3. July 6, 1883 - Dec. 21, 1901 Reel 4. Jan. 4, 1902 - March 3, 1906. Suspended publication Sept. 28, 1853- April 22, 1870; Jan. 1875 - March 4, 1876. Microform. Oklahoma City, Oklahoma State Historical Society. 4 microfilm reels; 35 mm).

Cherokee Emigration Rolls, 1817-1835. / transcribed by Jack D.Baker. (Oklahoma City, OK : Baker Pub. Co., 1977).

Cherokee Nation 1890 census: index of persons living under permit in the Cooweescoowee and Delaware Districts / Rosalie Wagner.(Vinita, OK: Northeastern Oklahoma Genealogical Society, 1986).

Cherokee Nation Births and Deaths, 1884-1901: abstracted from Indian Chieftain and Daily Chieftain newspapers / by Dixie Bogle (Vinita, OK: Northeast Oklahoma Genealogical Society, 1980).

Cherokee Nation Marriages, 1884-1901: abstracted from Indian

Chieftain and Daily Chieftain newspapers / by Dixie Bogle and Dorothy Nix. (Vinita, OK : Abraham Coryell Chapter NSDAR, [1980]).

Our People and Where They Rest / James and Maxine Tyner and Alice Timmons/12 Volumes (vol 1-8, Norman, OK: American Indian Institute; vol 9-12, Muskogee, OK: Chigau Press), 1968-1985. [Note: These are guides to cemeteries in Indian Territories of N.E. Oklahoma showing locations of graves by name, birth and death dates].

Cherokee Reservees / David Keith Hampton. (Oklahoma City, OK: Baker Pub. Co., 1979).

Genealogical Data extracted from "Muskogee Weekly Phoenix" Indian Territory / compiled by Sheri Siebold. (Muskogee, OK: Muskogee County Genealogical Society, 1985). Contents: v.1. 1888-1892.

Index to Marriages, First United States Court Northern District, Muskogee, Indian Territory, 1890-1907. (Oklahoma City, OK Oklahoma Genealogical Society, 1980, Series: Special publication (Oklahoma Genealogical Society) no. 6; LC 83-150507). v. 1. Marriage Books A, B, B-1, C (5 Jul 1890 - 19 Sep 1894) with abstracts of some marriages and divorces from inventory of Creek and Cherokee National Records, 1869-1894.

Index to Payment Roll for Old Settler Cherokee, 1896 / transcribed by Marybelle W. Chase. (Tulsa, OK: Author, 1989).

Cherokee Old Settler Annuity Roll 1851 /transcribed by Marybelle W. Chase from National Archives records regarding 1896 payment of Old Settlers. (Tulsa, OK: Author, 1989).

Index to The Cherokee Advocate. (Little Rock, AR : American Native Press Archives, University of Arkansas at Little Rock,

1987); books in files (2nd-3rd ser.). Contents: 2nd series (1870-1875) 3rd series v. 1-3 (1 Mar 1876 - 26 Mar 1879).

The Intruders: The Illegal Residents of the Cherokee Nation, 1866-1907 / Nancy Hope Sober. (Ponca City, OK: Cherokee Books, 1991. LC 90-84850).

Indians and Intruders/compiled by Sharon Standifer Ashton (Includes permits issued to non-citizens in the Cherokee Nation, 1874-1894). Order from the author: 3812 NW Sterling St, Norman, OK 73072-1240. Journal of Cherokee Studies.(Cherokee, N.C.: Museum of the Cherokee Indian. Quarterly).

Oklahoma Genealogical Society Quarterly. v.6, no.1 (Mar 1961)- (Oklahoma City, OK: Oklahoma Historical Society).

Southeastern Native American Exchange (S.E.N.A.) - (Mobile, AL: Jacqueline Hines, publisher. Quarterly. Address: P.O.Box 16124, Mobile, AL 36616-2424).

Talbot Library & Museum Genealogy Newsletter (Colcord, OK: Published by TL&M. Quarterly. Address: P.O. Box 349, Colcord, OK 74338-0349. Phone 918-326-4532).

The Cherokee Tracer. v. 1, no. 1 (Winter 1991)- (Tulsa, OK: Marybelle W. Chase, editor and publisher, 1991- Quarterly. Address: 5802 E. 22nd Pl, Tulsa,OK 74114).

The Chronicles of Oklahoma. 1 (Jan 1921)- (Oklahoma City, OK: Oklahoma Historical Society, Quarterly).

The Going Snake Messenger (Colcord, OK: Virgil Talbot, editor. Published by The Going Snake District Heritage Assn. Quarterly. Address: P. O. Box 349, Colcord, OK 74338-0349. Phone 918-326-4532).

Tulsa annuals. v. 1 (Sep 1966)- (Tulsa, OK : Tulsa Genealogical Society. Three times a year).

Twin Territories (Gore, OK: Frankie Sue Gilliam, publisher. Quarterly. Address: Rt. 2, Box 37-1, Gore, OK 74435. Phone 918-489-2217).

[Note: The nine periodicals listed immediately above provide an on-going supply of valuable family information for researchers. Some back issues are offered. I highly recommend you subscribe to them if at all possible].

Probate records... Northern District Cherokee Nation / Orpha Jewell Wever; indexed by Rosalie Wagner. (Vinita, OK: Northeast Oklahoma Genealogical Society, 1982-<1983>). Contents: v. 1. 1892-1904 v. 2. 1904-1908.

Those Who Cried, the 16,000, a record of the individual Cherokees listed in the United States official census of the Cherokee Nation conducted in 1835 / James W. Tyner. ([Norman, OK]: Chi-ga-u Inc., 1974).

History

[Note: These texts often contain family surnames not found on any official rolls]:

Advancing the Frontier, 1830-1860 / Grant Foreman. (Norman, OK: University of Oklahoma Press, 1933).

America's Exiles: Indian colonization in Oklahoma / Arrell Morgan Gibson. (Oklahoma City, OK: Oklahoma Historical Society, 1976. Series: The Oklahoma series, vol. III. LC 76-11417).

And Still the Waters Run / Angie Debo. (Princeton, NJ: Princeton University Press, 1940; reprint in 1984: Norman, OK: University of Oklahoma Press).

A History of the Indians of the United States / Angie Debo. [1st ed.]. (Norman, OK: University of Oklahoma Press, 1970. Series: Civilization of the American Indian series, v. 106. LC 73- 108802).

A Political History of the Cherokee Nation, 1838-1907 / Morris L. Wardell. 1st ed. (Norman, OK: University of Oklahoma Press, 1938. Series: Civilization of the American Indian series, v. 17).

Cherokee Beliefs & Practices of the Ancients: Out of the Flame/James Adair; edited and reprinted by Willena Robinson (Tulsa, OK: Cherokee Language & Culture, 1998). Order from: 4158 East 48th Place, Tulsa , OK 74135-4739.

Cherokee Cavaliers, forty years of Cherokee history as told in the correspondence of the Ridge-Watie-Boudinot family / Edward Everett Dale & Gaston Litton. 1st ed. (Norman, OK: University of Oklahoma Press, 1939). Series: Civilization of the American Indian series, v. 19).

Cherokee Nation of Indians / Charles C. Royce. (Chicago, IL Aldine Pub. Co., 1975. Series: Native American Library; A Smithsonian Institution Press Book. LC75-20708).

Cherokee Indian Removal from the Lower Hiwassee Valley/Robert C. White.(Cleveland, TN, 1973).

Cherokees of the Old South: A People in Transition/ Henry Thompson Malone. (Athens, GA: University of Georgia Press, 1956).

Cherokee Old Timers/James Manford Carselowey. (Tulsa, OK: Oklahoma Yesterday Publications, 1980).

Cherokee Removal, Before and After / William L. Anderson (Athens, GA: University of Georgia Press, 1991).

Cherokee Tragedy: The Ridge Family and the Decimation of a People / Thurman Wilkins. 2nd ed., rev. (Norman, OK: University of Oklahoma Press, 1986. Series: Civilization of the American Indian series, v. 169. LC 85-20260).

Cherokees: An Illustrated History / Billy M. Jones and Odie B. Faulk. (Muskogee, OK: The Five Civilized Tribes Museum, 1984).

Cherokee Footprints, Volume I, The Principal People "Ani-Yunwiya." /Charles O. Walker. The author.

Cherokee Footprints, Volume II, Home and Hearth/ Charles O. Walker. The author.

Cherokee Sunset: A Nation Betrayed/Samuel Carter III. (Doubleday, 1976).

Chief Bowles and the Texas Cherokees / Mary Whatley Clarke. 1st ed. (Norman, OK: University of Oklahoma Press, 1971. Series: Civilization of the American Indian series, v. 113).

Dawn of the Tennessee Valley and Tennessee History /Samuel C. Williams. (Johnson City, TN: Watauga Press, 1937).

Fire and the Spirit: Cherokee Law from Clan to Court/Rennard Strickland. (Norman, OK: University of Oklahoma Press, 1975).

Footsteps of the Cherokees: A Guide to the Eastern Homelands of the Cherokee Nation/Vicki Rozema.(Winston Salem, N.C. , 1998. John F. Blair, Publisher).

Hard times in Oklahoma: The Depression Years / Kenneth E. Hendrickson, Jr. (Oklahoma City, OK: Oklahoma Historical Society, 1983. Series: The Oklahoma Series. LC 83-060262).

Heart of the Eagle: Dragging Canoe and the Emergence of the Chickamauga Confederacy/by Brent Yanusdi Cox. (Chenanee

Publishers 1999). ISBN 0-9667177-0-8. Order from Chenanee, 2043 Algee Lane, Milan, TN 38358.

History of Hamilton County and Chattanooga/ Zella Armstrong. (Chattanooga: Lookout Mountain Publishing, 1931-40).

Indian Removal: The Emigration of the Five Civilized Tribes of Indians / Grant Foreman. (Norman, OK: University of Oklahoma Press, 1932. Series: Civilization of the American Indian Series, v.2).

Myths of the Cherokee and Sacred Formulas of the Cherokees /James Mooney. (Nashville, TN: Charles Elder, Bookseller, 1972. Reprint of 19th and 7th annual reports of Bureau of American Ethnology).

James G. Thompson: [This is a daybook and personal papers of trader who operated trading post on Arkansas River, 1832-1835]/Mary & Mavis Kelsey.(College Station, TX: Texas A & M University, Sterling Evans Library, 1988).

New Echota Letters / Jack Frederick Kilpatrick and Anna Gritts Kilpatrick. (Dallas, TX: Southern Methodist University Press, 1968. Selections from the newspaper Cherokee phoenix, 1828-33, including contributions of S. A. Worcester and the newspaper's editor, E. Boudinot).

Occupying the Cherokee Country of Oklahoma/ Leslie Hewes. (Lincoln, NE: University of Nebraska Press, 1978.).

Oklahoma Place Names / George H. Shirk. (Norman: University of Oklahoma Press, 1981).

Old Frontiers, The Story of the Cherokee Indians from Earliest Times to the Date of Their Removal to the West, 1838 / John P. Brown. (Kingsport, TN: Southern Publishers, 1938).

Passports of Southeastern Pioneers 1770-1823 / Dorothy Williams Potter. (Baltimore, Maryland: Gateway Press, 1982).

Red over Black, Black Slavery Among the Cherokee Indians / R. Halliburton, Jr. (Westport, CT: Greenwood Press, 1977. Series: Contributions in Afro-American and African studies, no. 27).

Red Clay and Rattlesnake Springs: A History of the Cherokee Indians of Bradley County, Tennessee / James F. Corn. (Cleveland, TN: Walsworth Publishing Co, reprinted 1984).

Sequoyah/ Grant Foreman. (Norman, OK: University of Oklahoma Press, 1938).

Sequoyah: The Cherokee Genius/ Stan Hoig.(OK City, OK: The Oklahoma Historical Society, 1995).

Starr Tracks: Belle and Pearl Starr/Phillip W. Steele. (Gretna, LA: Pelican Books, 1992).

Tennessee's Indian Peoples: From White Contact to Indian Removal, 1540-1840/Ronald N. Satz. (Knoxville, TN, 1979).

The Last Cherokee Warriors/Phillip W. Steele. (Gretna, LA: Pelican Books, 1993).

The Cherokees / Grace Steele Woodward. [1st ed.]. (Norman, OK: University of Oklahoma Press, [1963], Series: Civilization of the American Indian series, v. 65. LC 63-8986).

The Five Civilized Tribes: Cherokee, Chickasaw, Choctaw, Creek, Seminole / Grant Foreman. 1st ed. (Norman, OK: University of Oklahoma Press, 1934. Series: Civilization of the American Indian series, v. 8).

The Eastern Band of Cherokees, 1819-1900. / John R. Finger. (Knoxville, TN: University of Tennessee Press, 1984. LC 83-10284).

The Cherokee Crown of Tannassy. / William O. Steele. (Winston-Salem, N.C.: J. F. Blair Publisher, 1977).

The Cherokee Indians and Those Who Came After: Notes for a History of Cherokee County, North Carolina, 1835-1860 Nathaniel C. Browder. [New ed.]. (Hayesville, NC: Browder, 1973 i.e. 1974. LC 74-25553).

The Papers of Chief John Ross / edited and with an introduction by Gary E. Moulton. (Norman, OK: University of Oklahoma Press, 1985. 2 v.). Contents: v. 1. 1807-1839 v. 2. 1840-1866.

The Cherokee People / Thomas E. Mails (New York, N.Y: Marlowe And Co. 1996; ISBN 1-56924-762-5).

The Cherokee Freedmen: From Emancipation to American Citizenship/Daniel Littlefield, Jr.(Westport, CT: Greenwood Press, 1978).

The Removal of the Cherokee Indians from Georgia, 1827-1841 / Wilson Lumpkin. (New York, A. M. Kelley, 1971. 2 v. in 1. Reprint of the 1907 ed.).

The Texas Cherokees, A People Between Two Fires, 1819-1840 / Dianna Everett. 1st ed. (Norman, OK: University of Oklahoma Press, 1990. Series: The Civilization of the American Indian series, v. 203).

Trail of Tears, the Rise and Fall of the Cherokee Nation. / John Ehle. 1st ed. (New York: Doubleday, 1988).

"The Wahnenauhi Manuscript: Historical Sketches of the Cherokees, together with some of their Customs, Traditions, and Superstitions" / [Wah-ne-nau-hi (Mrs. Lucy Lowrey Hoyt Keys)]; edited by Jack Frederick Kilpatrick. Smithsonian Institution. Bureau of American Ethnology. Bulletin 196, Anthropological papers, no. 77).

The Cherokee Indian Nation: A Troubled History / Duane H. King.

(Knoxville: University of Tennessee Press, 1981, 2nd Printing).

The American Indian in North Carolina / Douglas L. Rights. (Durham: Duke University Press, 1947).

Walking the Trail: One Man's Journey Along the Cherokee Trail of Tears/Jerry Ellis. (Dell Publishing, 1993).

From 1819 to 1838, the American Board of Commissions for Foreign Missions maintained schools and churches at several localities in the eastern Cherokee Nation: Brainerd, Candy's Creek, Hightower, Creek Path, Carmel and New Echota. Rev. Samuel Worcester is the best known of the resident missionaires, primarily for his work with the Cherokee Nation's first newspaper, the Cherokee Phoenix. Records that were kept by the missions, often including lists of students, are located in the Houghton Library at Harvard University, Cambridge, Massachusetts.

CHEROKEE BOOK SOURCES

(All of the following take orders by phone)

Talking Leaves Book Store, P.O. Box 519C, Cherokee, N.C.28719, Phone 704-497-6044.

Cherokee Publications, P.O. Box 430-N, Cherokee, NC 28719, Phone 704-488-8856.

The Cherokee Nation Gift Shop, Tahlequah, Oklahoma, Phone 918-456-2793.

Cherokee Heritage Center, P.O. Box 515, Tahlequah, OK 74465-0515, Phone 918-456-6007.

Museum of the Cherokee Indian, Cherokee, N.C. Phone 704-497-3481.

Cherokee Nation Capitol, Tahlequah, Oklahoma
built in 1867.

OKLAHOMA
TAHLONTEESKEE
WESTERN CHEROKEE CAPITOL, 1829-39, AND COURT GROUND FOR CHEROKEE NATION. NAMED FOR THE CHIEF WHO SECURED THE ESTABLISHMENT OF DWIGHT MISSION IN ARKANSAS TER. HIS BROTHER, JOHN JOLLY, SERVED AT THIS CAPITOL AS CHIEF; AND SAM HOUSTON OFTEN VISITED HERE. IT WAS CHIEF JOLLY WHO HAD GIVEN HOUSTON THE FAMOUS NAME "THE RAVEN"--COLONAH--AN OLD, CHEROKEE WAR TITLE.
OKLAHOMA HISTORICAL SOCIETY
MANUFACTURED BY
WILLIS GRANITE PRODUCTS
GRANITE OKLAHOMA

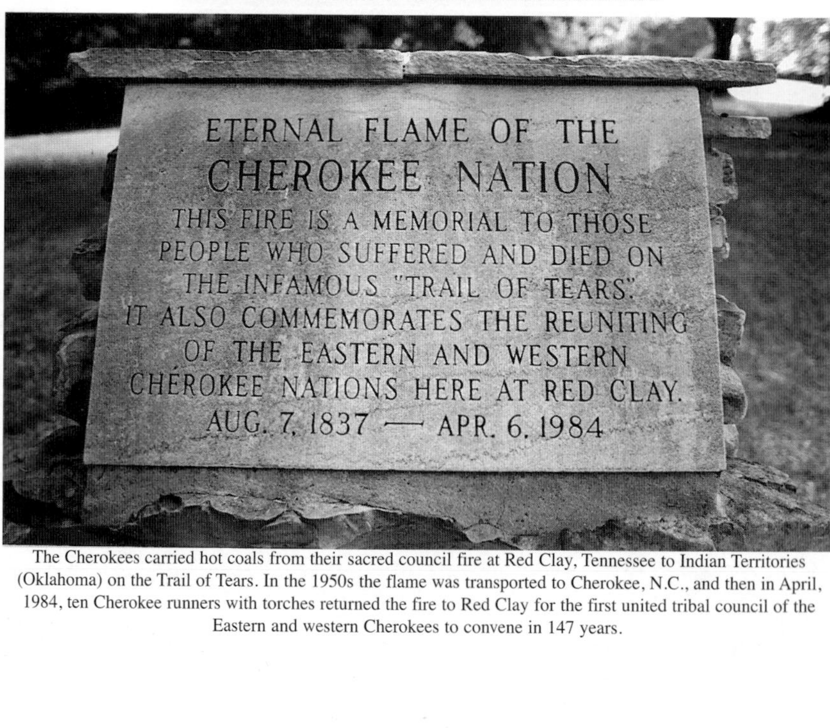
ETERNAL FLAME OF THE
CHEROKEE NATION
THIS FIRE IS A MEMORIAL TO THOSE
PEOPLE WHO SUFFERED AND DIED ON
THE INFAMOUS "TRAIL OF TEARS."
IT ALSO COMMEMORATES THE REUNITING
OF THE EASTERN AND WESTERN
CHEROKEE NATIONS HERE AT RED CLAY.
AUG. 7, 1837 — APR. 6, 1984

The Cherokees carried hot coals from their sacred council fire at Red Clay, Tennessee to Indian Territories (Oklahoma) on the Trail of Tears. In the 1950s the flame was transported to Cherokee, N.C., and then in April, 1984, ten Cherokee runners with torches returned the fire to Red Clay for the first united tribal council of the Eastern and western Cherokees to convene in 147 years.

56,000- 57,000 - acre Cherokee Indian Reservation known as Qualla Boundary nestled deep in the heart of the Great Smoky Mountains, Cherokee, N.C. Inset photo (top right) highlights the spectacular Eagle Dance, a part of America's favorite outdoor drama "Unto These Hills" performed each summer at Qualla's mountainside theatre. (Lower inset) Cherokee basket maker Alice Walkingstick demonstrates her craft for a youngster in the Oconaluftee Village, a replica of a Cherokee community of the 1750 period.

Gravesite of respected Cherokee leader Tsunu-lahun-ski, whom the whites called Junaluska and his wife Nicie near Robbinsville, N.C. Junaluska was credited with saving the life of Andrew Jackson at the Battle of Horseshoe Bend and although Jackson swore an everlasting friendship with him, Jackson betrayed the trust. Afterwards, Junaluska said: *"If I had known that Jackson would drive us from our homes, I would have killed him myself that day at Horseshoe."*

Nantahala Mountains of North Carolina, hiding place of Tsali and a band of refugees who escaped arrest during the removal. According to most accounts, including those in Eastern Cherokee literature, it was the gallant self-sacrifice of Tsali, his son and brother that led to freedom for these few hundred Cherokees who were allowed to remain in North Carolina.

56,000- 57,000 - acre Cherokee Indian Reservation known as Qualla Boundary nestled deep in the heart of the Great Smoky Mountains, Cherokee, N.C. Inset photo (top right) highlights the spectacular Eagle Dance, a part of America's favorite outdoor drama "Unto These Hills" performed each summer at Qualla's mountainside theatre. (Lower inset) Cherokee basket maker Alice Walkingstick demonstrates her craft for a youngster in the Oconaluftee Village, a replica of a Cherokee community of the 1750 period.

Gravesite of respected Cherokee leader Tsunu-lahun-ski, whom the whites called Junaluska and his wife Nicie near Robbinsville, N.C. Junaluska was credited with saving the life of Andrew Jackson at the Battle of Horseshoe Bend and although Jackson swore an everlasting friendship with him, Jackson betrayed the trust. Afterwards, Junaluska said: *"If I had known that Jackson would drive us from our homes, I would have killed him myself that day at Horseshoe."*

Nantahala Mountains of North Carolina, hiding place of Tsali and a band of refugees who escaped arrest during the removal. According to most accounts, including those in Eastern Cherokee literature, it was the gallant self-sacrifice of Tsali, his son and brother that led to freedom for these few hundred Cherokees who were allowed to remain in North Carolina.

Today, Cherokees everywhere still celebrate a number of their own traditional festivals and also take part in modern, plains-type inter-tribal pow-wows which are distinguished by a variety of colorful dress and dance. In the upper photo, Cherokee Dancer Two Crows Thomas proudly poses with 11 year old Lacy Johnson who only recently learned that she is a Cherokee descendant.

Festivals are great social and educational gatherings that include visiting friends and family, competitive or inter-tribal dancing, ball games, cultural exhibits, crafts and plenty of traditional food. Here, the author's wife Robin McClure and friend, Levi Walker, take a break from dancing at the Cherokee Homecoming Festival in Rome, Georgia.

Casual festival wear for Cherokee males is usually the traditional Cherokee Tear shirt, also called a "ribbon shirt," as worn here by internationally known river cane flutist and singer Tommy Wildcat, Cherokee Nation of Oklahoma. On the following page, lovely Cherokee Ahnawake Clinch is wearing a traditional Cherokee Tear dress.

(Upper photo by Pete McClure: Following page photo by Aubrey Watson).

Casual festival wear for Cherokee males is usually the traditional Cherokee Tear shirt, also called a "ribbon shirt," as worn here by internationally known river cane flutist and singer Tommy Wildcat, Cherokee Nation of Oklahoma. On the following page, lovely Cherokee Ahnawake Clinch is wearing a traditional Cherokee Tear dress.

(Upper photo by Pete McClure: Following page photo by Aubrey Watson).

Native American Newspapers

Obviously, Indian newspapers can keep you up to date on the latest happenings within Native America- local and other tribal events, health, politics, editorials, education and more. But researchers often overlook the fact that they also sometimes contain a bounty of valuable historical and genealogical information. Some also carry language lessons and other important social issues. There are four Cherokee newspapers:

The Cherokee Advocate is the official monthly newspaper of the Cherokee Nation of Oklahoma. $12.50 annually within Oklahoma, $10 for senior citizens; $15 and $12.50 for seniors outside Oklahoma.// P.O. Box 948, Tahlequah, OK. 74465.

The Cherokee Observer is the only "independent" Cherokee Newspaper. Published monthly; $12.50 annually US, $25.00 outside the US.// P.O. Box 1301, Jay, OK. 74346-1301.

The Cherokee One Feather is published weekly by the Tribal Council of the Eastern Band of Cherokees. $25 year within the US.// P.O. Box 501, Cherokee, NC 28719.

The United Keetoowah Band News is published monthly by the United Keetoowah Band of Cherokee Indians of Oklahoma. $10 annually within the US. // P.O. Box 746, Tahlequah, OK 74465- 0746.

News from Indian Country: The Nations Native Journal, is published twice monthly by Indian Country Communications, Inc. 7831 Grindstone Ave., Hayward, WI 54843. $50 year U.S. for 1st class.

Indian Country Today is the largest Indian newspaper in the United States , published weekly, and while it's primary focus is the Northern Plains, Northwest, Southwest and Midwest (all tribes), it also contains information of interest to Eastern natives including Cherokees. $58 year U.S. // 1920 Lombardy Drive, Rapid City, SD 57701.

SONG MORNING SONG

by Marijo Moore

A song escapes from the darkness
rising falling floating
words suppressed - not long forgotten.
Hearts beat in unison to the melody
soft sweet piercing tearing
scratching the flesh from the bones
like fingers sliding down mirrors.

It is the song of the Grandmothers
rising from the earth, falling with the rain,
floating on the lilies.
Pulling us deeper into ourselves
beyond thoughts past dreams
under memories
deep deep deeper.

Touching the linings of the souls
sewing the linings of the souls
to the spreading cloth of time.
Emptying calling haunting
rising falling floating
sweet soft soft sweet
piercing.

Song Morning Song
Song Celebration Song
Song Touching Song

Now . . .

Poet/author/artist Marijo Moore is of Eastern Cherokee, Irish and Dutch ancestry. Her published works include Returning to the Homeland-Cherokee Poetry and Short Stories, Crow Quotes, Stars are Birds, and Spirit Voices of Bones. She was chosen as North Carolina's 1998 Woman of the Year in the Arts and resides in the mountains of North Carolina.

A Brief History of the Cherokee People

by Lee Sultzman

The Desoto expedition is believed to have made the first European contact in 1540 when they met the "Chalaque" on the Tennessee River. Although Pardo revisited the area in 1566 and the Spanish maintained a small mining and smelting operation in the area until 1690, the Cherokee's location in the interior mountains kept them relatively isolated until after the settlement of Virginia in 1609. By 1629 English traders had worked their way west into the Appalachians and met the Cherokee. Contact became continuous with the founding of the Carolina colonies. Virginian Abraham Wood tried unsuccessfully to maintain his trade monopoly with the Cherokee and sent two men, James Needham and Gabriel Arthur, to the Cherokee Overhill capital at Echota in 1673, but the following year a group of Cherokee met with rival Carolina traders along the upper Savannah River. A treaty with South Carolina followed in 1684 beginning a steady trade in deerskins and Indian slaves. Although contact was limited initially to white traders, important changes began to occur within the Cherokee as a result. Leadership shifted from priest to warrior, and warriors became hunters for profit.

Increasing dependence on trade goods also drew the Cherokee to the British as allies in their wars against the French and Spanish between 1689 and 1763. Cherokee relations with their neighbors were not always friendly before contact. They raided Spanish settlements in Florida during 1673 and fought the coastal tribes of the Carolinas, but European trade and competition aggravated these rivalries and destabilized the region. By 1680 most of the tribes had gotten their first firearms and the Cherokee had fortified their larger villages. Constant fighting with the Catawba erupted in the east followed by a growing friction with the Creek and Choctaw to the south. To the west there was a traditional hostility with the Chickasaw (also a British ally). To the north, the struggle between the French, Dutch, and English in the fur trade started the Beaver Wars and a period of conquest by the Iroquois League which spread across the Great Lakes and the Ohio Valley.

In 1660 large groups of Shawnee were driven south by the Iroquois. The Cherokee allowed one group to settle in South Carolina and serve as a buffer between them and the Catawba. Other Shawnee were permitted to locate in the Cumberland Basin of Tennessee for a similar purpose against the Chickasaw. This self-serving hospitality was to earn the Cherokee nothing but grief. The Iroquois never forgot an enemy, and the Shawnee presence brought them south in raids against both the Shawnee and the Cherokee. Meanwhile, the Shawnee were becoming dangerous. In 1692 a Shawnee raid to capture slaves for trade with the English destroyed a major Cherokee village while its warriors were absent on a winter hunt. While both tribes still had common enemies (Iroquois, Catawba, and Chickasaw), this treachery destroyed any trust or friendship that had existed between the Cherokee and Shawnee. The following year a Cherokee delegation visited Charlestown demanding more firearms to fight their enemies. The situation had become so dangerous by 1705 that North Carolina was urging South Carolina to curtail the trade in Native American slaves or face a massive uprising.

Actually, warfare between allies and trading partners did not serve British interests, so they encouraged the peace that was finally arranged between the Cherokee and Iroquois in 1706. This respite allowed Cherokee warriors in 1708 to join the Catawba and Alibamu in an attack against the Mobile in southern Mississippi who were serving as middlemen for the new French trading posts in the region. 300 Cherokee warriors also served with the South Carolina army of Colonel James Moore against the Tuscarora in 1713, although some of the Lower Cherokee joined the Yamasee during the general uprising against the Carolinas in 1715. Peaceful relations resumed afterwards, and the Cherokee received a large quantity of guns and ammunition in exchange for their allegiance However, the peace with the Iroquois collapsed when the League attempted to dominate the Cherokee. When the Cherokee refused to comply with Iroquois demands, the raiding resumed.

Never forgetting the treachery of the Shawnee in 1692, the Cherokee decided to rid themselves of their now-unwelcome guests. To do this, they allied with the Chickasaw (enemies with similar feelings about the Shawnee) to inflict a major defeat in 1715 on the Shawnee of the Cumberland Basin. The Chickasaw alliance and war with the Shawnee brought the Cherokee to the attention of the French and their Algonquin allies north of the Ohio River. The result was a steady stream of war parties directed south against them. The Cherokee were in the dubious position of fighting the pro-British Iroquois and the pro-French Algonquin at the same time, but they held their own, despite devastating smallpox epidemics in 1738 and 1753 which killed almost half of them. The epidemics were also devastating to the Cherokee priests who, unable to cure the disease, lost most of their remaining influence. A second Chickasaw alliance in 1745 forced the remaining Shawnee north across the Ohio River and then succeeded in defeating the French-allied Choctaw in 1750.

Meanwhile, a treaty, signed in 1721 and thought to be the first land cession by the Cherokee, regulated trade and established a boundary between the Cherokee and the British settlements. Despite this agreement, settlement from the Carolinas was rapidly invading the lands of the Lower Cherokee east of the Appalachians and tempting the Cherokee to switch their loyalty to the French. This option had become available to them after the French made peace with the Alibamu and built a trading post at Fort Toulouse near Montgomery, Alabama in 1717. French traders were also reaching the Overhill Cherokee by following the Cumberland River from its mouth near the Ohio. The Chickasaw, however, still made travel on the Tennessee River by the French far too dangerous. All of this trade could easily have tied the Cherokee to the French if they had been able to compete with the British, but they could not. French goods were generally inferior and more expensive, and the British had the naval power to blockade Canada in times of war (King George's War 1744-48) and halt the supply. More important, the British valued their alliance with the Cherokee and worked hard to maintain it. Colonel George Chicken was sent by the British government in 1725 to regulate Cherokee trade and prevent the possibility of their turning to the French. He was followed by Sir Alexander Cuming who visited the major Cherokee towns and convinced them to select a single chief to represent them with the British. Cuming even escorted a Cherokee delegation to England for an audience with George II. In the treaty signed at Charleston in 1743, the Cherokee not only made peace with the Catawba, but promised to trade only with the British. Two years later, the Cherokee also concluded a peace with the Wyandot (an important French ally north of the Ohio), only to learn that the Wyandot and other French tribes were secretly plotting to break free from the French trade monopoly. At this point, the Cherokee apparently decided the French would not be an improvement over the British. While the French were permitted to build a trading post in their homeland, this was a close as the Cherokee ever came to changing sides. However, the British still had serious doubts about Cherokee loyalty.

Pressed to acquire new land to compensate for their growing losses to white settlement, the Cherokee and Creek were almost forced into a war with each other (1752-55). At stake was control of a hunting territory in northern Georgia which the two tribes had formerly shared. After the decisive battle at Taliwa (1755), the Cherokee emerged as the winner, and this new territory probably allowed them to support the British at the outbreak of the French and Indian War (1755-63). Although the Cherokee signed a treaty in 1754 confirming their alliance and allowing the construction of British forts in their territory to defend the colonies, the lingering suspicion remained they were sympathetic to the French. Incidents between Cherokee and white settlers during 1758 were hastily covered over by another treaty, but the cooperation collapsed in 1759. Almost 100 Cherokee accompanying a Virginia expedition against the Ohio Shawnee lost their provisions while crossing a river and were abandoned by their white "allies." Angry at this treatment, the Cherokee helped themselves to some of the Virginians' horses and were attacked. After killing more than twenty Cherokee, the Virginians scalped and mutilated the bodies. They later collected a bounty for the scalps.

While their chiefs rushed to arrange restitution to "cover the dead," outraged Cherokee warriors launched a series of retaliatory raids against outlying settlements. Blaming French intrigue rather than Virginia treachery, Governor Littleton of South Carolina raised an 1,100 man army and marched on the lower Cherokee settlements. Stunned to discover the British were attacking them, the lower Cherokee chiefs quickly agreed to peace. Two warriors accused of murder were handed over for execution, and 29 chiefs were surrendered as hostages at Fort Prince George on British suspicions of their hostile intentions. Satisfied with these arrangements, Littleton left, but the Cherokee were furious. His army had barely reached Charleston when the Cherokee War (1760-62) exploded with full fury. Settlers were massacred at Long Canes, and a militia unit was mauled near Broad River. In February of 1760, the Cherokee attacked Fort Prince George in an attempt to free the hostages, killing the fort's commander from ambush. The fort's new commander promptly executed the hostages and fought off the assault. Fort 96 also withstood an attack, but lesser outposts were not so fortunate, and the war quickly expanded beyond Littleton's resources.

He appealed for help from Lord Jeffrey Amherst, the British commander in North America (who despised Indians, friend or foe). With the French defeated, the entire British army in North America was available for use against the Cherokee. In May Amherst sent 1,200 Highlanders and Royals under Colonel Montgomery to the area. Montgomery's approach to Indian warfare: no male prisoners, but spare women and small children. The war did not go well for the British. After burning several abandoned lower Cherokee towns, Montgomery met with ambush and defeat when he attempted to push deeper into Cherokee territory. After a long siege, Fort Loudon in eastern Tennessee fell during August, and the garrison was massacred. In early 1761, the incompetent Montgomery was replaced by Colonel James Grant. Ignoring Cherokee attempts to make peace, Grant enlisted the help of Catawba scouts in June, and soon afterwards his 2,600 man army captured 15 middle Cherokee towns and destroyed the food the Cherokee needed for the coming winter. Faced with starvation if the war continued, the Cherokee signed a treaty with the South Carolina in September that ceded most of their eastern lands in the Carolinas. A second treaty was signed with

Virginia in November. The Cherokee maintained their part of the agreement and did not participate in the Pontiac uprising (1763) but did suffer another smallpox epidemic that year. They still benefitted somewhat when the rebellion forced the stunned British government to temporarily halt all new settlement west of the Appalachians. Within a few years, colonial demands forced the British to reverse this policy, and begin negotiations with the Iroquois. Land cessions by the Iroquois at Fort Stanwix (1768) opened large sections west of the Appalachians to settlement. Their generosity also included land in West Virginia, eastern Tennessee and Kentucky claimed by the Cherokee, and this forced the British to negotiate new boundaries with the Cherokee at the Treaty of Hard Labor (1768).

As white settlers poured across the mountains, the Cherokee tried once again to compensate themselves with territory taken by war with a neighboring tribe. This time their intended victim was the Chickasaw, but this was a mistake. Anyone who tried to take something from the Chickasaw regretted it, if he survived. After eleven years of sporadic warfare ended with a major defeat at Chickasaw Oldfields (1769), the Cherokee gave up and began to explore the possibility of new alliances to resist the whites. Both the Cherokee and Creek attended the 1770 and 1771 meetings with the Ohio tribes at Sciota but did not participate in Lord Dunnmore's War (1773-74) because the disputed territory was not theirs. On the eve of the American Revolution, the British government scrambled to appease the colonists and negotiate treaties with the Cherokee ceding land already taken from them by white settlers. To this end, all means, including outright bribery and extortion, were employed: Lochaber Treaty (1770); and the Augusta Treaty (1773) ceding two million acres in Georgia to pay for debts to white traders. For the same reasons as the Iroquois cession of Ohio in 1768, the Cherokee tried to protect their homeland from white settlement by selling land they did not really control. In the Watonga Treaty (1774) and the Overhill Cherokee Treaty (Sycamore Shoals) (1775), they sold all of eastern and central Kentucky to the Transylvania Land Company (Henderson Purchase).

Despite the fact that these agreements were a clear violation of existing British law, they were used later to justify the American takeover of the region. The Shawnee also claimed these lands but, of course, were never consulted. With the Iroquois selling the Shawnee lands north of the Ohio, and the Cherokee selling the Shawnee lands south, where could they go? Not surprisingly, the Shawnee stayed and fought the Americans for 40 years. Both the Cherokee and Iroquois were fully aware of the problem they were creating. After he had signed, a Cherokee chief reputedly took Daniel Boone aside to say, "We have sold you much fine land, but I am afraid you will have trouble if you try to live there."

Not all of the Cherokee honored these agreements. Tsi'yu-gunsini, sometimes seen as Cheucunsene or Kunnesee, (Dragging Canoe) and the Chickamauga refused and kept raiding the new settlements. At the outbreak of the Revolution, the Cherokee received requests from the Mohawk, Shawnee, and Ottawa to join them against the Americans, but the majority of the Cherokee decided to remain neutral in the white man's war. The Chickamauga, however, were at war with the Americans and formed an alliance with the Shawnee. Both tribes had the support of British Indian agents who were still living among them (often with native wives) and arranging trade. During 1775 the British began to supply large amounts of guns and ammunition and offer bounties for American scalps. In July 1776, 700 Chickamauga attacked two American forts in North Carolina: Eaton's Station and Ft. Watauga. Both assaults failed, but the raids set off a series of attacks by other Cherokee and the Upper Creek on frontier settlements in Tennessee and Alabama.

The frontier militia organized in response made little effort to distinguish between hostile and neutral Cherokee except to notice that neutrals were easier to find. During September the Americans destroyed more than 36 Cherokee towns killing every man, woman and child they could find. Unable to resist, the Cherokee in 1777 asked for peace. The Treaties of DeWitt's Corner (May) and Long Island (or Holston) (July) were signed at gunpoint and forced the Cherokee to cede almost all of their remaining land in the Carolinas. Although this brought peace for two years, the Chickamauga remained hostile and renewed their attacks against western settlements in Tennessee, Alabama, and Kentucky during 1780. After more fighting, the second Treaty of Long Island of Holston (July

1781) confirmed the 1777 cessions and then took more Cherokee land.

Through all of this, the Chickamauga fought on but were forced to retreat slowly northward, until by 1790 they had joined forces with the Shawnee in Ohio. After the initial Indian victories of Little Turtle's War (1790-94), most of the Ohio Chickamauga returned south and settled near the Tennessee River in central Tennessee and northern Alabama. From here, they had the unofficial encouragement of the Spanish governments of Florida and Louisiana and began to attack nearby American settlements. One of these incidents almost killed a young Nashville attorney/land speculator named Andrew Jackson, which may explain his later attitude regarding the Cherokee.

Dragging Canoe died in 1792, but a new round of violence exploded that year with the American settlements in central Tennessee and northern Alabama. After two years of fighting with Tennessee militia, support from other Cherokee declined, and the Chickamauga's resolve began to weaken. Following the American victory at Fallen Timbers (1794), the last groups of the Ohio Chickamauga returned to Tennessee. Meanwhile, the Spanish government had decided to settle its border disputes with the United States by diplomatic means and ended its covert aid to the Cherokee. After a final battle near Muscle Shoals in Alabama, the Chickamauga realized it was impossible to stop the Americans by themselves. By 1794 large groups of Chickamauga had started to cross the Mississippi and settle with the Western Cherokee in Spanish Arkansas. The migration was complete by 1799, and open warfare between the Cherokee and Americans ended.

The Keetoowah (Western Cherokee or Old Settlers) had their origin with a small group of pro-French Cherokee that moved to northern Arkansas and southeastern Missouri after the French defeat by the British in 1763. The Spanish welcomed them and granted land. Toward the end of the American Revolution in 1782, they were joined by a group of pro-British Cherokee. With the migration of the Chickamauga (1794-99), the Keetoowah became formidable and a threat to the Osage who originally claimed the territory. Cherokee and Osage warfare was fairly common in 1803 when the United

States gained control of the area through the Louisiana Purchase. With continued migration, the Western Cherokee steadily gained at the expense of the Osage, and by 1808 over 2,000 Cherokee were established in northern Arkansas.

The Turkey Town treaty (1817) was the first formal recognition of the Western Cherokee by the United States. Under its terms, 4,000 Cherokee ceded their lands in Tennessee in exchange for a reservation with the Western Cherokee in northwest Arkansas. With this new immigration during 1818-19, the number of Western Cherokee swelled to over 6,000. However, the Osage continued to object to the Cherokee presence, and the Americans were forced to build Fort Smith (1817) and Fort Gibson (1824) to maintain peace.

Reconstructed Fort Gibson, Indian Territories (Oklahoma).

White settlers of the Arkansas territory were soon demanding the removal of both the Cherokee and Osage. In 1828 the Western Cherokee agreed to exchange their Arkansas lands for a new location in Oklahoma. The boundaries were finally determined in 1833, although it took until 1835 to get the Osage to agree.

Meanwhile, the Cherokee homeland in the east was rapidly being whittled away by American settlement reflected by a series of treaties: Hopewell 1785; Holston 1791; Philadelphia 1794; and Tellico in 1798, 1804, 1805, and 1806. The final cession of ten million acres in 1806 by Doublehead (Chuquilatague) outraged many of the Cherokee and resulted in his assassination as a traitor by the faction led by Major Ridge (Kahnungdatlageh -"the man who walks the mountain top"). A new, mixed-blood leadership of Ridge and John Ross (Guwisguwi - blue eyes and 1/8 Cherokee) seized control determined not to yield any more of the Cherokee homelands while introducing major cultural changes. With a unity made possible by the departure of the more traditional Cherokee to Arkansas, in less than 30 years the Cherokee underwent the most remarkable adaptation to white culture of any Native American people. By 1817 the clan system of government had been replaced by an elected tribal council. A new capital was established at New Echota in 1825, and a written constitution modeled after that of the United States was added two years later.

Many Cherokee became prosperous farmers with comfortable houses, beautiful cultivated fields, and large herds of livestock. Christian missionaries arrived by invitation, and Sequoyah invented a syllabary that gave them a written language and overnight made most of the Cherokee literate. They published a newspaper, established a court system, and built schools. An inventory of Cherokee property in 1826 revealed: 1,560 black slaves, 22,000 cattle, 7,600 horses, 46,000 swine, 2,500 sheep, 762 looms, 2,488 spinning wheels, 172 wagons, 2,942 plows, 10 sawmills, 31 grist mills, 62 blacksmith shops, 8 cotton machines, 18 schools, and 18 ferries. Although the poor Cherokee still lived in simple log cabins, Chief John Ross had a $10,000 house designed by a Philadelphia architect (See photograph in color images section). In fact, many Cherokee were more prosperous and 'civilized' than their increasingly envious white neighbors.

Although the leadership of the eastern Cherokee steadfastly maintained their independence and land base, they felt it was important to reach an accommodation with the Americans. They refused Tecumseh's requests for Indian unity in 1811, ignored a call for war from the Red Stick Creek in 1813, and then fought as American allies during the Creek War (1813-14). Eight hundred Cherokee under Major Ridge were with Jackson's army at Horseshoe Bend in 1814, and according to one account, a Cherokee warrior (Junaluska) saved Jackson's life during the battle. If Jackson was grateful, he never allowed it to show. At the Fort Jackson Treaty ending the war (1814), Jackson demanded huge land cessions from both the Cherokee and Creek. As allies, the Cherokee must have been stunned at this treatment, and reluctantly agreed only after a series of four treaties signed during 1816 and 1817.

The Cherokee government afterwards became even more determined not to surrender any more land, but things were moving against them. In 1802 Cherokee land had been promised by the federal government to the state of Georgia which afterwards refused to recognize either the Cherokee Nation or its land claims. By 1822 Georgia was pressing Congress to end Cherokee title within its boundaries. $30,000 was eventually appropriated as payment but refused. Then bribery was attempted but exposed, and the Cherokee responded with a law prescribing death for anyone selling land to whites without permission.

With the election of Jackson as president in 1828, the Cherokee were in serious trouble. Gold was discovered that year on Cherokee land in northern Georgia, and miners swarmed in. Indian removal to west of the Mississippi had been suggested as early as 1802 by Thomas Jefferson and recommended by James Monroe in his final address to Congress in 1825. With Jackson's full support, the Indian Removal Act was introduced in Congress in 1829. There it met serious opposition from Senators Daniel Webster and Henry Clay who were able to delay passage until 1830. Meanwhile, Jackson refused to enforce the treaties which protected the Cherokee homeland from encroachment. During the two years following his election, Georgia unilaterally extended its laws to Cherokee territory, dividing up Cherokee lands by lottery, and stripping the Cherokee of legal protection. Georgia citizens were free to kill, burn, and steal. With the only alternative a war which would result in annihilation, John Ross decided to fight for his people's rights in the United States courts.

The Cherokee won both cases brought before the Supreme Court: Cherokee Nation vs. Georgia (1831) and Worcester vs. Georgia(1832), but the legal victories were useless. Jackson's answer: "Justice Marshall has made his decision. Let him enforce it." Without federal interference, Georgia and Tennessee began a reign of terror using arrest, murder and arson against the Cherokee. Ross was arrested, and the offices of the Cherokee Phoenix were burned in May 1834. The mansion of the wealthiest Cherokee, Joseph Vann, was confiscated by the Georgia militia, and the Moravian mission and school was converted into a militia headquarters. When Ross traveled to Washington to protest, Jackson refused to see him. Instead overtures were made to Major Ridge, his son John Ridge, and nephew Elias Boudinot (Buck Oowatie), editor of the Phoenix (Cherokee newspaper). The hopelessness of the situation finally convinced these men to sign the Treaty of New Echota (December 1835) surrendering the Cherokee Nation's homeland in exchange for $5,000,000, seven million acres in Oklahoma, and an agreement to remove within two years (See Appendix 3).

Known as the Treaty Party (Ridgites), only 350 of 17,000

In 1835, the Chatsworth mansion of the wealthiest Cherokee, Joseph Vann, was confiscated by the Georgia militia because Vann had unknowingly violated Georgia law by hiring a white man to work for him. The Moravian mission and school at nearby Spring Place was converted into a militia headquarters. Above photos (c.1950) show the once stately mansion abandoned and deteriorating. Today, the restored homeplace is a State Historic Site (See Color section at center of book).
Photos courtesy of GA.Dept. of Natural Resources.

Cherokee actually endorsed the agreement. Threatened by violence from their own people, they and 2,000 family members quickly gathered their property and left for Oklahoma. The treaty was clearly a fraud, and a petition of protest with 16,000 Cherokee signatures was dispatched to Washington to halt ratification. After violent debate, Jackson succeeded in pushing it through the Senate during May by the margin of a single vote. The Cherokee Nation was doomed. For the next two years, Ross tried every political and legal means to stop the removal, but failed. When the deadline arrived in May 1838, 7,000 soldiers under General Winfield Scott (virtually the entire American Army) moved into the Cherokee homeland. The Cherokee found that their reward for 'taking the white man's road' was to be driven from their homes at gunpoint. It was the beginning of the Nunahi Duna Dio Hilu I or 'the trail where they cried.' History would call it the Trail of Tears.

Forced to abandon most of their property, the Cherokee were herded into hastily-built stockades at Rattlesnake Springs near Chattanooga and several others throughout the Cherokee Nation. Little thought had been given to these, and in the crowded and unsanitary conditions, measles, whopping cough and dysentery took a terrible toll throughout the summer. After most of the Cherokee had been collected, relocation by boat began in August, but drought had made the Tennessee River unusable. At this point, Cherokee desperation contributed to the disaster. Not wishing to remain until spring in the lethal stockades, Ross petitioned the government to allow the Cherokee to manage their own removal.

Permission was delayed until October. When it finally came, several large groups of Cherokee departed into the face of an approaching winter. They were marched west without adequate shelter, provisions, or food. The soldiers were under orders to move quickly and did little to protect them from whites who attacked and robbed the Cherokee of what little they had left. Two-thirds were trapped in southern Illinois by ice on the Mississippi and forced to remain for a month without shelter or supplies. As many as 4,000, including the wife of John Ross, died en route. Many had to be left unburied beside the road.

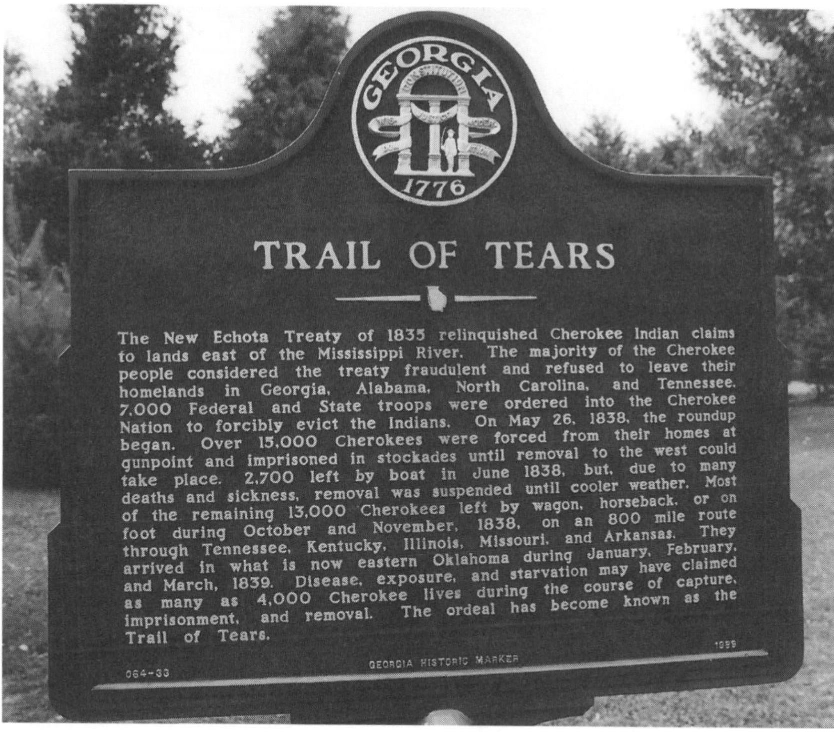

GEORGIA
1776
TRAIL OF TEARS
The New Echota Treaty of 1835 relinquished Cherokee Indian claims to lands east of the Mississippi River. The majority of the Cherokee people considered the treaty fraudulent and refused to leave their homelands in Georgia, Alabama, North Carolina, and Tennessee. 7,000 Federal and State troops were ordered into the Cherokee Nation to forcibly evict the Indians. On May 26, 1838, the roundup began. Over 15,000 Cherokees were forced from their homes at gunpoint and imprisoned in stockades until removal to the west could take place. 2,700 left by boat in June 1838, but, due to many deaths and sickness, removal was suspended until cooler weather. Most of the remaining 13,000 Cherokees left by wagon, horseback, or on foot during October and November, 1838, on an 800 mile route through Tennessee, Kentucky, Illinois, Missouri, and Arkansas. They arrived in what is now eastern Oklahoma during January, February, and March, 1839. Disease, exposure, and starvation may have claimed as many as 4,000 Cherokee lives during the course of capture, imprisonment, and removal. The ordeal has become known as the Trail of Tears.
GEORGIA HISTORIC MARKER
064-33

Some Cherokee avoided the removal. Under the provisions of the 1817 and 1819 treaties, 400 Qualia of Chief Yonaguska who lived in North Carolina were United States citizens and owned their land individually. Because they were not members of the Cherokee Nation and subject to removal, they were allowed to stay. Several hundred Cherokee escaped and hid in the mountains. The army used other Cherokee to hunt them. Tsali and two of his sons were captured and executed after they had killed a soldier trying to capture them. In 1842 the army gave up the effort, and the fugitive Cherokee were allowed to remain in an "unofficial" status. Formal recognition came in 1848 when Congress agreed to recognize the Eastern Cherokee provided North Carolina would do likewise. It was not until 18 years later (1866) that the legislature of that state approved a statute granting them the right to remain.

Currently, more than 8,000 of 11,000 enrolled Eastern Cherokee live and work in the mountains of western North Carolina on communal, corporate land purchased by them and known as Qualla

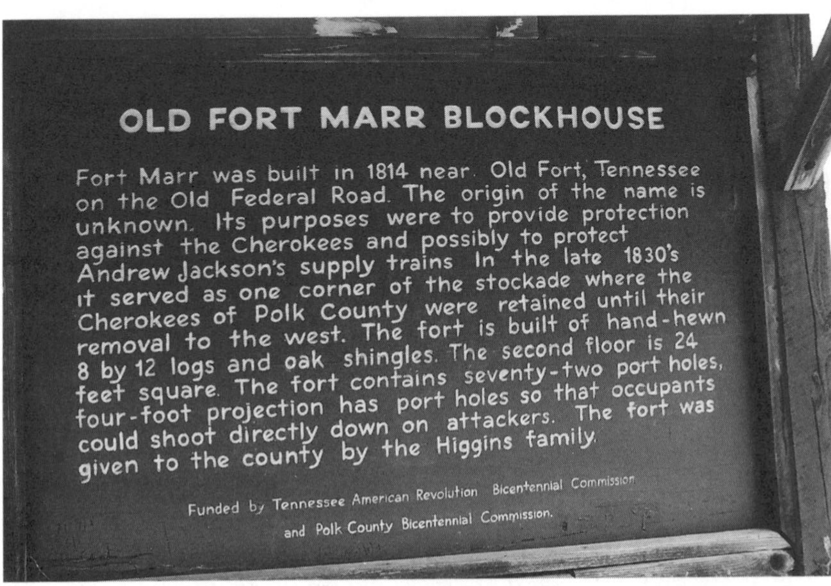

OLD FORT MARR BLOCKHOUSE
Fort Marr was built in 1814 near. Old Fort, Tennessee on the Old Federal Road. The origin of the name is unknown. Its purposes were to provide protection against the Cherokees and possibly to protect Andrew Jackson's supply trains In the late 1830's it served as one corner of the stockade where the Cherokees of Polk County were retained until their removal to the west. The fort is built of hand-hewn 8 by 12 logs and oak shingles. The second floor is 24 feet square. The fort contains seventy-two port holes. four-foot projection has port holes so that occupants could shoot directly down on attackers. The fort was given to the county by the Higgins family.
Funded by Tennessee American Revolution Bicentennial Commission
and Polk County Bicentennial Commission.

Old Fort Marr Blockhouse relocated to nearby Benton, Tennessee served as a stockade for the Cherokees during the mortal summer of 1838. Conditions inside were horrible as there were no provisions for sanitation. Many died here while waiting their turn for removal to the west.

Boundary. The 56,000 - acre reservation covers parts of five North Carolina counties.

Family friend Charley George of the Eastern Cherokee Band adds face paint to author's wife Robin McClure during a spring festival.

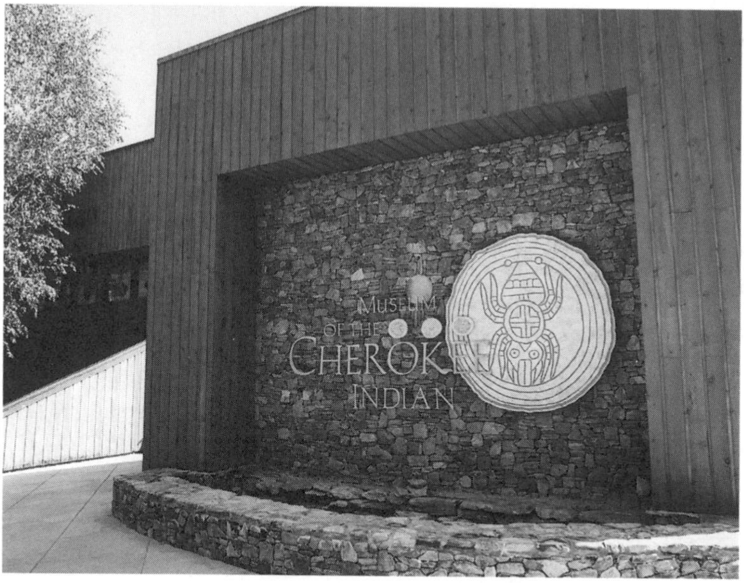

Modern Museum on the Qualla Boundary Reservation, Cherokee, North Carolina.

Many other Cherokee alienated themselves from their tribesmen and fled into various parts of the southeast to become assimilated into white communities. Still others took advantage of Article 12 of the New Echota treaty which allowed those wanting to stay in the east to do so if they met certain criteria. The Siler Cherokee Payment roll includes the names of 1750 Cherokees still living in the states of North Carolina, Tennessee, Georgia and Alabama in 1851 who were entitled to a per capita payment pursuant to acts of Congress in 1850-51. Today, many of the enrolled members of two Cherokee tribes in Georgia and three in Alabama - all officially recognized by Indian Affairs Commissions of their states - are descended from the Siler enrollees and other individual landowners under the 1817-19 treaties.

At the same time as the Trail of Tears, another group of Cherokee was being forcibly removed to Oklahoma from Texas. In 1807, after the Louisiana Purchase, the Spanish government was nervously watching the American expansion toward Texas and requested a number of tribes to resettle in eastern Texas as a buffer against the Americans. The first Cherokee settlement in the region was at Lost Prairie in 1819, and it received a land grant in 1822. After a successful revolt by the Texans in 1835, a treaty confirming the Cherokee title failed ratification in the Texas legislature during 1836 despite the strong support of President Sam Houston. White Texans pressed for the removal, and in July of 1839 three Texas regiments attacked the Cherokee of Chief Bowl and forced them across the Red River into Oklahoma. The irony of the Cherokee situation in Oklahoma in 1839 should not be lost. No matter what course chosen: war, accommodation, surrender, or flight; their fate had been the same.

Of the Five Civilized Tribes, the Creek, Choctaw and Seminole received similar treatment during removal, although the Chickasaw had foreseen what was coming and prepared better. Following removal, all had major problems, but the Cherokee had the most bitter internal divisions. Gathered for the first time in 50 years, the Cherokee in Oklahoma were ready for civil war during the spring of 1839. 6,000 Western Cherokee (Old Settlers) from Arkansas and Texas had been living there since 1828 and defending themselves from the Osage, Kiowa, Wichita, and Comanche. They had maintained their traditional government of three chiefs without written laws. Suddenly 14,000 Eastern Cherokee (New Settlers) arrived in their midst with an elaborate government, court system, and a written constitution, but the newcomers were bitterly divided between 2,000 Ridgites (Treaty Party) and 12,000 Rossites who had just lost 4,000 of their people on the Trail of Tears.

Violence was not long in coming. On June 22, Major Ridge, John Ridge, and Elias Boudinot were murdered. Stand Watie, Boudinot's brother and Major Ridge's nephew, was the only leader of the Treaty Party to escape. The assassinations effectively silenced the Treaty Party, but the hatreds endured. This left only two contending groups: west and east. The Western Cherokee refused to accept any of the new changes, while the more numerous Eastern Cherokee considered themselves superior and would not compromise. The first meeting of these factions failed to reach agreement. At a second meeting, Ross could only obtain the signature of one western chief but proceeded anyway to organize a government. The majority of the western Cherokee and the Treaty Party refused to recognize it. For the next six years there was civil war over borders and jurisdiction.

The situation became so bad that Congress proposed dividing the Cherokee into two tribes. This was incentive enough for the Cherokee to set aside their differences and unite under the Cherokee Nation, an accomplishment recognized by treaty with the United States in 1846. The wounds from removal and reunification never healed completely, but the Cherokee adjusted well enough to enjoy what they consider to have been their golden age during the 1850s. On the eve of the Civil War in 1861, the Cherokee Nation was controlled by a wealthy, mixed-blood minority which owned black slaves and favored the South. The vast majority of the Cherokee did not have slaves, lived simple lives and could have cared less about the white man's war, especially the Old Settlers. John Ross leaned toward the South, but mindful of the divisions within the Cherokee, refused the early offers by Albert Pike to join the Confederacy. When Union soldiers withdrew during the summer of 1861, the Confederate army occupied the Indian Territory. The Cherokee Nation voted to secede from the United States in August 1861, and a formal treaty was signed at the Park Hill home of John Ross between the Cherokee Nation and the new Confederate government. Four years later, this agreement was to cost them very dearly.

Americans are usually surprised to learn that the Civil War was bitterly contested between the Native Americans in Oklahoma. For the Cherokee, it was very much a war of brother against brother. 3,000 Cherokee (usually New Settlers) enlisted in the Confederate army while 1,000(Old Settlers) fought for the Union. In the east 400 North Carolina Cherokee, virtually every able-bodied man, served the South. Cherokee Civil War Units included: First Cherokee Mounted Rifles (First Arkansas Cherokee); First Cherokee Mounted Volunteer (Watie's Regiment, Cherokee Mounted Volunteers); Second Regiment, Cherokee Mounted Rifles, Arkansas; First Regiment, Cherokee Mounted Riflemen; First Squadron, Cherokee Mounted Volunteers (Holt's Squadron); Second Cherokee Mounted Volunteers (Second Regiment, Cherokee Mounted Rifles or Riflemen); and Cherokee Regiment(Special Service).

Cherokee units fought at Wilson Creek (1861) and Pea Ridge (1862). There were few large battles in Oklahoma, but they were brutal. In November 1861, a combined force of 1,400 Cherokee, Chickasaw, Choctaw, and Texas cavalry commanded by Colonel Douglas Cooper attacked a refugee column of 4,000 pro-Union Creek trying to reach safety in Kansas. Over 700 refugees were killed during the three-day battle before reason took hold. After two assaults against the Creek, the Cherokee refused to participate in a third and withdrew. Meanwhile, the Cherokee allegiance to the Confederacy faltered. Following the Confederate defeat at Pea Ridge, John Ross switched sides to the Union. Actually Ross allowed himself to be captured in 1862 and spent the rest of the war in Philadelphia. John Drew's Mounted Rifle regiment also deserted and was reorganized as a regiment in the Union army, but other Cherokee units under Stand Watie remained loyal to the Confederacy.

The fighting in Oklahoma degenerated into the same vicious guerrilla warfare that prevailed among the white settlers of Kansas and Missouri. Stand Watie, who became a Confederate general, was a leader of the Treaty Party and personally hated John Ross. After

Monument to Gen. Stand Watie in courtyard of Cherokee Nation Capitol Building, Tahlequah, OK. The inscription reads:

GEN. STAND WATIE

ONLY FULL BLOOD INDIAN Brig.Gen. IN THE CONFEDERATE ARMY. THIS BRAVE CHEROKEE WITH HIS HEROIC REGIMENT RENDERED INESTIMABLE SERVICES TO THE CONFEDERATE CAUSE OF Ind. Terr. BORN IN GA. DEC 12, 1806. DIED IN CHER.NAT. SEPT 9, 1871. A TRIBUTE TO HIS MEMORY BY OKLA DIV UNITED DAUGHTERS OF THE CONFEDERACY. "LEST WE FORGET."

Ross switched in 1862 and went east, Stand Watie was elected principal chief of the Cherokee Nation. He captured the Cherokee capital at Tahlequah and ordered Ross' home burned. The fighting produced hatreds that, added to the earlier differences, endured long after the war was over.

Many Oklahoma Indians fled north to escape the fighting. Kansas eventually had more than 7,000 refugees from the Indian Territory which it could not house or feed. Many froze to death or starved. Heavily involved in the fighting throughout the war, the Cherokee Nation lost more than 1/3 of its population. No state, north or south, even came close to this. On June 23, 1865, Stand Watie was the last Confederate general to surrender his command to the United States.

Afterwards, the victorious federal government remembered the services of General Stand Watie to the Confederacy. It also remembered the 1861 vote by the Cherokee legislature to secede from the United States. These provided the excuse to invalidate all previous treaties between the Cherokee and United States. John Ross died in 1866, and in new treaties imposed in 1866 and 1868, large sections of Cherokee lands were taken for railroad construction, white settlement (1889), or the relocation of other tribes. The Cherokee Nation never recovered to the prosperity it had enjoyed before the Civil War. As railroads were built across Cherokee lands, outlaws discovered that the Indian territory, especially the Cherokee Nation, was a sanctuary from federal and state laws. Impoverished by the war, the Cherokee also began to lease lands to white tenant farmers. By 1880, whites outnumbered Indians in the Indian Territory.

In 1885 a well-intentioned, but ill-informed, Senator Henry Dawes of Massachusetts decided that holding of land in common was delaying the progress of Indians toward "civilization." Forming an alliance with western Congressmen who wished to exploit Indian treaty lands, he secured passage of the General Allotment (Dawes) Act in 1887 which ultimately cost Native Americans 2/3 of their remaining land base. The Five Civilized Tribes of Oklahoma were exempt from allotment, but came under tremendous pressure to accept it. Until the 1880s, cattle from the Chisholm and Texas trails routinely grazed on the lands of the Cherokee Outlet before going to Kansas railheads. The Cherokee earned a good income from this

Final Resting Place of Cherokee Chief John Ross
Ross Cemetery, Tahlequah Oklahoma

enterprise until it was halted without explanation by the Commissioner of Indian Affairs in 1890. It should also be noted that the Oklahoma Territory was organized that same year from the western half of the Indian Territory, and there may have been some connection! After the Cherokee were forced to sell, the land was made available for white settlement.

The Dawes commission attempted to persuade the Five Tribes to accept allotment in 1893, but they refused. This led to the passage of the Curtis Act (1895) which dissolved tribal governments and forced allotment during 1901. Grafting(swindles) of Indian lands became a massive and unofficially sanctioned form of theft in Oklahoma. Of the original seven million acres granted the Cherokee in the New Echota Treaty, the Cherokee Nation kept less than 1/3 of 1 percent. As compensation, the Cherokee became citizens in 1901 and were finally allowed to vote. An attempt by the Five Tribes to form their own state of Sequoyah in eastern Oklahoma failed in 1905, and the Cherokee Nation was officially dissolved on March 3, 1906. The following year Oklahoma was admitted as the 46th state. The present government of the Cherokee Nation was formed in 1948 after passage of the Wheeler-Howard Indian Reorganization Act (1934). In 1961 the Cherokee Nation was awarded $15,000,000 by the U.S. Claims Commission for lands of the Cherokee Outlet.

Original Location

The southern Appalachian Mountains including western North and South Carolina, northern Georgia and Alabama, southwest Virginia, southern West Virginia and the Cumberland Basin of Tennessee and Kentucky.

Current Locations

Three tribes of Cherokee currently have federal recognition. The Cherokee Nation of Oklahoma and the United Keetoowah Band of Cherokees have members distributed across the United States, but they are concentrated in eastern Oklahoma. The Eastern Band of Cherokee still maintain their reservation in western North Carolina. Six other tribes of Cherokee have state recognition; the Northern

Cherokee Nation of the Old Louisiana Territory has recognition from both Missouri and Arkansas. The remaining five state recognized tribes are headquartered in Georgia and Alabama. All six of these tribes have enrolled members in most states. Various other groups claim Cherokee heritage, but have no official recognition.

Population

European epidemics introduced into the southeastern United States in 1540 by the Desoto expedition are estimated to have killed at least 75% of the original native population. How much the Cherokee suffered from this disaster is unknown, but their population in 1674 was about 50,000. A series of smallpox epidemics (1729, 1738, and 1753) cut this in half, and it remained fairly stable at about 25,000 until their removal to Oklahoma during the 1830s. The American Civil War was the next disaster and cost the Cherokee 25% of their population. The 1990 census listed 308,132 persons (15,000 full-blood) who identified themselves as Cherokee. Of these, 95,435 were concentrated in eastern Oklahoma while 10,114 eastern Cherokee lived on or near the North Carolina reservation. Cherokee tribal governments have fairly liberal membership standards, and some estimates exceed 370,000, which would make the Cherokee the largest Native American group in the United States.

Tribal Name

The most familiar name, Cherokee, comes from a Creek word "Chelokee" meaning "people of a different speech." In their own language the Cherokee originally called themselves the Aniyunwiya (or Anniyaya) "principal people" or the Keetoowah (or Anikituaghi, Anikituhwagi) "people of Kituhwa." Although they usually accept being called Cherokee, many prefer Tsalagi from their own name for the Cherokee Nation (Tsalagihi Ayeli). Other names applied to the Cherokee have been: Allegheny (or Allegewi, Talligewi) (Delaware), Baniatho (Arapaho), Ca†xi (or Cayaki) (Osage and Kansa), Chalaque (Spanish), Chilukki (dog people) (Choctaw and Chickasaw), Entarironnen (mountain people) (Huron), Gatohu† (Creek), Kittuwa (or Katow†) (Algonquin), Matera (or Manteran) (coming out of the ground) (Catawba), Nation du Chien (French), Ochietarironnon (Wyandot), Oyatageronon (or Oyaudah, Uwatayoronon) (cave people) (Iroquois), Shanaki (Caddo), Shannakiak (Fox), Tcaike (Tonkawa), and Tcerokieco (Wichita).

Language

Iroquoian, but Cherokee differs significantly from other Iroquoian languages.

Sub-tribes

Originally, the Cherokee were divided into three divisions depending on location and dialect (east to west):
Lower, Middle, and Over-the-Hill.

Other Distinct Bands

Atali, Chickamauga, Etali, Onnontiogg, and Qualia.

Villages

The number following a particular name indicates more than one of the same name.

Lower Settlements:

Echota, Estatoee (2), Keowee (2), Kulsetsiyi (or Sugartown) (3), Oconee, Qualatchee (2), Tomassee (2), Toxaway, Tugaloo, Ustanali (6).

Middle Settlements:

Cowee, Coweeshee, Ellijay (4), Itseyi (3), Jore, Kituhwa, Nanyahala, Nucassee, Stikayi (3), Tawsee, Tekanitli, Tessuntee, Tikaleyasuni, Watauga (2), Yunsawi.

Overhill Settlements:

Chatuga (3), Chilhowee, Cotocanahut, Echota (5), Hiwassee (2), Natuhli, Nayuhi (4), Sitiku, Tahlasi, Tallulah (2), Tamahli (2), Tellico (4), Tanisi (Tennessee) (2), Toquo, Tsiyahi (3), Ustanali.

Other Settlements
(Alphabetically by Location):

Aguaquiri, Amahyaski, Amakalali, Amohi, Anisgayayi (NC), Anuyi, Aquohee (NC), Aracuchi, Atsiniyi, Aumuchee, Ayahliyi, Big-island (TN), Briertown (NC), Broomtown, Brown's Village, Buffalo Fish, Canuga (2) (NC/SC), Catatoga (NC), Chagee (SC), Chattanooga (TN), Cheesoheha (SC), Chewase (TN), Chicherohe (GA), Chickamauga (TN), Conisca, Conontoroy, Conoross (SC), Cooweescoowee, Coyatee (TN), Crayfish Town (GA), Creek Path (AL), Crowmocker (AL), Crow Town (AL), Cuclon, Cusawatee (GA), Dulastunyi (NC), Dustavalunyi (NC), Ecochee (GA), Elakulsi (GA), Etowah (or High Tower Forks) (2) (GA), Euforsee, Fightingtown (GA), Frogtown (GA), Guasuli, Gulaniyi, Gusti (TN), Gwalgahi (or Guhlaniyi) (Natchez) (NC), Halfway Town (TN), Hemptown (GA), Hickory Log (GA), Ikatikunahita (GA), Ivy Log (GA), Johnstown (GA), Kalanunyi (NC), Kanastunyi (NC), Kansaki (4) (NC/GA/TN), Kanutaluhi (GA), Kawanunyi (TN), Kuhlahi (GA), Kulahiyi (GA), Leatherwood (GA), Long Island (TN), Lookout Mountain (GA), Naguchee (GA), Nanatlugunyi (TN), Nickajack (TN), Niowe, Noewe, Nowe, Nununyi (NC), Ocoee (TN), Oconaluftee (NC), Olagatano, Ooltewah (TN), Oothcaloga (GA), Paint Town (NC), Pine Log (GA), Quacoshatchee (SC), Qualla (NC), Quanusee, Quinahaqui, Rabbit Trap (GA), Red Bank (GA), Red Clay (TN), Running Water (TN), Saguahi, Sanderstown (AL), Selikwayi (GA), Seneca (SC), Setsi (NC), Skeinah (or Devil Town (GA), Soquee (GA), Spike Bucktown (or Spike Town) (NC), Spring Place (GA), Standing Peach Tree (GA), Sunanee (GA), Sutali (GA), Tagwahi (3) (TN/NC), Takwashnaw, Talahi, Talaniyi (GA), Talking Rock (GA), Tanasqui, Tasetsi (GA), Taskigi (3) (TN/NC), Tausitu, Tikwalitsi (NC), Tlanusiyi (NC), Tocax, Torsalla, Tricentee, Tsilaluhi (GA), Tsiskwahi (NC), Tsistetsiyi (TN), Tsistuyi (TN), Tsudinuntiyi (NC), Tucharechee, Tuckaseegee (2) (NC/GA), Turkeytown (AL), Turniptown (NC), Turtletown (GA), Tusquittah (NC), Two Runs (GA), Ustisti, Valleytown (NC), Wahyahi (NC), Wasasa (AL), and Willstown (AL).

Culture

According to some accounts, before the coming of the Europeans, the Cherokee were forced to migrate to the southern Appalachians from the northwest after a defeat at the hands of the Iroquois and Delaware. Some Delaware traditions also support this, but the Iroquois have no memories of such a conflict. While there is probably some historical basis, it is difficult to imagine a tribe as large and powerful as the Cherokee being forced to move anywhere, although they may have lost some territory in the north to the Susquehannock, Erie, or Delaware. Considering their language differences with other Iroquoian groups, the Cherokee probably have been a distinct group for a considerable period. It seems more reasonable to assume that the Cherokee had occupied their mountain homeland for a long time before the arrival of the Europeans.

At the time of contact, the Cherokee were a settled, agricultural people living in approximately 200 fairly large villages. The typical Cherokee town consisted of 30 to 60 houses and a large council house. Homes were usually wattle and daub, a circular framework interwoven with branches (like an upside-down basket) and plastered with mud. The entire structure was partially sunken into ground. In later periods, log cabins (one door with smokehole in the bark-covered roof) became the general rule. The large council houses were frequently located on mounds from the earlier Mississippian culture, although the Cherokee themselves did not build mounds during the historic period. Used for councils, general meetings, and religious ceremonies, the council houses were also the sites of the sacred fire, which the Cherokee had kept burning from time immemorial.

Like other Iroquoian peoples, kinship and membership in seven matrilineal clans (originally there were fourteen) were determined through the mother, although the women's role never achieved the importance that it enjoyed among the Iroquois League in New York. In most ways, the Cherokee more closely resembled the Creek and other southeastern tribes, including the celebration of the Busk, or Green Corn festival. Agriculture relied heavily on the "three sisters" (corn, beans, and squash), supplemented by hunting and the gathering of wild plants. Cherokee villages were largely independent in daily matters, with the whole tribe only coming together for ceremonies or times of war. Leadership was divided according the circumstances: "red" chiefs during war and "white" chiefs in times of peace.

The Cherokee were the only Iroquoian-speaking member of the five Civilized Tribes of the southeast United States. Although it is difficult to ascertain what privilege in treatment they received for being classified as "civilized," their achievements were remarkable and accomplished almost entirely through their own efforts. During the early 1800s, the Cherokee adapted their government to a written constitution. They established their own courts and schools, and achieved a standard of living that was the envy of their white neighbors. Particularly noteworthy was the invention of written language by Sequoyah (George Gist) in 1821. Using an ingenious syllabary of 86 characters, almost the entire Cherokee Nation became literate within a few years. A Cherokee newspaper, the Phoenix, began publication in the native language in February 1828. Prominent Cherokees are too numerous to list but include Senator Robert Owen and Will Rogers. Despite all they have endured, the Cherokee level of education and living standard ranks among the highest of all Native American tribes.

WORKS CITED

Bahti, Tom, Southwestern Indian Tribes. Las Vegas, Nevada: KC Publications, 1989.

Brown, John P. Old Frontiers: The Story of the Cherokee Indians from Earliest Times to the Date of Their Removal to the West, 1838. Kingsport, Tennessee: 1938.

Burt, Jesse, and Ferguson, Robert B. Indians of the Southeast: Then and Now. Nashville, Tennessee and New York: Abingdon Press, 1973.

Catlin, George, Letters and Notes on the North American Indians. Indianapolis, Indiana: The Indian Question CD-ROM, Objective Computing, 1994.

Colema, R. V. First Frontier, New York and London: Charles Scribner's Sons, 1948.

Connell, Evan S. Son of the Morning Star: Custer and the Little Big Horn. San Francisco: North Point Press, 1984.

Cotterill, Robert S. The Southern Indians: The Story of the Civilized Tribes Before Removal. Norman: University of Oklahoma Press, 1954.

Debo, Angie, A History of the American Indians. Norman: University of Oklahoma Press, 1983.

Debo, Angie, The Road to Disappearance: A History of the Creek Indians. Norman: University of Oklahoma Press, 1941.

DeRosier, Arthur H. Jr. The Removal of the Choctaw Indians. Knoxville: University of Tennessee Press, 1970.

Dowd, Gregory E. A Spirited Resistance: The North American Indian Struggle for Unity, 1745-1815. Baltimore: John Hopkins University Press, 1992.

Drake, Benjamin, Life of Tecumseh and His Brother the Prophet With a Historical Sketch of the Shawanoe Indians. Cincinnati: E. Morgan & Co. 1841.

Dutton, Bertha P. American Indians of the Southwest. Albuquerque: University of New Mexico Press, 1983.

Edmunds, R. David, The Shawnee Prophet. Lincoln: Universty of Nebraska Press, 1983.

Ehle, John, Trail of Tears: The Rise and Fall of the Cherokee Nation. New York: Doubleday, 1988.

Encyclopedia of Native American Tribes. New York and Oxford: Facts On File Publications, 1988.

Fiedel, Stuart J. Prehistory of the Americas. Cambridge, New York, New Rochelle, Melborne, Sidney: Cambridge University Press, 1987.

Finger, John, The Eastern Band of Cherokee in the 20th Century. Lincoln: University of Nebraska Press, 1991.

Foreman, Grant, The Five Civilized Tribes. Norman: University of Oklahoma Press, 1989.

Foreman, Grant, Indian Removal: The Emigration of the Five Civilized Tribes of Indians. Norman: University of Oklahoma Press, 1932.

Foreman, Grant, A History of Oklahoma. Norman: University of Oklahoma Press, 1945.

Frazer, Robert W. Forts of the West. Norman: University of Oklahoma Press, 1965.

Gibson, A. The Chickasaw. Norman: University of Oklahoma Press, 1971.

Grant, Bruce, Concise Encyclopedia of the American Indian. New York: Wings Books, 1958.

Graymont, Barbara, The Iroquois, Frank W. Porter III, General Editor. New York and Philadelphia: Chelsea House Publishers, 1988.

Graymont, Barbara, The Iroquois in the American Revolution. New York: Syracuse University Press, 1972.

Green, Michael D. The Creek, Edited by Frank W. Porter, III. New York and Philadelphia: Chelsea House,1989.

Handbook of North American Indians, 15 Volumes. Washington, D.C.: Smithsonian Institution, 1990.

Hodge, Frederick W. Handbook of American Indians, 2 Volumes. New Jersey: Rowman and Littlefield, 1975.

Horowitz, David. The First Frontier: The Indian Wars and America's Origins, 1607-1776. New York: Simon and Shuster, 1978.

Hudson, Charles M. The Southeastern Indians. Knoxville: University of Tennessee Press, 1976.

Hyde, George E. Indians of the Woodlands: From Prehistoric Times to 1725: Norman: University of Oklahoma Press, 1962.

Jablow, Joseph. Indians of Illinois and Indiana. New York: Garland Publishing, 1974.

Josephy, Alvin M. The Patriot Chiefs: A Chronicle of American Indian Resistance. New York: The Viking Press, 1958.

Kappler, Charles J. Indian Affairs: Laws and Treaties, Volume II (Treaties). Indianapolis, Indiana

Kehoe, Alice B. North American Indians: A Comprehensive Account. Englewood Cliffs, New Jersey: Prentice-Hall, 1981.

Leitch, Barbara A. A Concise Dictionary of Indian Tribes of North America. Michigan: Reference Publications, 1979.

Marriott, Alice, and Rachlin, Carol K. American Epic: The Story of the American Indian. New York: G.P. Putnam's Sons, 1969.
Mathews, John Joseph, The Osages: Children of the Middle Waters. Norman: University of Oklahoma Press, 1961.
Mathews, John Joseph, Wah'kon-tah: The Osage and the White Man's Road. Norman: University of Oklahoma Press, 1932.
McCary, Ben C., Indians in Seventeenth-Century Virginia. Charlottesville: University Press of Virginia, 1957.
McReynolds, Edwin C. The Seminoles. Norman: University of Oklahoma Press, 1957.
Merrell, James H. The Catawbas, Edited by Frank W. Porter, III. New York and Philadelphia: Chelsea House, 1989.
Merrell, James H., The Indians' New World: Catawbas and Their Neighbors from European Contact to the Era of Removal. Chapel Hill:
University of North Carolina Press, 1989.
Milanich, Jerald T. & Hudson, Charles, Hernando De Soto and the Indians of Florida. Gainsville: University of Florida Press, 1993.
Native America in the Twentieth Century: An Encyclopedia, Edited by Mary B. Davis. New York: Garland Publishing, 1994.
Native North Americans, Edited by Daniel L. Boxberger. Dubuque, Iowa: Kendall/Hunt Publishing Company, 1990.
Newcomb, William W. Jr. The Indians of Texas: From Prehistoric to Modern Times. Austin: University of Texas Press, 1961.
Parkman, Francis, France and England in North America, 2 Volumes. New York: The Viking Press, 1983.
Perdue, Theda, The Cherokee, Edited by Frank W. Porter, III. New York and Philadelphia: Chelsea House, 1989.
Russell, Howard S. Indian New England Before The Mayflower. Hanover, New Hampshire: University Press of New England, 1980.
Schoolcraft, Henry R., Information Respecting the History, Condition and Prospects of the Indian Tribes of the United States. Philadelphia: J.
B. Lippencott & Co. 1860.
Southeastern Indians Since the Removal Era, Edited by Walter L. Williams. Athens: University of Georgia Press, 1979.
Stiggins, George, Creek Indian History: A Historical Narrative of the Genealogy, Traditions and Downfall of the Ispocoga or Creek Indian
Tribe of Indians, Introduction and Notes by William Stokes Wyman, Edited by Virginia Pounds Brown. Birmingham, Alabama:
Birmingham Public Library Press, 1989.
Stoutenbaugh, John Jr. Dictionary of the American Indian. New York: Wing Books, 1990.
Swanton, John R. Indians of the Southeastern United States. Washington, D.C.: Smithsonian Institution, 1946, reprinted 1978.
Swanton, John R. The Indian Tribes of North America. Washington, D.C.: Smithsonian Institution, 1952, reprinted 1969.
Tebbel, John, The Compact History of the Indian Wars. New York: Hawthorne Books, 1966.
Waldheim, Carl, Atlas of the North American Indian. New York and Oxford: Facts On File Publications, 1985.

Weslager, C.A. The Delaware Indians: A History. Brunswick, New Jersey: Rutgers University Press, 1972.
Woodward, Grace Steele. The Cherokees. Norman: University of Oklahoma Press, 1963.
Wright, J. Leitch, Jr. The Only Land They Knew: The Tragic Story of the American Indian in the Old South. New York and London: The Free Press, 1981.
Yenne, Bill, The Encylopedia of North American Indian Tribes: A Comprehensive Study of Tribes from Abitibi to the Zuni. Greenwich,
Connecticut: Bison Books, 1986.

Sequoyah, inventor of the Cherokee syllabary, built this one-room log cabin in 1829 as his home shortly after his move to Indian Territories. When the cabin and surrounding grounds near Sallisaw became the property of the state of Oklahoma in 1936, the cabin was enclosed in a protective stone building built by the WPA.
Photo Courtesy of Archives and Manuscripts Division, Oklahoma Historical Society

Sequoyah Birthplace Museum near Vonore, Tennessee features the art, language, myths and legends of Cherokee life in modern state-of-the-arts exhibits.

Cherokee Memorial on the grounds of Sequoyah Birthplace Museum is the common burial site for the remains of 18th century Cherokees relocated from sites of former towns along the Little Tennessee River flooded by the construction of Tellico Reservoir.

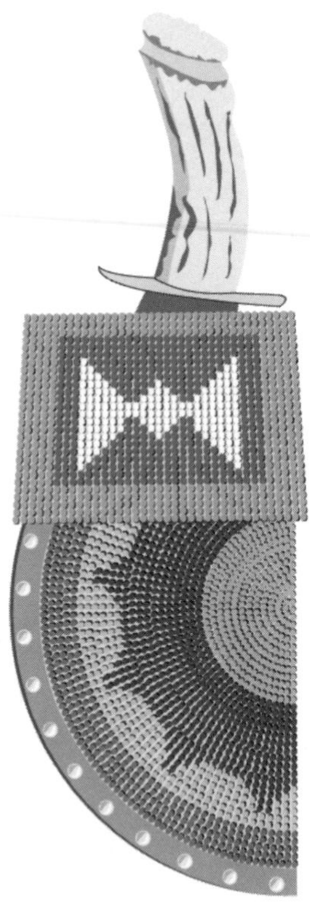

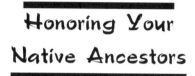

Honoring Your Native Ancestors

It is my personal opinion that every Cherokee descendant has a moral obligation to respect and honor their distinguished heritage, and to make a definitive effort to pass the tradition on to future generations. Since the first foreigner set foot on Native American soil where our people had lived since time immemorial, there has been a concerted effort by some to assimilate all Native Americans into the dominant race; yet to portray them, at best, as inferior human beings, and purge all traces of their customs and beliefs. As mentioned earlier, attitudes are slowly changing, but the very idea of a "different" people with a different culture living among them still is unacceptable to many of European descent despite knowing the land they live on today was stolen from native people.

At the time of the expulsion of the Cherokee people from their native homelands in the southeast, they were not itinerant barbarians as the government leaders of the day would have us believe. Instead, most were a settled people developing constitutional governments, establishing churches and schools, and farming by usual frontier standards. In the words of Grant Foreman, the Dean of American Indian Historians:

"They loved their streams and valleys, their hills, their forests, their fields and herds, their homes and firesides, families and friends; they were rooted to the soil. The trees that shaded their homes, the cooling spring that ministered to every family, friendly watercourses, familiar trails and prospects, busk grounds, and council houses were their property and their friends; these simple possessions filled their lives; their loss was cataclysmic."

Unfortunately, we cannot miraculously change the cruel and unnecessary hardships suffered upon our forebears, but it would be both unthinkable and immoral for us not to do everything in our power to remember, honor and respect them. This is not meant to imply that you should abruptly change your lifestyle and show up at work tomorrow sporting buckskins and moccasins. There are many ways to pay homage and express your pride, depending on individual circumstances. Joining an organized cultural group or reputable tribe and regularly taking part in their events is admirable and desirable for some, but time constraints and distance understandably prevents this for others.

Showing a genuine interest by acquiring a reasonably good understanding of Cherokee history can, in itself, be a means of memorial. Armed with this, you will be surprised at the myriad ways you can contribute to perpetuating the remembrance of your ancestors. Civic groups, schools, and especially organizations like the Boy and Girl Scouts will be quick to enlist you to help them learn about Cherokee life and culture. Others tracing their own native ancestors will seek you out to share the benefits of your experience.

There are a number of very worthwhile organizations dedicated to preserving and furthering Cherokee tradition in which you can provide needed financial support, either by membership fees or donations, or if your funds are limited, most also welcome volunteer workers for a variety of beneficial projects.

The Trail of Tears Association is a non-profit corporation working in a cooperative agreement with the National Park Service to protect, promote and preserve two of the routes taken by the Cherokee people during their removal and catastrophic journey to the west. Their goals include promoting awareness of the trail's legacy, including the effects of the U.S. Government's Indian Removal Policy on the Cherokees and other tribes. Assistance and support are needed from individuals and groups who wish to learn, educate others and preserve this important part of Native history. Your state may have a local chapter Charter memberships (available only for a limited time) are $15.00 per year and are tax deductible. Contact them at: 1100 N. University, Suite 133, Little Rock, AR 72207-6344.

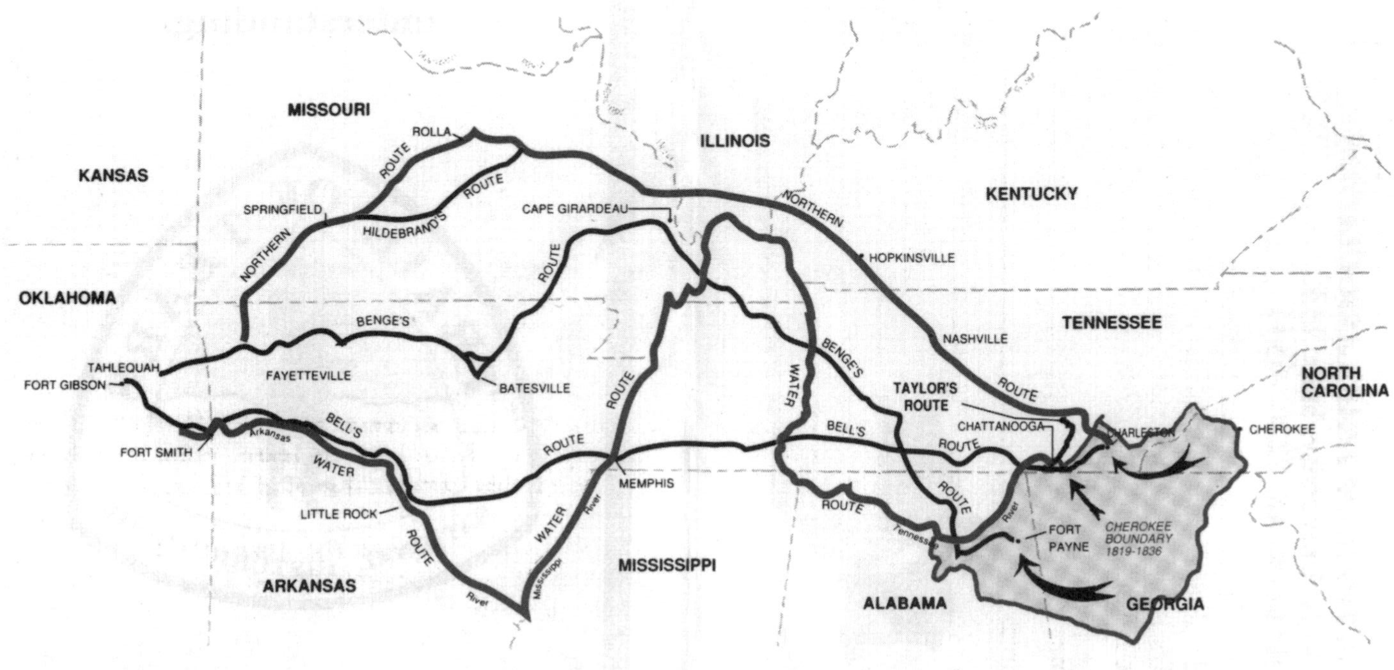

Land and Water Routes Used During Cherokee Removal to the West on the Trail of Tears.

The Cherokee National Historical Society operates The Cherokee Heritage Center which includes the Museum and bookstore, Tsalagi Theatre and Rural Museum Village at Tahlequah, Oklahoma. Their fine efforts to perpetuate the educational and cultural activities of the Cherokee people are indispensable. Supporting memberships at various levels from Youth ($5 annually) to regular ($30 annually) to Charter Archives benefactors are available: CNHS, P.O. Box 515, Tahlequah, OK 74465, Phone 918-456-6007.

The Cherokee Cultural Society of Houston is a non-profit group dedicated to building community, preserving Cherokee heritage, perpetuating Cherokee Culture and building the future of the Cherokee people. Volunteers produce the Cherokee Messenger newsletter which includes news articles, family histories, poetry, recipes and other items of interest. Annual membership dues are $20: Address: P.O. Box 1506, Bellaire, TX 77402-1506, Phone 713-668-9998.

National Museum of the American Indian, a part of the Smithsonian Institution, was created by a Congressional Act in 1989. It is the first national museum to be run by an American Indian and, upon completion, will house the finest collection of native artifacts in the world. Their stated purpose is to change forever the way people view Native Peoples of this hemisphere...to correct misconceptions, to end prejudice, to stop injustice and to demonstrate how Indian cultures are enriching the world. Numerous membership categories are available. For more information, write: NMAI, National Campaign, Smithsonian Institution, Washington, D.C. 20560.

Many states have non-profit organizations designed to provide a number of services to it's Native American citizens. The most popular of these in my own home state of Tennessee is shown here and I urge you to search for and support similar organizations in your area:

Native American Indian Association of Tennessee conducts and promotes seminars, institutes, educational programs and public information activities to raise the level of consciousness of the non-Indian population in the state of Tennessee to a fuller awareness of the past history and current status of Native American Indians. They also sponsor, promote and provide social services and other forms of assistance to American Indians who are in need and locate public and private agencies that can provide health, education, welfare, employment and other services. Membership fees are $10 annually and they do accept tax deductible contributions. NAIA, 211 Union St., Nashville, TN 37201.

The American Indian College Fund raises funds from the private sector primarily for scholarships, the most pressing and immediate need. With the help of a challenge grant from the National Endowment for the Humanities, AICF is building a Native Studies Endowment to maintain and strengthen Native studies programs at each of the colleges. Through a volunteer public education campaign, AICF works to increase public awareness of values and traditions of tribal cultures as well as the higher education needs of Native Americans. For information on how you can take part: AICF, 1111 Osage St., Bldg D, Suite 205A, Boulder, CO 80204.

The Native American Rights Fund is a non-profit legal organization devoted to defending and promoting the legal rights of all Indian people. NARF attorneys, most of whom are native Americans, defend tribes who otherwise cannot bear the financial burden of of obtaining justice in the courts in the United States. It focuses on guaranteeing that national and state governments live up to their legal obligations mainly through work in the courtroom. Here, NARF invokes laws enacted by these same government bodies to give strength and substance to promises that have been empty for too many years. Overall, this emphasis helps individual Native Americans advance toward controlling their own destinies and assuring their own survival. Contact them by telephone at 303-447-8760. Donations are tax deductible.

The Cherokees of California, Inc. is a non-profit, tribal organization whose primary purpose is to preserve and pass on Cherokee traditions, history and language to future generations. They have on-going programs across the state of California which has the highest population of Cherokee people outside Oklahoma. All who have an interest in renewing ties to their Tsalagi heritage are invited and there is plenty of volunteer work to be done. Contact them at P.O. Box 2372, Marysville, CA 95901.

When the Memories of Your Loved Ones are Dishonored, Do Something!

One of the most important things you can do as an individual or as a family to honor those who came before you is to stand up and be counted when issues arise that affect either the well being or consciences of any Native People. I've always noticed that few people are willing to express opinions that differ from the prejudices of their social environment, but change can come only when enough people do something about obvious injustices that occur. Discussing displeasures only in private, being complacent or waiting for someone else to do it simply doesn't work! Letter writing campaigns and phone calls to elected officials, lectures to local groups, and voicing outrage about insensitive actions on the part of anyone to local print media and radio and television station representatives can have a positive effect if enough people will just do it.

A good example of the type of event I'm talking about here is illustrated in the following adaptation of a guest editorial about Andrew Jackson that appeared under my byline in numerous newspapers, including Indian Country Today, the nation's largest Indian newspaper. How it fits as a means of openly "honoring" your beloved ancestors should become quite obvious . . .

(Article reprinted as it appeared in newspapers, 1996)

Andrew Jackson:
Hero or Hatchet Man?

by
Tony Mack (McClure), Ph.D.

The often apathetic attitudes of the Tennessee State Historic Society are showing again. Newspapers across Tennessee recently carried a publicity release touting a soon-to-be-released commemorative United States stamp that will feature Nashville's famous equestrian statue of Andrew Jackson superimposed in front of the Tennessee capitol building. Tennessee Governor Don Sundquist, U.S. Postmaster General Marvin Runyon, U.S. Senator Bill Frist, Martha Ingram, Chairman of the Tennessee 200 Bicentennial Commission, and other state officials unveiled the stamp design on the steps of the Tennessee Capitol building last week. In Runyon's words, *"Here, the character of the people have joined to create a national treasure," and he goes on to hail Jackson's spirit as "valiant"*. Governor Sundquist saw fit to add, *" This is a worthy symbol of that celebration* [referring to Tennessee's bicentennial, the event the stamp is supposed to comemmorate] *and a fitting tribute to Tennessee and her people."*

Once again, they are asking the citizens of America, who are finally beginning to realize that much of the history heralding some of our predecessors as great heros was really nothing more than hogwash, to pay homage to *"Old Hickory."* Will they never learn that in deciding whom our real heros are; indeed, who we would like to see "commemorated," as such, most of us have finally become intelligent and caring enough to weigh the effects of one's crimes against the effects of their virtues?

No one can dispute that Andrew Jackson was an elected President of the United States. His accomplishments, though questionable, as a leader in the battle of New Orleans also are well recorded. But also written in those annals of our time are indisputable facts which confirm that he was guilty of bribery, fraud, blatant racism and possibly murder! Do the decision makers in Nashville honestly believe we should simply ignore these attributes in choosing our heros? Or are they just having yet another laugh behind our backs because they are able, time and again, to brainwash us into revering whomever they choose. If this seems ridiculous, consider that as recently as two years ago, Tennessee's highly acclaimed "Tennessee Treasures" traveling museum featured Jackson as its main attraction, and that for decades every twenty-dollar bill in your paycheck has carried his portrait!

Andrew Jackson a murder? Decide for yourself after considering some well-documented facts. By virtue of a fraudulently acquired treaty which Jackson himself orchestrated, he pushed the *Indian Removal Act of the 1830's* through Congress. The results of this obviously immoral and unethical act may well exceed in weight of grief and pathos any other passage in American history; even the well-known exile of the Arcadians falls far behind it in its record of death and misery.

The law required the removal of native Cherokees from the very lands where their ancestors lay buried. Those who did not comply voluntarily were forced to do so. General Winfield Scott's army troops, armed with rifles and bayonets, searched out every remote cabin in the Cherokee country of the great Smoky mountains to seize and bring in all occupants. Families at the dinner table were startled by the sudden appearance of unexpected, armed intruders into their homes who drove them with blows and swearing along weary miles of footpaths that led to hastily built stockades. They arrested men at work in their fields of corn; they dragged women from their spinning wheels and small children from their play. It was common, according to published testimonials, that as these terrified people glanced back for one last look at their paltry, but cherished holdings, they saw their shelters in flames - fired by white settlers who followed on the heels of the soldiers, uncontested, to loot and pillage their cattle, stock, and other meager, personal belongings. Even graves were searched and robbed of valuables deposited with the dead.

According to statements in the military archives, one soldier whom they had assigned to this disgusting task stated years later, *"I fought through the civil war and have seen men shot to pieces and slaughtered by thousands, but the Cherokee Removal was the cruelest work I ever knew."*

A full century before the world would know the hate and greed of a race led by a man named Adolph Hitler, a comparative ethnic cleansing had begun right here in our Southeastern mountains . . .in the land of the free. A strategic expurgation of the impure from the midst of the pure, in the settler's eyes, identical to what would later ensue in a far away place called Bosnia.

From October 1838 through March 1839, which encompassed the cruelest months of winter, a grim, forced march of an entire nation was ordered. In an attempt to weather the 1200-mile journey from their familiar homelands in the Tennessee and Georgia Mountains to designated anomalous territories in Eastern Oklahoma, more than 4,000 men, women and children perished from hunger, disease and exposure. The single blanket and paltry salt-pork rations that government agents had issued them proved insufficient to sustain life for many, especially the sick, the aged, and small children who already were ill-prepared for such an odyssey. Thus, the lamentable *Trail of Tears* became one of the most shameful blights in the history of humankind and should have forever stamped a mutation into the reputation of Andrew Jackson, one of Tennessee's favorite sons, and all who had a part in it.

In the words of John Burnett, A U.S. Army interpreter during the forced march, *"Murder is murder . . .Somebody must explain the four-thousand silent graves that mark the trail of the Cherokees to their exile."* Yet, it is 1996, over a century and a half later; no one has ever explained, and today we face still another insult. We are to witness the memories of the men, women and children who died so needlessly at Jackson's hand further desecrated by the issuance of a United States Commemorative stamp that features him!

It is commonly known that attitudes are slow to change and it is no wonder, considering the insensitivities of so many. In a recent reprint series in several southeastern newspapers entitled "History" by historians John Hedge Whitfield and S.C. Williams, one article headlined *History: Settlers Strike Hard at the Cherokees* is an account of white reprisals that followed the "Cherokee invasion" of the Holston and Watauga settlements of Tennessee during the Revolutionary period. The author ends his commentary with the statement:

" It should be a matter of pride to all Tennesseans to know that so many inhabitants of the Tennessee Country played important parts in the war with the Cherokees."

It seems totally incongruous that in an era of bicentennial celebration for the state of Tennessee and so many years after the infamous "Trail of Tears" tragedy that an official state historical society or individual historians would dare have the impudence to suggest that we should be proud of the atrocities that any of our European ancestors inflicted upon the native Americans (in this case, the Cherokees) who rightfully occupied this land we now call Tennessee. These so called "settlers' or "early pioneers" were in fact intruders who immorally and unlawfully invaded the ancestral lands of an Indian nation who resided here long before those instruments we know as the Constitution and Bill of Rights were even thought of. Incredibly, even the name "Tennessee"belonged to the Cherokees, as it is an adaptation from their language!

Only after all peaceful pleas for recognition of their rights failed; only after their villages were attacked and their citizens maimed and murdered did the Cherokees retaliate with force against the repeated intrusions. From that day forward in history, the Cherokees have been largely regarded as savages. Even the writings that recorded the conflicts tend to confirm this; they were *"great victories"* if the settlers won, but *"massacres"* when the Indians prevailed.

Regrettably, there are still those among us, especially historical institutions and politicians, who insist on perpetuating the myths about what actually happened in those days, and relentlessly imposing on us, our children and their children, gross misrepresentations about the heroism and greatness of some participants. Are we to supposed to totally disregard other wicked and inexcusable criminal acts of Andrew Jackson during his presidency: refusing to allow anti-slavery pamphlets to be distributed in the U.S. Mail; refusing to carry out his lawful duties as President by refusing to enforce Supreme Court rulings when the state of Georgia violated Native American rights on territories guaranteed by federal treaties; or his destablization of the nation's currency by transferring taxpayer's monies out of the Bank of the United States into "pet" banks to give more aid and comfort to wealthy bankers loyal to him?

Will it never end? Have Americans reached such a state of low self esteem with callous, "I don't give a damn if it doesn't affect me attitudes," that we are willing to allow the continuation of this brainwashing forever?

The inexcusable treatment of Native Americans throughout the history of this entire country is well recorded and equally as tragic. Besides the nefarious Cherokee "Removal," the Sand Creek, Sappa Creek and Wounded Knee massacres by the U.S. Army serve as just three more shameful examples of almost 400 years of unrelenting savagery against the indigenous people of America, the most genocidal action by one race against another in the history of man. Even the World War II holocaust in which seven million Jews were exterminated by the Germans doesn't begin to compare with what was done more slowly to Native Americans by American "settlers" and the United States Army. Soldiers and "settlers," we remind you, that still today, *they tell us we should be proud of?*

Obviously, we cannot and should not live in the past. Nevertheless, it is only right that our country should forever bear the disgrace and suffer the retribution of its wrongdoing. We should forgive the responsible parties, but we must never, ever forget! If there is to ever be a complete healing process, instead of taking pride in the atrocities committed by our forebears, we should do everything possible to insure that such brutal, inhumane, criminal acts never happen again. Dispelling delusions which suggest that any of these people had any right whatsoever to do what they did is a first step. And refusing to recognize the perpetrators as "valiant" patriots in any form is a profound responsibility that we all share.

Prevarications of this type will never be corrected until we as individuals have the guts to stand up and say, "NO MORE," when we realize that, by today's standards, one of our so-called heroes would be considered little more than a thug. So what if he was president or governor or whatever. Right is right and wrong is wrong, even if the man did hold the highest office in the land! Is it not inherently wrong either to believe or say what is popular just to satisfy our peers, when in our hearts we know that something is morally or ethically wrong? And don't you agree that passing this garbage on to our children, generation after generation after generation is unforgivable?

In an effort to understand how men like Andrew Jackson and others of that time thought, indeed how incredulously some people still think, it might be enlightening to consider this information gleaned from highly respected Native American Journalist Tim Giago: Five days after the perfidious Wounded Knee Massacre of 1890 in which 300 unarmed men, women and children of the Lakota nation were murdered by the U.S. Army, L. Frank Baum, in his newspaper, the *Aberdeen South Dakota Saturday Pioneer wrote:*

"The Pioneer(newspaper) has before declared that our only safety depends upon the total extermination of the Indians. Having wronged them for centuries we had better, in order to protect our civilization, follow it up by one more wrong and wipe these untamed and untamable creatures from the face of the earth."

Ironically, ten years after penning this dispassionate editorial, this same man who seriously advocated the genocide of an entire race of Americans while publicly admitting that it was wrong, wrote one of the most widely acclaimed classics of all time. It was called *"The Wonderful Wizard of Oz."* So, wolves in sheep's clothing are all about us. Nevertheless, we still seem to exalt them as heroes and partake of their wares, even when we are fully aware of their vices! Surely, sufficient time has passed and enough learning has taken place for attitudes like this to change. Yet, so long as "respected historians," history books, influential government officials and historical organizations still can convince enough of us to take pride in the treacherous acts of our forefathers and to recognize them as great statesmen, man's inhumanity to man is destined to continue.

Was Andrew Jackson really a hero or was he a hatchet man? Regardless of your race, can you explain to your children why a man who committed such despicable horrors should be honored today on commemorative stamps, with publically displayed statues, in mobile museums, on the nation's money. . . or anywhere else in this country? Think about it.

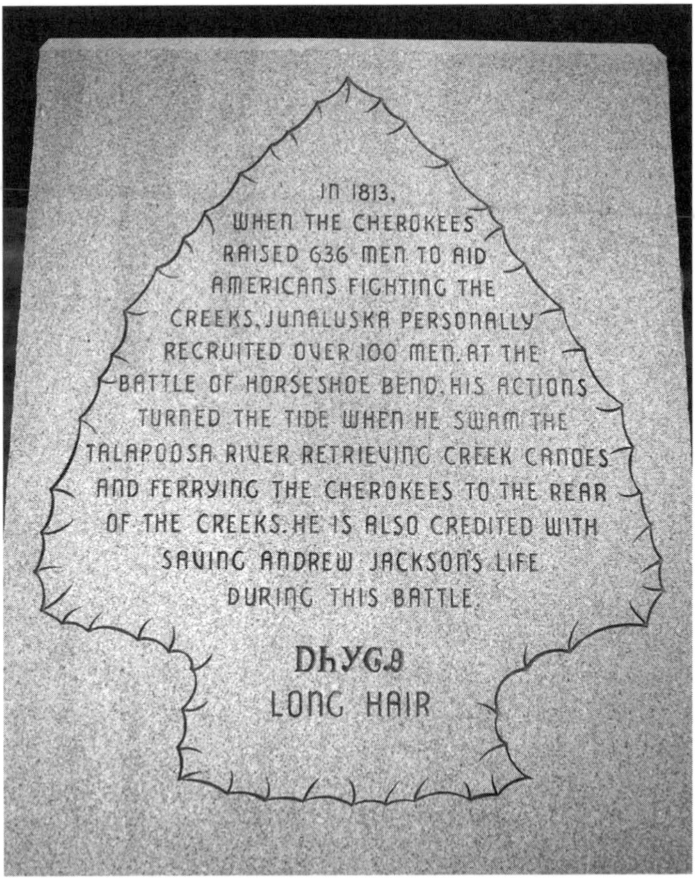

One of several markers at Junaluska's gravesite, Robbinsville, North Carolina.

The Eastern Band of Cherokee Indians

The Honorable Joyce C. Dugan, Principal Chief
The Honorable Gerard Parker, Vice-Chief

Jack E. Gloyne
Chairman
Birdtown Township

Billy Brown
Vice-Chairman
Snowbird &
Cherokee Co. Township

Tribal Council Members

Jim Bowman
Snowbird &
Cherokee Co. Township

Delores B. Davis
Yellowhill Township

Alan B. Ensley
Yellowhill Township

Steve George
Wolfetown Township

Bill Lambert
Birdtown Township

Henson Littlejohn
Wolfetown Township

Woodrow W. Lossiah
Big Cove Township

Teresa Bradley McCoy
Big Cove Township

Regina Ledford Rosario
Painttown Township

Marion Teesateskie
Painttown Township

February 15, 1996

Tony Mack McClure
434 Distribution Parkway
Collierville, Tennessee 38017

Dear Mr. McClure,

Thank you for your work of January 29, 1996 regarding the "Tennessee Bicentennial Stamp Design". It is disheartening to see a design which so clearly overlooks the important contributions Native Americans have made to the state of Tennessee. Andrew Jackson is controversial and his actions as President are often interpreted as "valiant", a fact, which has offended Native people, myself included.

The words you so eloquently put to paper are feelings shared by the Cherokee community. As a Cherokee leader, I feel we must work together to correct these myths perpetuated by professional historians and politicians. Finding the best method to convey this message of disapproval is the challenge we face. I will pursue a variety of avenues to address the concerns of Native People and also the people of Tennessee. The first is to inform the Cherokee Nation of Oklahoma and the Five Civilized Tribes which were affected by Jackson's removal policy. I will also work to insure a more accurate historical account of the Removal Policy is portrayed in Museums, Historical Societies and publications through our division of Cultural Resources. The frustrations from this type of misrepresentation

Qualla Boundary • P.O. Box 455 • Cherokee, N.C. 28719
Telephone: (704) 497-2771 or 497-4771
Telefax: (704) 497-2952

of the facts must force us to action within our communities but must also provide us with the strength to attempt positive change.

Letters and writings such as yours strengthen my resolve that the Cherokee community has many friends and supporters. Through this network we can affect positive change. I hope your writing receives the public attention it deserves. Your concerns are shared and I shall do all within my power to rectify this situation.

With kind regards, I am

Sincerely,

EASTERN BAND OF CHEROKEE INDIANS

Joyce C. Dugan

Joyce C. Dugan
Principal Chief

Enrollment Information

If you are conducting family research with a goal of gaining tribal membership in one of the three federally recognized Cherokee tribes (Cherokee Nation of Oklahoma or United Keetoowah Band headquarted in Tahlequah Oklahoma or the Eastern Band of Cherokees in Cherokee, Qualla Boundary, North Carolina), it is important to know the following: To register as a member of the Cherokee Nation of Oklahoma one must prove direct decendancy from a person of Cherokee Blood enrolled by DAWES during the period of 1898 to 1914 (An in-depth explanation of this role appeared earlier). Direct descendancy refers to **mother, father, or grand-parents of any generations.** Unfortunately, aunts, uncles, brothers etc. DO NOT qualify. Simultaneous applications for "Certificate of Degree of Indian Blood" and "Cherokee Nation Membership" are required. There is no minimum blood quantum required. Birth certificates, death certificates, and Court Records are some of the means of proving direct descendancy from a person listed on the DAWES Roll. Note that tribal agencies DO NOT accept Federal Census Records as proof of Indian blood.

It is your burden to prove to the Cherokee Nation that you are entitled to be registered in their community as a member and according to their rules. Regardless of the fact that the DAWES roll was a U.S. Government orchestrated requirement, if your ancestor is not listed on it, you simply won't be allowed to enroll, even if you have positive proof that you are 100 percent Cherokee! Welcome to the world of government bureaucracy. If your descendant IS listed on the DAWES ROLL, and you desire to attempt enrollment in the Cherokee Nation of Oklahoma, applications may be obtained from:

Cherokee Nation,
Tribal Register
Tahlequah, OK. 74465
Phone 918-456-0671

Enrollment requirements for the United Keetoowah Tribe and Eastern Band of North Carolina are even more stringent. Until just recently an applicant for enrollment in the eastern band was required to prove direct decendancy from a person who was listed on the Baker Roll of 1924 and have a minimum 1/16 blood quantum.

After Feb 15, 1996, ENROLLMENT IN THE EASTERN BAND WAS RESTRICTED TO NEWBORNS ON THE RESERVATION, however this is always subject to change.

For current information, contact:
Eastern Band of Cherokee Indians
Tribal Enrollment Office
Council House
Cherokee, N.C. 28719

Enrollment in the United Keetoowah Tribe of Oklahoma under UKB Membership Ordinance 90 UKB 9-16, 16 September 1990, provides that any descendant of 1/4 Cherokee Indian blood of any enrollee on the 1949 UKB Base Roll, **or on any other historical Cherokee Roll,** shall be eligible for enrollment in the UKB. Final determination of Cherokee Indian blood quantum rests with the UKB Tribal Council. For applications, call or write:

United Keetoowah Band
of Cherokee Indians of Oklahoma
P.O. Box 746
Tahlequah, Ok. 74465-0746
Phone (918) 456-5491

Over the years, the "rolls rules," have led to the formation of a few non-federal tribes in various parts of the country. Some of these are officially recognized by the legislated Indian Affairs

Commissions of their individual state governments. You might want to consider pursuing membership there if you do not have the required Dawes or Baker rolls connection for the federal tribes. Just keep in mind that they will be asking what you can do for them, instead of what they can do for you. Benefits are almost non-existent, save some educational scholarship considerations and limited housing assistance for the needy , and they are available only to legal residents of the state where the tribe is located. I also strongly recommend that you check out the credentials, goals, policies and tribal enrollment requirements of any non-federal tribe you consider applying to. The common denominator for authenticity, credibility and approval by state governments seems to be an absolute requirement for proving descent from a Cherokee ancestor and the government rolls are the vehicles for this in all cases that I have researched. In some rare instances, I am told, certified family documents will be considered.

There are many groups without any form of recognition that claim Cherokee descent, some of which even call themselves "tribes" and award titles such as "chiefs, clan mothers, etc." Some of these are made up of very sincere people desiring a local place to exercise traditions of heritage, even if they are unable to document it. Nevertheless, others are headed by shysters interested more in the pocketbooks of their "tribesmen" and general public than anything else; thus, I cannot urge you enough to carefully investigate any such group that you consider becoming affiliated with.

In the first edition of this book, I listed every group I could find whose primary focus seemed to be respect for and interest in Cherokee culture. That was a mistake, because I later learned that one of them was advertising memberships in their "tribe" to include a "card certifying you as Indian with no paperwork required" for just $25; another was designating people as "chiefs" (and awarding them plains Indian names) without any requirement for proof of Cherokee blood.

Understand, it is not my purpose to be judgmental, but I find such practices very objectionable because they can have only a detrimental effect on real Cherokee people and culture. In view of these incidents, I elected to list in this edition only federal or state recognized tribes. The term "recognition" in this context is defined as recognition by a state Commission of Indian Affairs or similar department charged specifically with handling Indian affairs. The fact that a group may have a state charter as some type of non-profit corporation does not qualify in this regard.

In response to inquiries to all fifty state governments, the following six tribes were reported to have official recognition. Contact them directly for information:

Cherokee Tribe of Northeast Alabama
P.O. Box 41
Boaz, AL 35957

Echota Cherokee Tribe of Alabama
P.O. Box 25
Cooks Springs, AL 35052

Cherokee of Southeastern Alabama
510 S. Park Ave.
Dothan, AL 36301

Cherokee of Georgia Tribal Council
P.O. Box 227
Saint George, GA 31646

Georgia Tribe of Eastern Cherokees
P.O. Box 1993
Dahlonega, GA 30533

Northern Cherokee Nation of the Old Louisiana Territory
1012 Old Highway 63 North
Columbia, MO 65201

DID YOU KNOW?

During the Dawes enrollments, if an applicant's parents were full bloods of different tribes, their registration was based only on the mother's blood. They would be listed as one-half Indian. Freedmen were always enrolled with no Indian blood.

Some Advice on Recognition

Once you have learned about your Cherokee ancestors and documented the lineage, you might be quite content to simply savor the knowledge and silently pay homage in a private way. This, of course, is a matter of personal choice, but as mentioned earlier, many people will want to take a more active part. If so, can you expect to be accepted by other Cherokees with open arms? With some exceptions to be noted, the extent of recognition is largely up to you, and a few personal words of advice are offered.

It is important to keep in mind that the mayhem and discrimination of the past have not deterred the Cherokee from being an extremely proud and determined people. They are intensely protective and conscientious of the images portrayed of them by anyone, and particularly watchful of those who claim Cherokee heritage. Rest assured that if you show up at Big Cove on the Qualla Boundary professing to the locals that your grandmother was of Cherokee royalty, they will quickly dub you a "wannabee," regardless of your ancestry. If you insist on dressing in Kevin Costner costumes when you attend official Cherokee functions or when visiting predominant Cherokee communities, you will not want to hear the whispers that are sure to follow. If you use the fact that your distant grandmother was a Cherokee to justify setting yourself up as some kind of shaman or to operate sweat lodges for hire on some secluded farm, have no doubts - your actions will be highly frowned upon. And, if you obviously know little or nothing about Cherokee history or culture, your authenticity is sure to be seriously questioned. Rightly so!

The terms "new ager" and "wannabee" are heard much more nowadays than a few years ago, largely due to the actions of a few who exploit native culture with only profit motivations. Most of the people who practice these scams have no Indian blood at all, but this isn't always the case. Unfortunately, this sort of activity often results in the unjust stereotyping by some Cherokee Nation citizens of everyone not living within a recognized Cherokee community or possessing a federal tribal enrollment card. This is sad, particularly for bonafide Cherokee descendants whose only impetus is to show respect for their antecedents, profess pride in being of Cherokee blood, and to carry this noble heritage forward to future generations.

Genuine Cherokee descendants have no trouble dubbing those who are frauds as such, and most agree that using ancestry - real or otherwise - for exploitation is unforgivable. Nevertheless, the feelings of those who have no such intentions should also always be considered. By personal choice, some Cherokee descendants have no interest at all in federal recognition or its benefits. Others, perhaps million of them, are not qualified for federal registration because their ancestors either never enrolled , separated from their tribe, or were listed only on rolls prior to the final Dawes census. It is very unfair for any of these circumstances to affect their acceptance or esteem, yet one cannot avoid noticing a marked tendency by even some of the *leaders* of the federal tribes to refuse to acknowledge the credibility of any non federally recognized individual or tribe. While this attitude is insensitive, there are some obvious reasons for it. Retaining tribal sovereignty is a constant uphill battle for tribal managers and maintaining even minimal tribal services with drastically reduced, federally administered budgets is a task that few of us would care to inherit. There is no way to escape the fact that the addition of only a single individual to tribal rolls amounts to a further dilution of already meager available income or other treaty entitlements. Imagine multiplying this by scores of people - many of whom, given the opportunity, would exercise their right to share in benefits that they neither need nor deserve - and it is easier to comprehend the seemingly over-protective guardianship exhibited by leaders who have the awesome responsibility of insuring the welfare of their tribal members.

The advent of Indian gaming laws which allow gambling on Indian trust lands (where states approve) and a resulting per-capita share of profits from these ventures has brought an influx of "new" Indians out of the woodwork seeking federal recognition. While there are certainly exceptions, the motivations of most of these are quite clear, and it's safe to say that *honoring their heritage* usually doesn't fit into the picture. Both of the above situations have understandably increased the apprehensions of native governments and caused them to question the legitimacy of those claiming native heritage, especially organized groups. Still, it is grossly unfair to stereotype everyone because of the selfish acts of a few.

Ultimately, how well one is accepted and recognized by the vast majority of the Cherokee people depends on one simple word - respect. And the amount received will be in direct proportion to the amount given. Sure, you might occasionally run into a jerk with a racist attitude, but if you do, simply consider the source. Respect the people, their culture and traditions, and most of them will happily treat you as one of their own.

Contemporary Traditional Dress

Dressing in distinctive native attire at certain times is a great way to assert and exhibit ancestral pride, but it is very important to make these choices carefully, depending on the type of event you plan to attend. Cherokees scrutinize the dress of their own (especially dancers) more seriously than some people seem to realize, because they are so protective of image and desirous of accurate portrayals of their culture. There are differing views on the correctness of this; some believe that Cherokees should always wear the traditional Cherokee dress of some period, regardless of the occasion, and they are quick to criticize those who do not strictly adhere to this. Others argue that the tribal dress they wear should be a matter of personal choice, so long as their selection is not offensive. This is likely to be a subject of continued discussion, so I'll interject my opinion for whatever it's worth.

Some festivals are private, spiritual ceremonies which agreeably should be kept as pure and traditional as possible. But most powwows of today are publicized events open to the public that offer not only dance competitions among inter-tribal dancers, but also a trade place for vendors of every conceivable type of native mer-

At inter-tribal festivals (pow-wows), it is not unusual to see Cherokee people dressed in a variety of Native American regalia.

chandise. One day is often devoted exclusively to school age children and while they come to learn, they also want to participate and have fun. In these instances, I can see no harm in real Cherokees dressing in "anything Indian" so long as it accomplishes the task at hand - namely, getting the attention of children (and some adults for that matter). While they're standing in awe of whatever costume you are wearing and busily clicking photographs, it's very easy to say, *"My people of old really didn't wear clothes like these, but some Native Americans did, and we want you to have the opportunity to see them."*

If you doubt my philosophy here, try wearing a turban like the one Sequoyah is always pictured in (no offense intended), and sit a few yards away from another Cherokee wearing a colorful, full-feathered head-dress. Then compare the number of children who run excitedly in his direction with those who only look questionably at you in passing. You'll quickly see my point. The Cherokees of the Eastern Band in North Carolina are often criticized by other tribes because some of their tribal members dress in Plains costumes and head-dress to pose with tourists for pictures. It's simply a matter of economics - they're providing what the visitors want, and although one could argue that these are still "teaching" situations where it's best to be authentic, I maintain that first you have to get the "student's" attention. Explanations can come later. Besides, there are always plenty of people around in "correct" attire that you can point out as examples.

You'll also occasionally hear derogatory comments about white people -those with no native ancestry-dressing in Indian clothing and attending pow-wows. They are sometimes dubbed as "wannabees" or "white Indians," and often are even accused of trying to "steal" the spirituality of Native Americans. Here again, with the exceptions on exploitation noted earlier, I cannot disagree more. In this regard, the late Archie Sam, highly regarded Cherokee chief of the Medicine Springs Stomp Dance Ground near Gore, Oklahoma summed it up nicely in parts of a speech he gave during a University of Oklahoma symposium on December 12, 1976:

"It was prophesied a long time ago that Indians would turn away

from their heritage and ceremonies, and would become weak and lost. Still, when the prophets gazed into their crystal stones they saw in the far distant future a young generation rising who would appreciate the values of their heritage and ceremonies and would become a strong race of people. For this reason the traditional Cherokees are desperately trying to preserve their songs and dances. It was further prophesied that when a non-Indian understands the Indian way of life and its value system and dresses like an Indian, the Indians will have found a true friend. So today, at our ceremonial grounds, we have many non-Indian friends. I personally remember when the non-Indian neighbors would come to the ceremonial grounds to play ball and dance. They were accepted as friends. They were true friends of the Indians."

What is considered the traditional dress of the Cherokee today? Ironically, according to the Cherokee National Historical Society, this question was not officially decided until about 1970 when a young lady named Virginia Stroud was chosen as *Miss Indian America*. Realizing that few dated paintings existed of Cherokee women during the 19th century, except for those of some means who wore the high fashion gowns of white society, a special committee was appointed by the leaders of the Cherokee Nation of Oklahoma to study what Miss Stroud should wear to represent her people and heritage. A member of this committee, Mrs. Wynona Day , visited Cherokee, North Carolina searching for clues to traditional dress before the Trail of Tears. There, she came into possession of an old house dress over one hundred years old. This article was researched in old historical society documents and those in private collections and eventually authenticated as a model for the current Cherokee traditional ladies *"tear dress."* [Note: pronounced as in "tear an ad from the paper."]

These garments are called tear dresses because in days of old, scissors were rare and all the pieces were actually torn from a single length of fabric. All parts are either squares or rectangles and the decorative trim is usually a band of contrasting, solid colored fabric fashioned so that the dress material can show through. The cutwork is usually some variation of simple diamond and square

Robin McClure, the author's wife, in traditional Tear dress.

Author's mother Marian Haley in Tear dress and fellow Cherokee David Bell wearing Tear shirt.

shapes. Today, they also are adorned with bands of colored ribbons.

This same committee confirmed that traditional jewelry was usually made from copper, although some gold and silver was used when available. Pearls, shells , and mother of pearl disks were often worn as pendants and medallions. These were ornately carved or decorated with pierced scroll work. Beadwork frequently adorned bags and belts with motifs of stylized vines, flowers and leaves.

Today, when referring to dresses, the term "tear" is also pronounced as in *"trail of tears"* and they are said to symbolize that infamous journey. Men wear "tear" or "ribbon" shirts fashioned very similar to the style of 19th Century white settlers, but they do not include the usual drop shoulders, gathers, gussets, ruffles or muslim cloth commonly worn by frontiersmen. They are highlighted with bands of colored ribbons and loose hanging ribbon streamers which replaced hide or hair fringes of old. Today, some say these symbolize the hidden "tears" of our ancestors who were forcibly removed from their native homeland and the real tears of helpless sympathizers as they watched the ruthless actions of their own government.

At any type of Cherokee function today, it can be said that "Tear" attire is the most commonly worn and accepted traditional dress. Several examples are shown throughout this text, most of which were made by my dear friend and Godmother of sorts, Helen Altman, a Washo-Assiniboine. They are relatively easy to make and patterns can be acquired from Cherokee Publications, P.O. Box 430, Cherokee, NC 28719, Phone (828) 488-8856 or Crazy Crow Trading Post, P.O. Box 847, Pottsboro, TX 75076, Phone (800)786-6210.

Tuckaleeche Story, Alabama Indian Affairs Commissioner in traditional ceremonial tear dress.

Ahnawake Clinch

Honor by Learning the Mother Tongue

It has long been said that when a people lose their language, with it goes their identity. For many years, there was a steady decline in Cherokee speakers, owing in large part to a period when Cherokee school children were forbidden to speak their native tongue. Like so many other endeavors of the ruling, English speaking majority, this was just another part of the assimilation plan. Although this prohibition ended with the closure of regulated Indian boarding schools and similar religious mission schools, the students who attended them grew up unable to converse in Cherokee and passed the inability on to other generations. Fortunately, a turnabout has now occurred and virtually all schools with large Cherokee enrollments offer language classes today.

Of all the ways a Cherokee descendant can honor their ancestors, none is more admirable than to acquire some knowledge and usage of their mother tongue and the effort can be most enjoyable. Cherokee is a soft and beautiful language, characterized by a richness of vowel sounds and filled with a treasury of enduring musical names for the wondrous keystones of Mother Nature. Her mountains and rivers, beasts of the forests, and homes of indigenous people are known by such artful and melodic names as Tanisi, Chattahoochie, Nantahala, Awohali, Hiwasse, Oostanaula and Tellico. Now, before you fling this book across the room and exit screaming, recognize that it is not my intention to suggest you immediately embark on a full-fledged language learning venture, although such a goal should not be considered out of the question. Learning a few basic words such as greetings, the names of foods and animals, how people are referred to. i.e., man, woman, boy, girl, etc. can be an interesting and rewarding quest and it is much easier than you might think. You'll also be quick to see how much more receptive Cherokee people are if you can speak a few words in Tsalagi.

The Cherokee word for "hello," for example, is "o si yo" and is pronounced "oh-see-yo." See that wasn't hard at all was it? As a matter of fact, you probably already speak a little Cherokee and simply didn't know it. The word for "yes" is "uh huh"...... and that's exactly where the term originally came from - the Cherokee language!

To be fair, there are factors involved that can be difficult but none that can't be overcome with a little practice. For instance, there is no word in our language for "goodbye," (it's too permanent). Instead we use the phrase "do na da go hv i" (pronounced "doe- nah-dah-go-huh-ee") which translates to "until we meet again." And there are words with the same spelling that mean different things, differentiated only by emphasis of a certain syllable. . . ."a ma" (said as "ah mah" with the emphasis on "mah" meaning "water," as compared to the same spelling "a ma" with emphasis on "ah" instead of "mah" which means "salt." A similar example is the word "ka ma ma" (pronounced "kah mah mah") which can mean either butterfly or elephant, depending on the speaker's intentions, thus it would be necessary to be very selective should you find yourself in the awkward position of having to describe the varmint that has invaded your vegetable garden to a Cherokee policeman on the telephone. Chances are good that he would be reluctant to come with blue lights flashing if he understood you to say that an escaped butterfly from the visiting circus was eating your lettuce patch. Are you confused yet?

Seriously, learning a working vocabulary of often- used Cherokee words is relatively easy and while space or intent here does not allow for a full treatment of the subject, suffice it to say that my recommendation is to acquire a good English-Cherokee dictionary so you can see the words you most want to learn and an audio tape set to hear how they should be spoken. Armed with these, you can learn a word to two a day with ease right from the beginning and then increase the pace as time permits.

My wife Robin, who only recently decided that perhaps she should learn the meanings of some of the off-the-cuff remarks I sometimes make to her, names things around the house with Cherokee words and finds it to help tremendously. I have been advised, for instance, that our cannister that holds the oatmeal on the kitchen counter is now known as "so qui li" (said as "so qee lee") meaning "horse." Word and mental picture associations have long been a great self-training tool, but I must point out to you there is one downside. I've noticed that Robin now has a new name for me - "u ne gi di," pronounced "oo nay gee dee" (oo as in ooze, gee as in geese). It means "ugly," or hadn't you guessed?

While there are many available choices of the language aids mentioned above, most of which are excellent, I always recommend the works of my Cherokee friends Prentice and Willena Robinson. They have operated Cherokee Language and Culture in Tulsa, Oklahoma since 1974 and have helped thousands of people learn our language.

Among the many cultural products offered, their *"Easy to Use Cherokee Dictionary"* is exactly what the name implies. The introduction explains in very simple terms a brief history about the language, plus offers expert advice on how to pronounce the vowel sounds, consonant sounds and unique combinations of both. This is something you can grasp in five minutes. It gives an English word followed by its Cherokee equivalent, and goes a step further by showing how the word is written in the Sequoyah Cherokee syllabary which will be discussed shortly. See samples below.

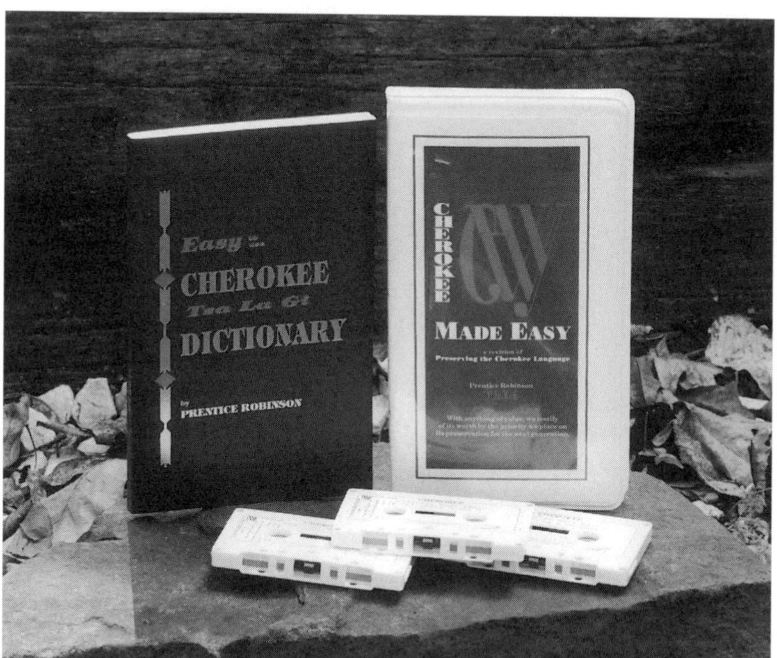

Easy to Use Cherokee Dictionary and 3 tape Audio Set.

heir	u ti ye hi	ᎤᏘᏰᎯ
held	a ye hv gi	ᎠᏰᎲᎩ
hell	tsv s gi no	ᏨᏍᎩᏃ
hello	o si yo	ᎣᏏᏲ
help	a (li) s de (lv) di	ᎠᎵᏍᏕᎸᏗ
helpful	a (li) s de li s gi	ᎠᎵᏍᏕᎵᏍᎩ
helping	a (li) s de li ha	ᎠᎵᏍᏕᎵᎭ
herd	u ni go di - ga na tla i	ᎤᏂᎪᏗᎦᎾᏝᎢ
helps	tsu na (li) s de lv di	ᏧᎾᎵᏍᏕᎸᏗ
hem	a yv qui dv - a sa no	ᎠᏴᏈᏛᎠᏌᏃ
hen	tsa ta ga - a gi si	ᏣᏔᎦᎠᎩᏏ
here	a ni	ᎠᏂ

Sample partial page from Prentice Robinson's "Easy to Use Cherokee Dictionary."

A three tape audio set features Prentice reciting a carefully selected array of commonly used Cherokee words and phrases and includes a written booklet of them. Each word or phrase is stated in English, followed by its Cherokee equivalent spoken three times. Although he is one-half Cherokee and was raised in a Cherokee speaking household, Prentice, being the southern gentleman that he is, speaks pretty much the same dialect as anyone in the south or southwest. In other words, he has no accent as is often found among people whose first language is something other than English. This is just one of several reasons that I always recommend his tapes over others I have reviewed. They're simply easier to understand and learn.

The Sequoyah Syllabary

Unlike English, all words in the Cherokee language are made up of 85 sounds (or syllables) and it was the world famous work of Sequoyah (George Gist or Guess) completed in 1821 that made his syllabary the first written language of any Indian tribe (see chart that follows). This was a remarkable feat, especially considering that Sequoyah could neither read or write English. A syllabary differs from an alphabet in that each character represents the sound of a syllable. Written Cherokee is especially unique in that it has no upper or lower case letters, no capitalization, and very little punctuation. There are no sounds for the English letters B F J P R V X or Th. (because no

Cherokee words include these sounds), and while Sequoyah originally also devised characters for numbers, the Cherokee council voted not to adopt them. The syllabary is so simple that when it was invented, most Cherokee speakers could have it memorized and be writing their own language within a matter of days. Elementary school children today can have it down pat in a few hours!

Using our earlier example of the word "o si yo," (meaning "hello" in English) and the English phonetics of how to pronounce it (oh see yo), refer to the Syllabary chart on the following page and notice that the characters used to make up the three sounds of the word are as follows:

o = Ꭳ
si = Ꮟ
yo = Ᏺ

The Robinson's have also devised a simple flash card set that can be very helpful in learning the syllabary.

All of the above products can be purchased by check or money order (sorry, no credit cards) as follows:

• Easy to Use Cherokee Dictionary - $20.00
•Cherokee Made Easy Three Tape Audio Set - $42.00
•Cherokee Syllabary Flash Card Set - $12.00
(Add $3 shipping for up to 2 items; $4 for all three.)

Mail order to:

Chu-nan-nee Books
P.O. Box 127
Somerville, TN 38068

Learn the Syllabary by Computer

If you have ventured into the infinite world of personal computers, my friend Marvin Plunkett, a member of the Cherokee Nation of Oklahoma, has teamed with other talented tribesmen (Marvin and Linda Summerfield and Robin Mayes) to develop a remarkably simple computer teaching program for the Sequoyah Syllabary that is nothing short of fantastic. Dubbed *"The Cherokee Companion,"* the idea for this software stemmed from the basic premise that learning the syllabary is a good first step in learning the Cherokee language because either reading or reciting Cherokee is nothing more than "naming" the characters of the written words. Once the syllables (sounds) and their written forms are mastered, learning words is much easier.

You will need Windows 3.x or above , a sound card and speakers (or headphones) to operate the program and if connected to an on-line service, you can download a FREE Demo - tutorial version directly from Marvin's website at http://intertribal.net. Plans are in the mill for this to eventually be a three-part program, however only Part One (and a neat, recent addition to it) is available at this writing.

Without fully explaining how the program works, when the program is installed, a computer keyboard laid out just like the one you are accustomed to using comes up across the bottom of your monitor screen. Instead of the English alphabet, however, the keys have the syllabary characters on them. The shift and cap-lock functions change the keyboard to different characters. Placing the cursor on any key and clicking the mouse causes that particular syllable to be audibly recited by the dynamic voice of Marvin Summerfield, a fluent Cherokee speaker and language editor of the *Cherokee Observer,* a monthly newspaper that features two pages of language studies in each issue.

The program includes a Cherokee True Type font, a talking syllabary chart, a talking syllabary typing tutor, a talking reader/writer and a few Cherokee words and phrases. When a word, or even an entire phrase is typed, a click of the mouse on the "reader" button causes it to be read back to you the same as touching a single character key. Terrific!

Recently added, the "Tah-Ah-Teh" Teacher teaches the syllabary in ten easy lessons that can be learned in just ten days! Plans for future parts include a built in dictionary (Prentice Robinson's, mentioned earlier) and a talking word processor. Part one retails for $45 which includes shipping in the U.S. **To order, call toll free. 1-800-323-6509.** Credit cards are accepted. Or mail your order to:

Profit Systems Software
Dept-CP
1641 NW Rutter Lane
Roseburg, OR 97470-1949

Whether you are a serious student of the Cherokee language or only want to learn a few words and phrases, I highly recommend all of the aids mentioned in this chapter. Just imagine how wonderful it would make both of you feel if, by some divine grace, you could walk up to your great-great grandmother today and say to her *"e li si gv ge yu hi"* (a-lee-see guh-gay-you-hee) ....Grandmother, I love you!

Understanding Traditional Cherokee Stomp Dance and Music

Modern pow-wows are characterized mostly by the colorful dress, music and dances unique to tribes other than those with Eastern woodlands origins. Of course, Indians from all nations now take part in these festivals which are held regularly all across the country, and this is especially true since the advent of dance competitions. Names like jingle dance, fancy dance, fancy shawl and grass dance are commonplace, and because of their popularity and widespread exposure at events open to the public, the average citizen today believes these are traditional to all tribes. The ceremonial dance of the Cherokee, however, is significantly different, and a basic knowledge of this important aspect of the culture is a necessary part of venerating those who came before.

In the traditional "stomp dance" as it is known, there is no stately display of feathered regalia, no electrical lighting or amplified sound, and there are no vendors or demonstrations. Dances are held in Oklahoma and Cherokee, North Carolina throughout the year and are central to the community life of both the Cherokee and Creek and people with Natchez Indian heritage. The stomp provides a vital link with a religious and cultural past that for many years almost totally disappeared. When Christian missionaries were first invited into Cherokee country in the east, they viewed these ancient rituals as heathen, partly because they did not attempt to understand them, but more because they conflicted with their ideas of religion. They made every attempt to convince our people to abandon the old ways, teaching in their churches that it was wrong, even akin to witchcraft. That attitude still prevails today in some rare cases, but a group of traditional Cherokee-Natchez, primarily of the Keetoowah Nighthawk Society, refused to convert and in the early 1900s the stomp again became a regular event in the full-blood communities of Oklahoma.

Cherokees dance single file around a sacred fire which has been kept burning since time immemorial It is said that hot ashes from the old fire in the east accompanied the people on the Trail of Tears to their new home in Oklahoma. The moral code or law the Cherokees had always lived by required the fire to be kept burning; that they be kind to each other and live in harmony with nature. It is no different today. Cherokees believe that when the fire shines into the heavens at night, the smoke carries their songs skyward; thus the Great Spirit knows his children have not forgotten him and will bless and watch over them as he did their forefathers.

Only the men are allowed to sing and dancers follow a lead singer-adults nearest the fire with children on the outside. Some wear special, homemade costumes, but most wear conventional, everyday clothing. Behind the lead singer, women dressed in long skirts with terrapin shell rattlers or shakers strapped to their ankles make the "music." The shells, filled with small river pebbles, synchronize the beat of the song and provide rhythm with each stomp of their feet. Occasionally, small water drums and gourd rattles provide additional sounds. Male dancers sometime shout, clap their hands, or make animal noises as they repeat what the leader calls out.

Keetoowahs gather at dusk for Cherokee Stomp Dance, 1917.
Photo Courtesy Archives and Manuscript Div. OK Historical Society.

"Music" in the Stomp Dance is made by women wearing Terrapin Shell Shakers (rattlers) filled with river pebbles on each ankle. When Terrapins are in short supply, small Carnation evaporated milk cans make good substitutes.

Stomp dances are always held at night because Cherokees believe the Great Spirit can see their sacred fire better at night. The "Long Dance" usually comes first in which the chants of the songs ask for a spiritual blessing to provide the strength necessary to dance all night. Next is a series of three dances reserved only for the members of the particular grounds and after that, the "Friendship Dance" is called so all can participate. It is not unusual to see people from every race attending; except on rare occasions when a stomp is designated as private, visitors are welcome.

By tradition, women having their menstrual period are not allowed to participate. Some stomps also still include the old tradition of ritual pipe smoking (yes, only standard tobacco is used), or ritual purification by the taking of the "black drink" or "medicine," as it is called, prior to the start of dancing, or in some cases, just after it ends. This is a natural "tea" or decoction prepared by designated medicine men of the stomp grounds and designed to cause a person to vomit within two or three minutes after ingestion, thus cleansing the interiors of the body. A person must always face east while he drinks it. In the old days, the emetic was made from a combination of cedar, horsemint and old tobacco, or from dried, baked leaves of either Yaupon or Cassine Holly. Today, it is more apt to be composed of the red root of Cherokee huckleberry (also called snakeroot), and flint weed (a red willow). Pine and cedar leaves are sometimes added to the pot of water when the mixture is boiled.

To the uninformed observer, many of the dances appear to be the same, but each is unique with its own name and its own song or songs. Some of the dances are purely social, but others are designed to re-enact historical events or provide instructions about the surrounding environment and the things in it. In the old days, they were primarily for instruction as opposed to recreation, but now there is a healthy mix of the two. In fact, the entire event can be considered a mixture of ethnic religion and recreation, similar in some respects to old time camp meets in white communities. Stomp dance ground members often bring covered dishes and cook a whole hog on an open pit. Any form of alcohol is strictly prohibited. Some of the dances honor specific animals and have names like the Bear, Buffalo, Eagle, or Quail dance. Participants in these often mimic the actions and movements of the animals and contrary to the opinions and teachings of the old missionaries (and a few modern ones) the animals themselves are not being worshiped. The creator is being sent thanks for including them among the people and for all the necessities of life they provide.

The songs, cumulatively referred to as the "Great Spirit songs" are always sung in the Cherokee language. Many of the words, however, are not definable today; they are only phonetic sounds that have no real meaning. Long ago, the words did have meanings, but were used only in religious songs. Basically, it can be safely stated that all of the songs used now, except those designed specifically for fun or recreational dances, are prayers of a type, similar to what is heard in conventional gospel songs. One word that can be understood, *"Ya lo sa le hey"* meaning "God" or "Great Spirit," is noticeably prevalent.

After dancing all night, just before it is time for the sky to lighten in the east, the leader calls for the "Drunk Dance" in which everyone dances like they are spiritually drunk with joy; it is in effect, a celebration. They have danced all night and can now applaud the accomplishment. In this dance only, the women are allowed to take off their shell shakers and sing. As the sun approaches on the horizon, the last dance - the Old Folks' Dance- is held and everyone takes part. Afterwards, all but the fire-keeper head for home. It is his duty to preserve the ashes for rekindling at the next stomp.

As of 1999, there are two ceremonial stomp dance grounds, *Gateo Unalas Deske,* still active in Oklahoma. Stokes ground and the Redbird Smith ground have regularly scheduled dances. On Qualla Boundary Cherokee reservation in North Carolina, stomps are conducted by grounds chief Walker Calhoun. If you are interested in attending any of these, inquire at the respective tribal headquarters for dates and locations.

A young full-blood who is almost single-handedly keeping this unique and important part of Cherokee culture alive outside of Oklahoma and North Carolina is my good friend and Cherokee brother, Tommy Wildcat. A few years ago, Tommy and his twin sister Tammy of Park Hill, Oklahoma started a group, mainly from their own family, called the "Cherokee Dancers of the Fire." They now conduct educational stomp dance demonstrations throughout the country at universities, cultural gatherings and Indian festivals with the admirable goals of promoting understanding between races and preserving ancient ways and dances. Three generations of their family participate, including Tommy and Tammy's father, Mr. Tom Webber Wildcat, now in his late 70's.

In addition to being an accomplished stomp dance leader, Tommy is a well known river-cane flutist, singer and recording artist who has appeared in numerous television specials and movies. His positive messages about the stomp dance and Cherokee culture are financed in large part by the sales of his wonderful recordings that feature the traditional music of the ancients. They are listed here for your perusal and highly recommended as a means of further cultural enlightenment and enjoyment.

Tommy Wildcat

Cherokee Stomp Dancers of the Fire: A collection of traditional Cherokee Stomp Dance songs that have been sung around the sacred fire since ancient times. Tommy and Tammy Wildcat collaborated with their father to produce this offering (Cassette tape).

Cherokee Voices - Songs 'N' Flutes: Tommy accompanies himself on flute as he sings traditional Cherokee songs as well as his favorite hymns including *Amazing Grace,* in the Cherokee language.
Sing-a-long phonetics are included. (Cassette tape).

Cherokee Flute - A Warrior's Spirit: This recording features traditional Cherokee river cane flute music accompanied by the ancient water drum in honor of Cherokee clan mothers. (Cassette or CD).

Cherokee Flute - Flames of Fire: Songs of comfort and healing using a wormy Chestnut flute accompanied by the natural sounds of night crickets. Dedicated in honor of Cherokee elders. (Cassette or CD).

Actual River Cane Flute: When the earliest Europeans came across the Cherokee people living in the Great Smoky Mountains, it is said that flute players came out of the Cherokee villages to meet them playing harmonic tunes to soothe their ears. Today, Tommy Wildcat continues this tradition using the same type of flutes used by the ancients. Each flute is personally handmade by Tommy using river cane (bamboo) gathered by his family along the Illinois River in his native Oklahoma.

Above cassette tapes are $12 each; CD's and River Cane flutes are $17 each, shipping included. Order directly from the following address. Performance engagements by either Tommy or the Cherokee Dancers of the Fire can also be made by contacting:

Tommy Wildcat
A Warrior's Spirit Productions
P.O. Box 66, Dept. TM
Park Hill, OK 74451
Phone 918-457-3409

Three generations of the well-known Wildcat Family, Cherokee Nation of Oklahoma, perform an educational demonstration Stomp Dance.

Epilogue:

Of Secrets Kept

In the sun-parched little town of Porum, Oklahoma along the Canadian River, the Cherokee woman listened intently as the white attorney sitting across the desk from her made inquiries about a time in her past she had hoped only she and close relatives would ever know of. Tears ran down her cheeks as she gave painful, but solemn answers. Her husband could have handled this better, she thought. He was a white man. Nevertheless, he was sick and unable to leave their cabin back in the quiet savanna, so she had come alone.

The year was 1907 and it was tumultuous times in the Cherokee Nation. The Dawes Commission was in the final stages of completing its devilish mandates, again setting aside solemn agreements made between the Indians and the white government. In violation of all the promises, Oklahoma Territory was destined for statehood. The communal land of the Cherokees would soon be gone forever, making way for railroads, ranches and businesses for the same people who had banished her ancestors to this country many years ago. Already, she had received her bantam Dawes land allotment of 110 acres, split in parcels in different places. But she knew she could no longer go whenever she pleased to the cane breaks along the river for basket reeds or to gather herbs that grew only in select places ordained by the creator.

When Katy Downing was born about 1851 in the Going Snake District up north, her life, though far from perfect, had been better. She didn't even know the name of her father who had died when she was just a moppet, but the old stories told by her mother, Darkey Buzzardflopper, were always wonderful, giving her a sense of family pride and imaginative glimpses of the Smoky mountains. the Cherokee's real homeland back east.

Her grandfather's name was Young Tiger Downing and from the many stories, his name was obviously fitting. His wife was Suzie Crittenden and they had lived on a little piece of land in a place called Georgia all their lives. So had her mother, even after her parents passed on . . . that is until the white soldiers came and took her and all of her nearby kin to a filthy stockade at Fort Marr across the mountain. They had to leave everything behind because the troops came without warning and left just as quickly, allowing unruly white men who had shadowed them to take whatever they wanted of their invaluable, but precious possessions.

All along the route of their exile to some yet undescribed, darkened place, many died and were committed back to the creator mostly in unmarked graves; several old and sick at a place called Blythe's Ferry where they crossed the Tanisi River. Two of their chiefs,Whitepath and Fly Smith, and some sick children were interred at Hopkinsville. And more in Illinois . . . and Missouri . . . and Arkansas. Thousands in all. Only loved ones in individual families knew for sure how many had left, or how many had arrived. They were sure of but one thing; their number had dwindled significantly during the merciless journey and in the year that followed, many more would succumb for lack of proper food and other necessities of life. There was no relief for the afflicted; not even a legendary talisman of times past to provide rescue.

Fortunately for Katy, her mother Darkey survived to give life to at least one more generation. Kah-tah-goo-ga, Katy was called as a lass, and it was so recorded by the government men whose leaders were decreed her people's masters. Darkey endured until Katy was eight years old, finally surrendering much too young to maladies induced by countless hardships and heartbreaks. Katy's remaining relatives were few, but they cared for her until her marriage to a Cherokee man named George Tehee. The union was good for a time, but again, kismet willed. Tehee was a good man, but their views differed, and they went their separate ways. Katy knew that subsisting alone would be hard for a woman in her thirties, but she gave it her best, tending her crops and orchards with help and advice from her uncle George Downing who lived nearby. Then one day in 1885, a stranger from Checotah in the Creek Nation stopped by her place to water his horse. He was a white man named James McClure en route to visit some relatives who lived just down the road in Briartown. He was a handsome sort, uncommonly courteous, and she couldn't avoid noticing the twinkle in his eyes as he glanced back at her when he rode away.

A couple of days later, he stopped by again on his return trip. Supper was on the table and she wondered if he had planned it that way. Earlier, she had noticed the figure of a man on a horse lingering way in the distance beyond the purple cone and thistle field. Smoke rising from the chimney was always a dead giveaway to vittles cooking at that time of year. It was October, still quite warm, and if not mere coincidence, the spiraling smoke seemed to be the signal that prompted the remote figure to start moving in her direction again.

He was the most polite man she had ever seen and the small talk was interesting. He told her about his cousin at Briartown. They even had the same name - James M. McClure. Their fathers were brothers, but the other James' father had married a Cherokee woman before they left Georgia, so he was a mixed blood and her welcome dinner guest was pure white. He came to the Creek Nation a few years earlier to work and had never gotten around to marrying.

Katy listened intently to all the tales he had to tell and found herself secretly hoping that he wouldn't just disappear, never to be seen or heard from again. It could get very lonesome in the remote areas along the Canadian, especially during the winter. Her work was a lot for a woman alone, too, though she was in her prime and headstrong.

As if by divine providence, the charming visitor asked her about possibly staying a few days and lending a hand around the place. The work he had back in Checotah was piecemeal anyway, he said. That is why he had come down to talk with his cousin; perhaps to find some work, but none was to be had there. He offered to work only for board for himself and his horse. Katy relished the idea, but wondered earnestly how it might look, given the fact she was still legally married. What would people say? Reputation was important, but so was companionship. And she had known far too much solitude since she and her husband had parted ways. She also knew reconciliation would never be, but divorce was up to the man in this culture and the stigma might make him avoid it. The help she could use, but another feeling inside her was inescapable, too. If she agreed to this, there would likely be more than a simple employer relationship. The howl of the lonely knows few bounds when eternal exile is feared and there are never any guarantees of tomorrow.

James McClure never made it back to Checotah, and that winter was the warmest one Katy had ever known. By Christmas, her belly was visibly swelling and she knew she was with child. On the one hand, she was happier than she could ever remember, but also could not put away somber thoughts of all that surely would be said about her. She was a full blood Cherokee living with a white man she wasn't married to; possibly could never marry. And now, she was carrying his child. Not long ago, her sister Nellie had ventured down this same path, having to give her newborn daughter the name of a man who was already married. And in spite of all of Katy's prying, the identity of her own father had been carried to the grave by her mother. Was this a contingency of something in the genes of the women in her family? Had fate resolved that because they were Indian and viewed as a lower class of humanity by the majority, they somehow could triumph only in moral degradation? Or had they, merely by ignoring the consequences, allowed the absence of needed affection to open the door to a secret vault that held more of a life than they had ever known before?

The harsh winter of Indian Territories quickly gave way to the new life of spring. The trees became green, the pastures rich, the waters calm. Katy's worries of peer discrimination were put aside by her resolve to stay close to home. Visitors were a rarity here, anyway. She seldom saw anyone outside of family. The joys in her life had been few, so she deserved to savor this part of her womanhood at all costs. Inside her a new soul was growing and its blood was her blood. That's all that mattered.

Her days were like a pleasant landscape; she welcomed the sights and sounds of fresh beauty. The birds were nesting in budding fruit trees and she loved the aroma of the freshly plowed earth as James prepared potato, corn and cotton fields. But there are always benign and malevolent rhythms in life. By June, Katy was heavy and it became almost impossible to complete necessary chores. Profuse sweats made breathing hard, limiting her energy. An incessant cough that James had developed back during the snows grew worse by the day until he could barely function. She began to realize that it was not something common. Trouble was on the horizon.

In July, James summoned Katy to his sickbed saying they had to make some hard decisions. He had seen this malady before and knew that few survived it. While the two of them could still travel, they would make a trip to the tobacco country in northwest Tennessee where some of his relatives could care for her when the baby came. He had a cousin there who was a lay preacher and knew that he would not turn them away.

In August 1886 at the farm home of David William and Mary McClure, just outside Palmersville, Tennessee, Katy gave birth to a healthy boy. She named him "Aulie," meaning "sweat" in the Cherokee language, and James chose "Floyd" as his middle name. Young David and his wife agreed to care for the child the same as their own until the outcome of James' affliction was known. To outrun the approaching winter, James and Katy made the long trip back to Oklahoma planning to return for Aulie Floyd as soon as possible.

But Katy's visions were not to be. James survived but was bedridden much of the time. New seasons came and went and times were harder than ever in the Cherokee Nation. It was all Katy could do to make ends meet. They sent any spare money they could muster to Tennessee for Aulie's board, but often there just wasn't any. Then Katy's sister Nellie passed away suddenly in the Flint district leaving no one to care for her four-year-old daughter, Nannie Griffin. There were but two choices; if Katy could not take her in, she would go to the Cherokee orphanage up north at Tahlequah. So, Nannie came to Texana and Aulie Floyd remained in Tennessee. It was a defeat in a battle she had not waged and a triumph for destiny, who had not even fought.

George Tehee never pursued divorce. He died in 1888. Five years later, rumors of termination of the Cherokee Nation and probable land allotment were rampant. James' health had improved some, so he and Katy finally married, hoping that intermarried whites would be accepted as Cherokee citizens when and if the land was allotted to individuals. In 1896, James went back to Tennessee to bring their child home. Katy stayed at home with Nannie. Instead of a warm welcome from his cousin, he was confronted by the sheriff who insisted that money for several years of boarding would have to be paid if he was to take his son back to Oklahoma. The boy had obviously been brainwashed by racist attitudes, too, and knowing his natural parents only as strangers about whom he evidently had heard the unthinkable, he made it quite clear that *"he didn't want to go live with "black" people."*

James returned to his beloved Indian wife in the Canadian River country bearing news that no mother should ever hear. Fears that had gnawed at her for the last ten years had now become realities. With no money for ransom, the fruit of her womb she had so longed for remained alien, possibly forever. Katy noticed a visible change in the person looking back at her from the old mirror in her bedroom that night. It was as if there were sudden prophecies of no more colorful flowers to please the eyes, laughter to excite, or contemplations of future pleasures. Through her favorite chink in the cabin wall, she watched through tears as the moon rose visibly blue and even the music and motion of the coyotes on the ridge behind the barn was noticeably different. Silhouetted against the lighted backdrop, the strides and wails of these minstrels of the dark signaled unusual caution as if already convicted for crimes not committed. Katy went to bed exhausted, physically and mentally. When sleep finally came it was vital, yet comatose . . . .a kind of death perhaps.

The woman sitting across the desk from attorney Clark looked much older than her fifty-six years. The sands of time had ridden through her life a victor; she had barely clung to the reins. Empathy, yet learned sustenance, was clearly visible, but through a veil of unavoidable tears. He knew how she must feel, but could offer little solace. She had opened her secret vault to him and the price was terrible. At age twenty one, her blood son had finally tried to learn more about who his blood parents really were, although through a lawyer, and only for a material reason. Nevertheless, he had a right to know all, like it or not, as did those he might father later. She knew that Aulie had been crowned with lies since the day he was born, but in the center of the crown, like a diamond, rested the only thing that mattered right then. Truth. And so it was written.

Katy Downing Tehee McClure died a widow on Jan 3, 1935. Years before, she was enrolled by both Dawes and Miller while James was denied Cherokee citizenship as an intermarried white. Neither she nor James ever saw their son Aulie Floyd again. He married, worked many years as farm manager for the Choctaw Planting Company, fathered nine children, and lived in Northwest Tennessee all his life. He made very effort to avoid being regarded as a mixed-blood and anything more than a slight mention of the circumstances of his birth was strictly forbidden. He would say only that he was the illegitimate son of a woman called "Tinnie" and that because he was misbegotten, the preacher who raised him as a "nephew" made him wear gum boots to church every Sunday. At his death in 1975 at the age of 89, he left instructions that one of his grandsons would receive a small, sealed cardboard box containing a vintage pipe he had smoked for many years and a worn out Schrade pocket knife used to clean it. The items rested on an old folded letter dated January 29, 1907 addressed to him from the law firm of Clark and Clark, Porum, Oklahoma. It must have been, to his way of thinking, the greatest thing of value he could bequeath to a grandson whose pride of heritage he knew was significantly different than his own. Incapable of forgiveness during his lifetime for having been "given away," he must also have known that by this gesture, his own singular blindness would be pardoned and finally, essential unity and understanding could begin. Aulie Floyd McClure was the beloved paternal grandfather of the author.

Aulie Floyd McClure, 1886-1975 (standing) pictured with his good friend Henry Nance in 1930. "Floyd" as he was always known, was farm manager for the old Choctaw Planting Co.

J. W. CLARK R.R. CLARK

CLARK & CLARK
ATTORNEYS
DAVIS BUILDING
PORUM, OKLAHOMA

1.29.1907

Mr. Floyd McClure
Palmersville, Tennessee

Dear Sir,

Referring to yours of 12th of January,last, we found James and Katie McClure, also known as Tehee, living at Texana. Mr. McClure could not come indue to illness but Mrs. McClure did come in and we find these to be the facts.

As you have been told she says that she and her husband James are your natural birth parents. At birth in 1886 you were left there in Tennessee to be cared for by your fathers cousin David and his wife Mary. He was a preacherand they agreed to do it because James was ill and believed he did not have long to live.

As to your question if you are illegitimite, Mrs.McClure says she was still married to her last husband when you were born, George Tehee, but she had not been living with him for some time. She and James married legally in 93. when his health improved and she showed her proof. She stated that when they were able they had sent money several times to help with your boarding but James and his cousin got into an affray about that when he come back to Tennessee about 10 years ago. He saidtheynevers sent it but your fathers cousin Robert McClure who lives here at Briartown can bear witness. James wanted to bring you back here but the Sheriff there said David had a right of raising for labor on his farm due to boarding you. He said you didnt want to come anyway because you thought we were all black people. There has been no contact since then.

We are obliged to inform you regarding the pending entitlement you inquire about, you have been misinformed because there is no land allotments to be had. In this matter any one eligible will receive an equal share of the money set by Congress. We do not know yet how much each share will be, but we believe you will be entitled and will be pleased to file the paperwork if you are still of interest knowing no land can accrue. Our commission is shown in the enclosed papers which you will need to fill out and return without delay.

Yours truly,

Clark & Clark.

And now, my grandmothers
the job is done . . .
So hear me - no more tears!
Once again, the rays of a warm
and welcome sun
shine brightly over Chu-nan-nee
burning the haze away.
The eagle is back
soaring high and free.
And the music of the wind
in your mountain valley
always reaches crescendo.
At Briartown, Porum and Texana
memories rein divine.
Of secrets kept, tears wept
no longer yours or mine.
When sands of time set free the truth
a pride of blood ensued
Now your kin will finally know
It all began with you.

Appendix 1

The American Genealogical Lending Library
a.k.a. Heritage Quest
Listing of Cherokee Microfilm
Available for Rental or Purchase

The American Genealogical Lending Library (Heritage Quest) was established to provide libraries, genealogical and historical societies, and individuals with a low-cost, efficient microform circulation and sales service. Nearly all microfilm and fiche titles may be purchased through Heritage Quest, while the same titles may be rented directly by Heritage Quest Members or without membership through interlibrary loan programs established in libraries throughout the nation. AGLL's microfilm holdings are 250,000 titles strong including the entire U.S. Federal Census (1790-1920) and is constantly expanding. With few exceptions, they have all microfilm pertaining to the Cherokee that is available in the National Archives. Instructions for microfilm rentals or purchase are given at the end of the following listings for Cherokee microfilm:

NATIVE AMERICAN CENSUS INDIAN TERRITORY 1860

M653-52 1860 Census: Washington, White, and Yell Counties in Arkansas; and Indian Lands

M653-54 1860 Census Slave Schedules: Johnson, Lafayette, Lawrence, Madison, Marion, Mississippi, Monroe, Montgomery, Newton, Ouachita, Perry, Phillips, Pike, Poinsett, Polk, Pope, Prairie, Pulaski, Randolph, St. Francis, Saline, Scott, Searcy, Sebastion, Sevier, Union, Van Buren, Washington, White, and Yell Counties in Arkansas and Indian Lands

T623-1843 1900 Indian Territory Census: Cherokee Nation (part: EDs 4-15, and ED 16, sheet 1)

T623-1844 1900 Indian Territory Census: Cherokee Nation (part:

	ED 16 sheet 2-end EDs 17-28, and ED 29, sheet; 1-20)
T623-1845	1900 Indian Territory Census: Cherokee Nation (part: ED 29, sheet 21-end, and EDs 30-41)
T623-1846	1900 Indian Territory Census: Cherokee Nation (con-t'd: ED 42-48, 189)
M595-23	Cherokee (North Carolina), 1915-22
M595-24	Cherokee (North Carolina), 1923-29
M595-25	Cherokee (North Carolina), 1930-32
M595-26	Cherokee (North Carolina), 1933-39

NATIVE AMERICAN - ENROLLMENT

Enrollment Cards of the Five Civilized Tribes, 1898-1914.

This microfilm publication reproduces the enrollment cards prepared by the staff of the Commission to the Five Civilized Tribes (Cherokee, Chickasaw, Choctaw, Creek, and Seminole) between 1898 and 1914. These records are part of the Records of the Office of Indian Affairs, Record Group 75, and are housed in the Archives Branch of the Federal Archives and Records Center, Fort Worth, Texas.

The Commission enrolled individuals as "citizens" of a tribe under the following categories: Citizens by Blood, Citizens by Marriage, New Born Citizens by Blood (enrolled under an act of Congress approved March 3, 1905, 33 Stat. 1071), Minor Citizens by Blood (enrolled under an act of Congress approved April 26, 1906, 34 Stat. 137), Freedmen (former black slaves of Indians, later freed and admitted to tribal citizenship), New Born Freedmen, and Minor Freedmen. Delaware Indians adopted by the Cherokee tribe were enrolled as a separate group within the Cherokee. Within each enrollment category, the Commission generally maintained three types of cards: "Straight" cards for persons whose applications were approved, "D" cards for persons whose applications were considered doubtful and subject to question, and "R" cards for persons whose applications were rejected. Persons listed on "D" cards were subsequently transferred to either "Straight" or "R" cards depending on the Commission's decisions. All decisions of the Commission were sent to the Secretary of the Interior for final approval.

An enrollment card, sometimes referred to by the Commission as a "census card," records the information provided by individual applications submitted by members of the same family group or household and includes notation of the actions taken. The information given for each applicant includes name, roll number (individual's number if enrolled), age, sex, degree of Indian blood, relationship to the head of the family group, parents' names, and references to enrollment on earlier rolls used by the Commission for verification of eligibility. The card often includes references to kin-related enrollment cards and notations about births, deaths, changes in marital status, and actions taken by the Commission and the Secretary of the Interior. Within each enrollment category, the cards are arranged numerically by a "field" or "census card" number which is separate from the roll number. The index to the final rolls, which is reproduced on roll 1 of this publication, provides the roll number for each person, while the final rolls themselves provide the census card numbers for each enrollee. No indexes have been located for the majority of the "D" and "R" cards.

Roll	Category	Census Card Number
M1186-1	Index to the Final Rolls	
M1186-2	Cherokee by Blood	1-805
M1186-3	Cherokee by Blood	806-1645
M1186-4	Cherokee by Blood	1646-2461
M1186-5	Cherokee by Blood	2462-3293
M1186-6	Cherokee by Blood	3294-4027
M1186-7	Cherokee by Blood	4028-4847
M1186-8	Cherokee by Blood	4848-5661
M1186-9	Cherokee by Blood	5662-6303
M1186-10	Cherokee by Blood	6304-7140
M1186-11	Cherokee by Blood	7141-7961
M1186-12	Cherokee by Blood	7962-8794
M1186-13	Cherokee by Blood	8795-9634
M1186-14	Cherokee by Blood	9635-10461
M1186-15	Cherokee by Blood	10462-11132
M1186-16	Cherokee Minors by Blood	1-824

Roll	Category	Census Card Number
M1186-17	Cherokee Minors by Blood	825-1582
M1186-18	Cherokee Minors by Blood	1583-2331
M1186-19	Cherokee Minors	2332-3034
M1186-20	Cherokee Minors	3035-3684
M1186-21	Cherokee Minors	3685-4005
M1186-22	Delaware	1-382;
	Delaware	D1-D50;
	Delaware	R1-R5;
	Cherokee by Marriage	1-188
M1186-23	Cherokee by Marriage	189-288;
	Cherokee Freedmen	1-382
M1186-24	Cherokee Freedmen	383-814
M1186-25	Cherokee Freedmen	815-1231
M1186-26	Cherokee Freedmen	1232-1595;
	Cherokee Freedmen Minors	1-93
M1186-27	Cherokee Freedmen Minors	94-542;
	Cherokee	D1-D267

Roll	Category	Census Card Number
M1186-28	Cherokee	D268-D1062
M1186-29	Cherokee	D1063-D1879
M1186-30	Cherokee	D1880-D2711
M1186-31	Cherokee	D2712-D3207
	Cherokee	R1-R336
M1186-32	Cherokee	R337-R1168
M1186-33	Cherokee Freedmen	D1-D388
M1186-34	Cherokee Freedmen	D389-D811
M1186-35	Cherokee Freedmen	D812-D1225
M1186-36	Cherokee Freedmen	D1226-D1342
	Cherokee Freedmen	R1-R304
M1186-37	Cherokee Freedmen	R305-R370
M1186-38	Cherokee Freedmen	R731-R1276

NATIVE AMERICAN ENROLLMENT

Final Rolls of Citizens and Freedmen of the Five Civilized Tribes in Indian Territory, 1907, 1914.

The rolls were prepared by the Commission and the Commissioner to the Five Civilized Tribes and submitted to the Secretary of the Interior for approval as provided by several acts of Congress. Both approved and disapproved names are included. Most rolls give name, age, sex, degree of Indian blood, and roll and census card number of each individual. This series is arranged by name of tribe and thereunder divided into rolls for citizens by blood, citizens by marriage, and freedmen.There are also rolls for the Delaware Cherokee. In many of the groups there are separate rolls for minor children and newborn babies.The names of the rolls are arranged numerically by roll numbers.

NATIVE AMERICAN ENROLLMENT

Applications for Enrollment of the Commission to the Five Civilized Tribes, 1898-1914. (Dawes)

D refers to dismissed or doubtful, M refers to Minor, R refers to refused.

Roll	Category	Census Card Number
M1301-174	Cherokee by blood	1-67
M1301-175	Cherokee by blood	68-150
M1301-176	Cherokee by blood	151-233
M1301-177	Cherokee by blood	234-323
M1301-178	Cherokee by blood	324-462
M1301-179	Cherokee by blood	463-553
M1301-180	Cherokee by blood	554-717
M1301-181	Cherokee by blood	718-865
M1301-182	Cherokee by blood	866-1020
M1301-183	Cherokee by blood	1021-1149
M1301-184	Cherokee by blood	1150-1294
M1301-185	Cherokee by blood	1295-1449
M1301-186	Cherokee by blood	1450-1611
M1301-187	Cherokee by blood	1612-1767
M1301-188	Cherokee by blood	1768-1914
M1301-189	Cherokee by blood	1915-2057
M1301-190	Cherokee by blood	2058-2198
M1301-191	Cherokee by blood	2199-2339
M1301-192	Cherokee by blood	2340-2504
M1301-193	Cherokee by blood	2505-2649
M1301-194	Cherokee by blood	2650-2804
M1301-195	Cherokee by blood	2805-2944
M1301-196	Cherokee by blood	2945-3055
M1301-197	Cherokee by blood	3056-3150
M1301-198	Cherokee by blood	3151-3275
M1301-199	Cherokee by blood	3276-3416

Roll	Category	Census Card Number
M1301-200	Cherokee by blood	3417-3550
M1301-201	Cherokee by blood	3551-3690
M1301-202	Cherokee by blood	3691-3838
M1301-203	Cherokee by blood	3839-3961
M1301-204	Cherokee by blood	3962-4100
M1301-205	Cherokee by blood	4101-4235
M1301-206	Cherokee by blood	4236-4345
M1301-207	Cherokee by blood	4346-4470
M1301-208	Cherokee by blood	4471-4608
M1301-209	Cherokee by blood	4609-4740
M1301-210	Cherokee by blood	4741-4855
M1301-211	Cherokee by blood	4856-4985
M1301-212	Cherokee by blood	4986-5124
M1301-213	Cherokee by blood	5125-5261
M1301-214	Cherokee by blood	5262-5400
M1301-215	Cherokee by blood	5401-5544
M1301-216	Cherokee by blood	5545-5675
M1301-217	Cherokee by blood	5676-5826
M1301-218	Cherokee by blood	5827-5970
M1301-219	Cherokee by blood	5971-6104

Roll	Category	Census Card Number
M1301-220	Cherokee by blood	6105-6270
M1301-221	Cherokee by blood	6271-6423
M1301-222	Cherokee by blood	6424-6587
M1301-223	Cherokee by blood	6588-6752
M1301-224	Cherokee by blood	6753-6941
M1301-225	Cherokee by blood	6942-7109
M1301-226	Cherokee by blood	7110-7266
M1301-227	Cherokee by blood	7267-7438
M1301-228	Cherokee by blood	7439-7633
M1301-229	Cherokee by blood	7634-7867
M1301-230	Cherokee by blood	7868-8015
M1301-231	Cherokee by blood	8016-8166
M1301-232	Cherokee by blood	8167-8315
M1301-233	Cherokee by blood	8316-8470
M1301-234	Cherokee by blood	8471-8630
M1301-235	Cherokee by blood	8631-8800
M1301-236	Cherokee by blood	8801-8968
M1301-237	Cherokee by blood	8969-9120
M1301-238	Cherokee by blood	9121-9290
M1301-239	Cherokee by blood	9291-9448

Roll	Category	Census Card Number
M1301-240	Cherokee by blood	9449-9532
M1301-241	Cherokee by blood	9533-9625
M1301-242	Cherokee by blood	9626-9741
M1301-243	Cherokee by blood	9742-9839
M1301-244	Cherokee by blood	9840-9943
M1301-245	Cherokee by blood	9944-10015
M1301-246	Cherokee by blood	10016-10075
M1301-247	Cherokee by blood	10076-10127
M1301-248	Cherokee by blood	10128-10183
M1301-249	Cherokee by blood	10184-10234
M1301-250	Cherokee by blood	10235-10299
M1301-251	Cherokee by blood	10300-10360
M1301-252	Cherokee by blood	10361-10455
M1301-253	Cherokee by blood	10456-10661
M1301-254	Cherokee by blood	10662-10729
M1301-255	Cherokee by blood	10730-10741
M1301-256	Cherokee by blood	10742-10750
M1301-257	Cherokee by blood	10751-10759
M1301-258	Cherokee by blood	10760-10769
M1301-259	Cherokee by blood	10770-10789
M1301-260	Cherokee by blood	10790-10808
M1301-261	Cherokee by blood	10809-10849
M1301-262	Cherokee by blood	10850-10910
M1301-263	Cherokee by blood	10911-10945
M1301-264	Cherokee by blood	10946-10994
M1301-265	Cherokee by blood	10995-11132
M1301-266	Cherokee minor (Act of 1906)	1-225
M1301-267	Cherokee minor (Act of 1906)	226-450
M1301-268	Cherokee minor (Act of 1906)	451-675
M1301-269	Cherokee minor (Act of 1906)	676-900
M1301-270	Cherokee minor (Act of 1906)	901-1125
M1301-271	Cherokee minor (Act of 1906)	1126-1350
M1301-272	Cherokee minor (Act of 1906)	1351-1590
M1301-273	Cherokee minor (Act of 1906)	1591-1820
M1301-274	Cherokee minor (Act of 1906)	1821-2049
M1301-275	Cherokee minor (Act of 1906)	2050-2275
M1301-276	Cherokee minor (Act of 1906)	2276-2425
M1301-277	Cherokee minor (Act of 1906)	2426-2650
M1301-278	Cherokee minor (Act of 1906)	2651-2875
M1301-279	Cherokee minor (Act of 1906)	2876-3100

Roll	Category	Census Card Number
M1301-280	Cherokee minor (Act of 1906)	3101-3325
M1301-281	Cherokee minor (Act of 1906)	3326-3550
M1301-282	Cherokee minor (Act of 1906)	3551-3750
M1301-283	Cherokee minor (Act of 1906)	3751-3945
M1301-284	Cherokee minor (Act of 1906)	3946-4005
M1301-285	Cherokee freedmen	1-225
M1301-286	Cherokee freedmen	226-450
M1301-287	Cherokee freedmen	451-666
M1301-288	Cherokee freedmen	667-890
M1301-289	Cherokee freedmen	891-1100
M1301-290	Cherokee freedmen	1101-1227
M1301-291	Cherokee freedmen	1228-1274
M1301-292	Cherokee freedmen	1275-1303
M1301-293	Cherokee freedmen	1304-1345
M1301-294	Cherokee freedmen	1346-1385
M1301-295	Cherokee freedmen	1386-1424
M1301-296	Cherokee freedmen	1425-1470
M1301-297	Cherokee freedmen	1471-1509
M1301-298	Cherokee freedmen	1510-1545
M1301-299	Cherokee freedmen	1546-1569

Roll	Category	Census Card Number
M1301-300	Cherokee freedmen	1570-1582
M1301-301	Cherokee freedmen	1583-1594;
	Cherokee freedmen minor	1-90
M1301-302	Cherokee freedmen minor	91-240
M1301-303	Cherokee freedmen minor	241-385
M1301-304	Cherokee freedmen minor	386-542
M1301-305	Cherokee intermarried white	1-160
M1301-306	Cherokee intermarried white	161-257
M1301-307	Cherokee intermarried white	257-288;
	Cherokee	D1-D76
M1301-308	Cherokee	D77-D191
M1301-309	Cherokee	D192-D297
M1301-310	Cherokee	D298-D388
M1301-311	Cherokee	D389-D493
M1301-312	Cherokee	D494-D604
M1301-313	Cherokee	D605-D717
M1301-314	Cherokee	D718-D791
M1301-315	Cherokee	D792-D847
M1301-316	Cherokee	D848-D929
M1301-317	Cherokee	D930-D995
M1301-318	Cherokee	D996-D1071

Roll	Category	Census Card Number
M1301-319	Cherokee	D1072-D1134
M1301-320	Cherokee	D1135-D1205
M1301-321	Cherokee	D1206-D1267
M1301-322	Cherokee	D1268-D1385
M1301-323	Cherokee	D1386-D1550
M1301-324	Cherokee	D1551-D1716
M1301-325	Cherokee	D1717-D1965
M1301-326	Cherokee	D1966-D2132
M1301-327	Cherokee	D2133-D2380
M1301-328	Cherokee	D2381-D2595
M1301-329	Cherokee	D2596-D2755
M1301-330	Cherokee	D2756-D2921
M1301-331	Cherokee	D2922-D3090
M1301-332	Cherokee	D3091-D3207;
	Cherokee	R1-R13
M1301-333	Cherokee	R14-R78
M1301-334	Cherokee	R79-R149
M1301-335	Cherokee	R150-R200
M1301-336	Cherokee	R201-R268
M1301-337	Cherokee	R269-R342
M1301-338	Cherokee	R343-R408
M1301-339	Cherokee	R409-R486
M1301-340	Cherokee	R487-R541
M1301-341	Cherokee	R542-R601
M1301-342	Cherokee	R602-R673
M1301-343	Cherokee	R674-R723
M1301-344	Cherokee	R724-R780
M1301-345	Cherokee	R781-R837
M1301-346	Cherokee	R838-R908
M1301-347	Cherokee	R909-R960
M1301-348	Cherokee	R961-R1035
M1301-349	Cherokee	R1036-R1063
M1301-350	Cherokee	R1064-R1105
M1301-351	Cherokee	R1106-R1152
M1301-352	Cherokee freedmen	D1-D682
M1301-353	Cherokee freedmen	D683-D741
M1301-354	Cherokee freedmen	D742-D792
M1301-355	Cherokee freedmen	D793-D855
M1301-356	Cherokee freedmen	D856-D903
M1301-357	Cherokee freedmen	D904-D957
M1301-358	Cherokee freedmen	D958-D1011

Roll	Category	Census Card Number
M1301-359	Cherokee freedmen	D1012-D1075
M1301-360	Cherokee freedmen	D1076-D1324
M1301-361	Cherokee freedmen	D1325-D2239;
	Cherokee freedmen	R1-R57
M1301-362	Cherokee freedmen	R58-R114
M1301-363	Cherokee freedmen	R115-R166
M1301-364	Cherokee freedmen	R167-R199
M1301-365	Cherokee freedmen	R200-R216
M1301-366	Cherokee freedmen	R217-R252
M1301-367	Cherokee freedmen	R253-R284
M1301-368	Cherokee freedmen	R285-R312
M1301-369	Cherokee freedmen	R313-R360
M1301-370	Cherokee freedmen	R361-R395
M1301-371	Cherokee freedmen	R396-R426
M1301-372	Cherokee freedmen	R427-R459
M1301-373	Cherokee freedmen	R460-R496
M1301-374	Cherokee freedmen	R497-R540
M1301-375	Cherokee freedmen	R541-R568
M1301-376	Cherokee freedmen	R569-R599
M1301-377	Cherokee freedmen	R600-R630
M1301-378	Cherokee freedmen	R631-R651
M1301-379	Cherokee freedmen	R652-R682
M1301-380	Cherokee freedmen	R683-R711
M1301-381	Cherokee freedmen	R712-R737
M1301-382	Cherokee freedmen	R738-R769
M1301-383	Cherokee freedmen	R770-R811
M1301-384	Cherokee freedmen	R812-R834
M1301-385	Cherokee freedmen	R835-R852
M1301-386	Cherokee freedmen	R853-R872
M1301-387	Cherokee freedmen	R873-R897
M1301-388	Cherokee freedmen	R898-R915
M1301-389	Cherokee freedmen	R916-R941
M1301-390	Cherokee freedmen	R942-R962
M1301-391	Cherokee freedmen	R963-R987
M1301-392	Cherokee freedmen	R988-R1010
M1301-393	Cherokee freedmen	R1011-R1033
M1301-394	Cherokee freedmen	R1034-R1057
M1301-395	Cherokee freedmen	R1058-R1100
M1301-396	Cherokee freedmen	R1101-R1271
M1301-397	Cherokee freedmen	R1272-R1276;
	Cherokee memo	(Act of 1900) 1-140
M1301-398	Cherokee memo	(Act of 1900) 141-315
M1301-399	Cherokee memo	(Act of 1900) 316-435

NATIVE AMERICAN - GENERAL

M142-1 Letter Book of the Arkansas Trading House, 1805-1810 [1948]. File Microcopies of Records in The National Archives: No.142.

NATIVE AMERICAN MILITARY

Note: ***All military records pertaining specifically to Indian Territory have been listed here. For more military records which may have included Native Americans, request the Heritage Quest Military Catalog (PCAT-23).***

NATIVE AMERICAN - MILITARY - 1784 to 1811

Index to Compiled Service Records of Volunteer Soldiers Who Served From 1784 to 1811.

This microfilm publication reproduces an alphabetical card index to the compiled service records of volunteer soldiers who served from 1784 to 1811. There are cross references for names that appear in the records under more than one spelling and for service in more than one unit or organization. The service records are microfilmed on M905.

M694-1	A - B	**M694-6**	M
M694-2	C	**M694-7**	N - R
M694-3	D - F	**M694-8**	S - Th
M694-4	G - Hi	**M694-9**	Ti - Z
M694-5	Ho - L		

NATIVE AMERICAN - MILITARY - 1784 to 1811

Compiled Service Records of Volunteer Soldiers Who Served From 1784 to 1811.

This microfilm publication reproduces the compiled service records of volunteer soldiers who served from 1784 to 1811. The records were compiled from original records maintained by the Office of the Adjutant General. They are grouped by category: U.S. organizations, state organizations, or territorial organizations. Thereunder they are arranged by unit, and thereunder alphabetically by surname. The records are indexed on M694.

M905-21 Indian Territory;
1st (Jordan's) Regiment, Militia;
2d (Bartholomew's) Regiment, Militia;
4th (Decker's) Regiment, Militia

M905-22 Lieutenant Berry's Detachment, Mounted Riflemen, Militia;
Captain DuBois' Co., Spies and Guides, Militia;
Indiana Territory Militia (Various Organizations);
Parke's Squadron, Light Dragoons, Militia;
Captain Robb's Co., Mounted Riflemen, Militia;
Major Robb's Detachment, Militia;
Captain Spencer's Co., Mounted Riflemen, Militia;
General Staff, Militia

NATIVE AMERICAN-MILITARY-CHEROKEE DISTURBANCES

M256-1 Index to Compiled Service Records of Volunteer Soldiers Who Served During the Cherokee Disturbances and Removal in Organizations From the State of North Carolina.

NATIVE AMERICAN-MILITARY-CHEROKEE DISTURBANCES

Index to Compiled Service Records of Volunteer Soldiers Who Served During the Cherokee Disturbances and Removal in Organizations from the State of Tennessee and the Field and Staff of the Army of the Cherokee Nation.

M908-1 Tennessee organizations A - K

M908-2 Tennessee organizations L - Y; Volunteer field and staff, Any of the Cherokee Nation, A - V

NATIVE AMERICAN-CHEROKEE-GENERAL

7RA01-1 Drennen Roll, or 1852 Cherokee Annuity Payment Roll.

7RA01-1, items 2-9. Drennen Roll of 1852, Citizens of the Cherokee Nation. Districts: Tahlequah, Flint, Going Snake, Delaware, Saline, Illinois, Skin Bayou (Sequoyah), Canadian.

7RA01-1, item 1. Index to the Drennen Roll of 1852, Citizens of the Cherokee Nation.

7RA06-1 Rolls of the Eastern Cherokee, 1848-1852. Copies of the 1848 Mullay Roll, the 1851 Siler Roll, a supplemental "Act of Congress Roll," and the 1852 Chapman roll are reproduced here.

7RA07-1 Index to 1880 Roll of Cherokee Indians.

Cherokee Nation

7RA51-1, item 1. 2 vols. of Index to Tompkins Roll of 1867, Freedmen, (7RA04-1).

7RA51-1, item 2. Wallace Roll of Cherokee Freedmen including Orphan Roll, 1880.

7RA51-1, item 3. Cherokee Colored Persons whose names appear on the Clifton roll, but are not on the authenticated Roll of 1880. Books 1 and 2.

7RA51-1, item 4. Index to Cherokee Freedmen, 1893.

7RA51-1, item 5. Wallace Roll Index to Cherokee Freedmen, 1890-1893.

7RA51-1, item 6. Wallace roll of Cherokee Census Roll of Freedmen, 1890-1893.

7RA51-2, item 1. Index to Cherokee Freedmen Roll of 1896.

7RA51-2, item 2. 1896 Census of Cherokee Freedmen.

7RA51-2, item 3. Index to Cherokee Freedmen Payment Roll, 1896-1897.

7RA51-2, item 4. Cherokee Freedmen Payment Roll, 1897.

7RA51-2, item 5. Census of Cherokee Freedmen, 1896.

7RA51-2, item 6. Admitted Cherokee Freedmen List, 1897.

7RA51-3, item 1. Kern-Clifton Roll of Cherokee Freedmen, 1897. Census of Authenticated Freedmen and their descendants.

7RA53-1, items 1-3. Indexes to Cherokee Nation: Intruder Cases; Intruders.

7RA53-8, item 6 Schedule of Awards by Appraisers of Intruders' Improvements in Cherokee Nation with Modifications.

7RA53-8, item 7. Cherokee Freedmen, List No. 1.

7RA53-8, item 8. Cherokee Freedmen, List No. 2.

M749-1 General Records of the Department of the Treasury (Record Group 56) Correspondence of the Secretary of the Treasury re: the Administration of Trust Funds for the Chickasaw and Other Tribes ("S" Series), 1834-1872.

NATIVE AMERICAN-CHEROKEE-CENSUS

T496-1 Census Roll, 1835, of Cherokee Indians East of the Mississippi. Index. The first treaty by which Indians ceded land east of the Mississippi River in exchange for land to the west was that of July 8, 1817, with the Cherokee Nation.

[Note: As of this writing, the Register of Cherokee Who Wished to Remain in the East, 1817-1819 (National Archives Film A-21) and the Cherokee Emigration Roll of 1817-38 (National Archives Film A-23) are not available from A.G.L.L. Documents from these two National Archives listings must be acquired as shown in the Quick Step chapter earlier in this book]. The major Cherokee removal, however, did not come until after the treaty of December 29, 1835. The census rolls for the Eastern Cherokee have been maintained with the removal records. The first, the Henderson Roll, 1835, is the roll made for those to be removed. It lists heads of families and gives information concerning each family and its property.

7RA04-1, items 1-9. Cherokee Census, 1867, Vol. 1-4. Districts: Vol. 1- Going Snake, Delaware; Vol. 4- Flint, Sequoyah, Kooweskoowe; Vol. 3- Canadian, Illinois; Vol. 2- Tahlequah, Saline.

7RA04-1 Tompkins Roll of 1867 Census of the Cherokee Nation. Contains Citizens and Freedmen of the Cherokee Nation.

7RA07-2 1880 Census Schedule 1, Pt.1 of the Cherokee Nation. Districts: Canadian (poor records), Kooweskoowe, Delaware, Flint.

7RA07-3 1880 Census Schedules 1, Pt.2 of the Cherokee Nation. Districts: Going Snake, Illinois, Saline, Sequoyah, Tahlequah.

7RA07-4, items 1-5 Cherokee Census of 1880, Schedules 2-6. Districts: Canadian, Kooweskoowe, Delaware, Flint, Going Snake, Illinois, Saline, Sequoyah, Tahlequah.

7RA08-1 Cherokee Census of 1890, Schedule 1, part 1. Districts: Canadian and Kooweeskoowe.

7RA08-2 Cherokee Census of 1890, Schedule 1, part 2. Districts: Delaware.

7RA08-3 Cherokee Census of 1890, Schedule 1, part 3. Districts: Going Snake, Illinois and Saline.

7RA08-4 Cherokee Census of 1890, Schedule 1, part 4. Districts: Sequoyah and Tahlequah District.

7RA08-5 Cherokee Census of 1890, Schedule 2-5. Sched. 2: Canadian Dist. missing. Sched. 3: Sequoyah Dist. missing.

7RA08-6 Cherokee Census of 1890, Schedule 6. Districts: Canadian, Kooweeskoowe, Delaware, Flint, Going Snake, Illinois, Saline, Sequoyah, Tahlequah.

7RA19-1 Cherokee Census of 1896. Districts: Canadian, Kooweeskoowe, Delaware, Flint, Going Snake, Illinois, Saline, Sequoyah, Tahlequah. Also contains census of adopted Whites, Delawares, Shawnees, and Freedmen.

7RA26-1, item 3. Shawnee - Cherokee Census, 1896 1904. Arranged roughly alphabetically by surname. Contains each individual's name, roll number, Cherokee number, age, sex, address, and some remarks about relation to others on roll, deaths, and different names used on other rolls.

7RA29-1 and **7RA29-2.** Cherokee Census of 1883. Contains 1883 Cherokee Payroll.

7RA54-1 Cherokee Freedmen Census Roll, 1893. Canadian, Kooweskoowe, Delaware, Flint, Going Snake, Illinois (part) Districts. Continued on film 7RA54-2.

7RA54-2 Cherokee Freedmen Census, 1893. Illinois (part), Saline, Sequoyah, Tahlequah Districts. Continuation of film 7RA54-1.

7RA55-1 1893 Cherokee (Cherokee Nation) Census of Intruders. Includes Canadian, Kooweskoowe, Delaware, Going Snake, Illinois and Sequoyah Districts.

Cherokee Census of 1883:

7RA56-1 Canadian, Kooweskoowe, Delaware, Flint Districts.

7RA56-2 Going Snake, Illinois, Saline, Sequoyah (Missing), Tahlequah Districts plus supplement.

7RA57-3 Cherokee Payment Roll of 1883. Tahlequah District and supplemental.

Cherokee Census of 1886:

7RA58-1 Canadian, Kooweeskoowe, Delaware, Flint Districts.

7RA58-2 Going Snake, Illinois, Saline, Sequoyah, Tahlequah Districts.

1890 Census of Cherokee Nation:

7RA60-1 Canadian and Kooweeskoowe Districts. Arranged alphabetically.

7RA60-2 Delaware, Flint and Going Snake Districts. Arranged alphabetically.

7RA60-3 Illinois, Saline, Sequoyah, Tahlequah Districts. Arranged alphabetically.

7RA71-1 Index to 1896 Cherokee Roll. This index does not include Freedmen.

7RA73-1, item 1. Index: Cherokee Delaware Census Roll, 1867.

7RA73-1, item 2. List of Names of the Delaware Indians Incorporated into the Cherokee Nation under of Agreement of Apr. 8th,1867.

7RA74-1 Lists of Delaware, Shawnee, and North Carolina Cherokees, 1867-1881.

7RA80-1, item 1. Payment to Destitute Cherokees, 1902.

7RA80-1, item 2. Payment to Intermarried Whites, Cherokee Nation, 1909-1910.

7RA81-1, item 1. Index: Cherokee Nation, 15 Dollar Payment, 1912.

7RA81-1 Index: Cherokees by Intermarriage. Index: Delaware Cherokees. Index: New Born Cherokee Freedmen. Index: New Born Cherokees by Blood.

Old Settler Cherokee Census Roll, 1895, and Index to Payment Roll, 1895:

T985-1 Index to Payment Roll for Old Settler Cherokee, 1896.

T985-2 Old Settler Cherokee Census Roll, 1895.

NATIVE AMERICAN-CHEROKEE-COURT

Dockets of Hearings on Intruder Cases, 1901-1909:

7RA53-2 No.1-350

7RA53-2 No.351-702

7RA53-3 No.703-806

7RA53-3 No.807-1304

Decisions of the U.S. Court, 1897-1899. - Cherokee Citizenship Judgments with General Opinion of Hon. Wm. M. Springer, Judge:

7RA98-1 Book 1.

7RA98-2 Book 2-3.

NATIVE AMERICAN-CHEROKEE-ENROLLMENT

7RA24-1 Index to Cherokee Rejected and Doubtful Dawes Enrollment Cards.

7RA25-1, item 1. List of Rejected Claimants, 1878-1880. Entries are arranged by type of decision and by case number.

7RA25-1, items 2-5. Lists of Persons Admitted to Citizenship.

7RA25-1 thru 7RA25-5. Cherokee Citizenship Commission Docket Books, 1880-1884 and 1887-1889.

Records Relating to Enrollment of the Eastern Cherokee, by Guion Miller, 1908-1910.

This publication includes Guion Miller's report and his supplemental report as well as the roll of Eastern Cherokee. In certifying the eligibility of the Cherokee, Miller used earlier census lists and rolls that had been made of the Cherokee between 1835 and 1884. Copies of the Chapman, Drennen, and Old Settler rolls of 1851 and the Hester roll of 1884, with the appropriate indexes, are reproduced as the final roll of this publication. M685-1 General Index to Eastern Cherokee Applications, vols. 1 and 2.

Report submitted by Guion Miller, Special Commissioner, May 28, 1909:

M685-2 Vols. 1-2, applications 1-6000

M685-3 Vols. 3-4, applications 6001-16000

M685-4 Vols. 5-7, applications 16001-31000

M685-5 Vols. 8-10, applications 31001-45857

M685-6 Roll of Eastern Cherokee, May 28, 1909, and report on exceptions, with supplemental roll, Jan. 5, 1910

Miscellaneous testimony taken before special commissioners, Feb. 1908 - Mar. 1909:

M685-7 Vols. 1-2

M685-8 Vols. 3-4

M685-9 Vols. 5-6

M685-10 Vols. 7-8

M685-11 Vols. 9-10

M685-12 Indexes and roll of Eastern Cherokee Indians, 1850, 1851, and 1884, and miscellaneous notes and drafts.

NATIVE AMERICAN-CHEROKEE-ENROLLMENT APPLICATIONS
Eastern Cherokee Applications of the U.S. Court of Claims, 1906-1909. (Guion Miller Roll).

The applications required each claimant to state full English and Indian names, residence, age, place of birth, name of husband or wife, name of tribe, and names of children. It also required information on the claimant's parents, grandparents, brothers, sisters, uncles, and aunts. The index to the applications is arranged alphabetically by name (either English or Indian) of claimant. The applications themselves should be searched by application number, NOT the Guion Miller roll number.

Roll - Application NR.		Roll - Application NR.	
M1104-2	46-136	**M1104-29**	2638-2743
M1104-3	137-224	**M1104-30**	2744-2841
M1104-4	225-331	**M1104-31**	2842-2947
M1104-5	332-420	**M1104-32**	2948-3049
M1104-6	421-514	**M1104-33**	3050-3147
M1104-7	515-596	**M1104-34**	3148-3250
M1104-8	597-681	**M1104-35**	3251-3342
M1104-9	682-778	**M1104-36**	3343-3442
M1104-10	779-859	**M1104-37**	3443-3540
M1104-11	860-964	**M1104-38**	3541-3647
M1104-12	965-1082	**M1104-39**	3648-3747
M1104-13	1083-1175	**M1104-40**	3748-3847
M1104-14	1176-1267	**M1104-41**	3848-3949
M1104-15	1268-1362	**M1104-42**	3950-4057
M1104-16	1363-1455	**M1104-43**	4058-4157
M1104-17	1456-1545	**M1104-44**	4158-4228
M1104-18	1546-1642	**M1104-45**	4229-4327
M1104-19	1643-1735	**M1104-46**	4328-4426
M1104-20	1736-1820	**M1104-47**	4427-4555
M1104-21	1821-1910	**M1104-48**	4556-4661
M1104-22	1911-2001	**M1104-49**	4662-4771
M1104-23	2002-2113	**M1104-50**	4772-4879
M1104-24	2114-2229	**M1104-51**	4880-4984
M1104-25	2230-2339	**M1104-52**	4985-5089
M1104-26	2340-2432	**M1104-53**	5090-5189
M1104-27	2433-2534	**M1104-54**	5190-5289
M1104-28	2535-2637	**M1104-55**	5290-5394

Roll - Application NR.		Roll - Application NR.	
M1104-56	5395-5492	**M1104-93**	9120-9219
M1104-57	5493-5591	**M1104-94**	9220-9317
M1104-58	5592-5690	**M1104-95**	9318-9416
M1104-59	5691-5789	**M1104-96**	9417-9515
M1104-60	5790-5889	**M1104-97**	9516-9615
M1104-61	5890-5989	**M1104-98**	9616-9715
M1104-62	5990-6089	**M1104-99**	9716-9815
M1104-63	6090-6189	**M1104-100**	9816-9900
M1104-64	6190-6289	**M1104-101**	9901-10000
M1104-65	6290-6391	**M1104-102**	10001-10100
M1104-66	6392-6481	**M1104-103**	10101-10200
M1104-67	6482-6580	**M1104-104**	10201-10300
M1104-68	6581-6683	**M1104-105**	10301-10400
M1104-69	6684-6787	**M1104-106**	10401-10500
M1104-70	6788-6888	**M1104-107**	10501-10600
M1104-71	6889-6991	**M1104-108**	10601-10700
M1104-72	6992-7091	**M1104-109**	10701-10800
M1104-73	7092-7202	**M1104-110**	10801-10900
M1104-74	7203-7302	**M1104-111**	10901-11000
M1104-75	7303-7403	**M1104-112**	11001-11100
M1104-76	7404-7504	**M1104-113**	11101-11200
M1104-77	7505-7604	**M1104-114**	11201-11300
M1104-78	7605-7704	**M1104-115**	11301-11400
M1104-79	7705-7771	**M1104-116**	11401-11500
M1104-80	7772-7904	**M1104-117**	11501-11600
M1104-81	7905-8006	**M1104-118**	11601-11700
M1104-82	8007-8115	**M1104-119**	11701-11806
M1104-83	8116-8216	**M1104-120**	11807-11900
M1104-84	8217-8316	**M1104-121**	11901-12000
M1104-85	8317-8416	**M1104-122**	12001-12100
M1104-86	8417-8516	**M1104-123**	12101-12200
M1104-87	8517-8617	**M1104-124**	12201-12350
M1104-88	8618-8720	**M1104-125**	12351-12500
M1104-89	8721-8818	**M1104-126**	12501-12650
M1104-90	8819-8918	**M1104-127**	12651-12800
M1104-91	8919-9019	**M1104-128**	12801-12950
M1104-92	9020-9119	**M1104-129**	12951-13100

Roll -	Application NR.	Roll -	Application NR.
M1104-130	13101-13250	**M1104-167**	18651-18800
M1104-131	13251-13400	**M1104-168**	18801-18950
M1104-132	13401-13550	**M1104-169**	18951-19100
M1104-133	13551-13700	**M1104-170**	19101-19250
M1104-134	13701-13850	**M1104-171**	19251-19400
M1104-135	13851-14000	**M1104-172**	19401-19550
M1104-136	14001-14150	**M1104-173**	19551-19700
M1104-137	14151-14300	**M1104-174**	19701-19850
M1104-138	14301-14450	**M1104-175**	19851-20000
M1104-139	14451-14600	**M1104-176**	20001-20150
M1104-140	14601-14750	**M1104-177**	20151-20300
M1104-141	14751-14900	**M1104-178**	20301-20450
M1104-142	14901-15050	**M1104-179**	20451-20600
M1104-143	15051-15200	**M1104-180**	20601-20750
M1104-144	15201-15350	**M1104-181**	20751-20900
M1104-145	15351-15500	**M1104-182**	20901-21050
M1104-146	15501-15650	**M1104-183**	21051-21200
M1104-147	15651-15800	**M1104-184**	21201-21350
M1104-148	15801-15950	**M1104-185**	21351-21500
M1104-149	15951-16100	**M1104-186**	21501-21650
M1104-150	16101-16250	**M1104-187**	21651-21800
M1104-151	16251-16400	**M1104-188**	21801-21950
M1104-152	16401-16550	**M1104-189**	21951-22100
M1104-153	16551-16700	**M1104-190**	22101-22250
M1104-154	16701-16850	**M1104-191**	22251-22400
M1104-155	16851-17000	**M1104-192**	22401-22550
M1104-156	17001-17150	**M1104-193**	22551-22700
M1104-157	17151-17300	**M1104-194**	22701-22850
M1104-158	17301-17450	**M1104-195**	22851-23000
M1104-159	17451-17600	**M1104-196**	23001-23150
M1104-160	17601-17750	**M1104-197**	23151-23300
M1104-161	17751-17900	**M1104-198**	23301-23450
M1104-162	17901-18050	**M1104-199**	23451-23600
M1104-163	18051-18200	**M1104-200**	23601-23750
M1104-164	18201-18350	**M1104-201**	23751-23900
M1104-165	18351-18500	**M1104-202**	23901-24050
M1104-166	18501-18650	**M1104-203**	24051-24200

Roll - Application NR.		Roll - Application NR.	
M1104-204	21201-24350	**M1104-241**	29751-29900
M1104-205	24351-24500	**M1104-242**	29901-30050
M1104-206	24501-24650	**M1104-243**	30051-30200
M1104-207	24651-24800	**M1104-244**	30201-30350
M1104-208	24801-24950	**M1104-245**	30351-30500
M1104-209	24951-25100	**M1104-246**	30501-30650
M1104-210	25101-25250	**M1104-247**	30651-30800
M1104-211	25251-25400	**M1104-248**	30801-30950
M1104-212	25401-25550	**M1104-249**	30951-31100
M1104-213	25551-25700	**M1104-250**	31101-31250
M1104-214	25701-25850	**M1104-251**	31251-31400
M1104-215	25851-26000	**M1104-252**	31401-31550
M1104-216	26001-26150	**M1104-253**	31551-31700
M1104-217	26151-26300	**M1104-254**	31701-31850
M1104-218	26301-26450	**M1104-255**	31851-32000
M1104-219	26451-26600	**M1104-256**	32001-32150
M1104-220	26601-26750	**M1104-257**	32151-32300
M1104-221	26751-26900	**M1104-258**	32301-32450
M1104-222	26901-27050	**M1104-259**	32451-32600
M1104-223	27051-27200	**M1104-260**	32601-32750
M1104-224	27201-27350	**M1104-261**	32751-32900
M1104-225	27351-27500	**M1104-262**	32901-33050
M1104-226	27501-27650	**M1104-263**	33051-33200
M1104-227	27651-27800	**M1104-264**	33201-33350
M1104-228	27801-27950	**M1104-265**	33351-33500
M1104-229	27951-28100	**M1104-266**	33501-33650
M1104-230	28101-28250	**M1104-267**	33651-33800
M1104-231	28251-28400	**M1104-268**	33801-33950
M1104-232	28401-28550	**M1104-269**	33951-34100
M1104-233	28551-28700	**M1104-270**	34101-34250
M1104-234	28701-28850	**M1104-271**	34251-34400
M1104-235	28851-29000	**M1104-272**	34401-34550
M1104-236	29001-29150	**M1104-273**	34551-34700
M1104-237	29151-29300	**M1104-274**	34701-34850
M1104-238	29301-29450	**M1104-275**	34851-35000
M1104-239	29451-29600	**M1104-276**	35001-35150
M1104-240	29601-29750	**M1104-277**	35151-35300

Roll	Application NR.	Roll	Application NR.
M1104-278	35301-35450	**M1104-315**	40851-41000
M1104-279	35451-35600	**M1104-316**	41001-41150
M1104-280	35601-35750	**M1104-317**	41151-41300
M1104-281	35751-35900	**M1104-318**	41301-41450
M1104-282	35901-36050	**M1104-319**	41451-41600
M1104-283	36051-36200	**M1104-320**	41601-41750
M1104-284	36201-36350	**M1104-321**	41751-41900
M1104-285	36351-36500	**M1104-322**	41901-42050
M1104-286	36501-36650	**M1104-323**	42051-42200
M1104-287	36651-36800	**M1104-324**	42201-42350
M1104-288	36801-36950	**M1104-325**	42351-42500
M1104-289	36951-37100	**M1104-326**	42501-42650
M1104-290	37101-37250	**M1104-327**	42651-42800
M1104-291	37251-37400	**M1104-328**	42801-42950
M1104-292	37401-37550	**M1104-329**	42951-43100
M1104-293	37551-37700	**M1104-330**	43101-43250
M1104-294	37701-37850	**M1104-331**	43251-43400
M1104-295	37851-38000	**M1104-332**	43401-43550
M1104-296	38001-38150	**M1104-333**	43551-43700
M1104-297	38151-38300	**M1104-334**	43701-43850
M1104-298	38301-38450	**M1104-335**	43851-44000
M1104-299	38451-38600	**M1104-336**	44001-44150
M1104-300	38601-38750	**M1104-337**	44151-44300
M1104-301	38751-38900	**M1104-338**	44301-44450
M1104-302	38901-39050	**M1104-339**	44451-44600
M1104-303	39051-39200	**M1104-340**	44601-44750
M1104-304	39201-39350	**M1104-341**	44751-44900
M1104-305	39351-39500	**M1104-342**	44901-45050
M1104-306	39501-39650	**M1104-343**	45051-45200
M1104-307	39651-39800	**M1104-344**	45201-45350
M1104-308	39801-39950	**M1104-345**	45351-45500
M1104-309	39951-40100	**M1104-346**	45501-45650
M1104-310	40101-40250	**M1104-347**	45651-45750
M1104-311	40251-40400	**M1104-348**	45751-45857
M1104-312	40401-40550		
M1104-313	40551-40700		
M1104-314	40701-40850		

M1104-1 Roll of Eastern Cherokee General index to Eastern Cherokee Applications, vols. 1 and 2. Application numbers 1-45

NATIVE AMERICAN-CHEROKEE-HISTORY

F-4495, 3 fiche. Tennessee Historical Records from Indian and Revolutionary Times up to 1883, Vol. 2, contains Cherokee Reservation Treaty Book 1, July 8, 1817; Genealogy of Ward Family of Tennessee; Historical sketch; Sullivan County pension abstracts. Comp. by Lucy Kate McGhee. Sullivan Co. Index.

NATIVE AMERICAN-CHEROKEE-PAYMENT

7RA26-1, item 1. Payroll, Delaware - Cherokee, 1896. "Payroll of Delaware Indians as disbursed, by D.W. Lipe, Treasurer of the Cherokee Nation." Some 1039 names on roll.

7RA81-2 and 7RA81-3. Duplicate Cherokee per Capita Payroll, 1912.

Cherokee Equalization Payment Rolls:

7RA82-1 Roll 1 (A - Z).

7RA82-2 1910-1915.

7RA82-4, item 1. Cherokee Equalization Payment Rolls, 1910-1914.

7RA82-4, item 2. Cherokee Equalization Payment Rolls, 1911-1914.

7RA82-4, item 3. Cherokee Equalization Money to Restricted Indians (Approved Roll), Feb. 13, 1914.

7RA82-4, item 4. Cherokee Equalization Money to Restricted and Unrestricted Indians, Dec. 12, 1912.

7RA91-1 Register of Cherokee Students, 1881-1882.

Cherokee Payment Roll (Lipe Roll):

7RA33-1 1880. Canadian - Sequoyah districts.

7RA33-2 1880. Tahlequah district.

7RA34-1 (Old Settlers Roll), 1896.

Cherokee Payment Rolls and Index (Starr Roll), 1894:

7RA38-1 Contains Index, Canadian, Kooweskoowe Districts.

7RA38-2 Contains Delaware, Flint, Going Snake, Illinois Districts.

7RA38-3 Contains Saline, Sequoyah, Tahlequah Districts and Orphans.

7RA38-4 Copy of Kooweskoowe, Delaware, and Flint Districts.

7RA38-5 Copy of Going Snake, Illinois, Saline, Sequoyah, and Tahlequah Districts, Orphans and Supplemental. Cherokee Payment Roll of 1890:

7RA59-1 Vol. 1-2. Canadian, Kooweeskoowe, Delaware, Flint Districts.

7RA59-2 Vol. 3-4. Going Snake, Illinois, Saline, Tahlequah, Sequoyah Districts.

NATIVE AMERICAN -DELAWARE CHEROKEE - GENERAL

7RA73-1, item 2. List of Names of the Delaware Indians Incorporated into the Cherokee Nation under Agreement of Apr. 8th, 1867.

7RA74-1 Lists of Delaware, Shawnee, and North Carolina Cherokees, 1867-1881.

7RA81-1, item 5. Index: Delaware-Cherokees.

NATIVE AMERICAN - DELAWARE CHEROKEE - CENSUS

7RA73-1, item 1. Index: Cherokee Delaware Census Roll, 1867.

NATIVE AMERICAN - DELAWARE CHEROKEE - PAYMENT

7RA26-1, item 1. Payroll, Delaware - Cherokee, 1896. "Payroll of Delaware Indians as disbursed, by D.W. Lipe, Treasurer of the Cherokee Nation." Some 1039 names on roll.

7RA26-1, item 2. Payroll, per Capita - Delaware, 1904. 1100 names.

NATIVE AMERICAN - SHAWNEE CHEROKEE - CENSUS

7RA26-1 1896 Census.

7RA26-1, item 3. Shawnee - Cherokee Census, 1896-1904. Arranged roughly alphabetically by surname. Contains each individual's name, roll number, Cherokee number, age, sex, address, and some remarks about relation to others on roll, deaths, and different names used on other rolls.

7RA74-1 Lists of Delaware, Shawnee, and North Carolina Cherokees, 1867-1881.

How to Rent or Buy Microfilm from A.G.L.L. (Heritage Quest)

Rental:

To receive a free two-month trial membership with rental privileges, call toll-free 1-800-760-2455. The price of each rental is $3.25 per roll or fiche title (Canadian price is $3.75). Orders for 10 or more items will be charged at $2.75 per film/fiche title (Canadian price is $3.25). An additional $3.00 per order is charged for shipping and handling. Return postage is paid by the borrower. Renewals are $3.25 per film/fiche title for the next 30-day use. If repeated renewals are needed, purchase of the film/fiche is suggested. Overdue items are charged as a renewal. Heritage Quest ships orders First Class or UPS for an additional $.50 per roll or fiche. There is no limit on the number of films/fiche that can be ordered. At the end of your trial membership you will receive an invoice for an annual membership fee of $39.95.

Purchase:

Microfilm rolls on diazo film are priced at $17.95 per roll for Heritage Quest Members and Institutions. Retail price is $24.95 per roll. Silver halide film can be ordered at $28.95 per roll. Retail is $33.95 per roll. Fiche is priced at $1.95 per card. Retail is $2.50 per card. Purchase prices include postage and handling charges. Payment should made be in the form of a check, credit card, or money order at the time the order is placed.

To receive a free CD ROM or catalog of available microfilm titles and other genealogical products, or to place an order, contact:

HERITAGE QUEST
P.O. Box 329
Bountiful, Utah 84011-0329
1-800-658-7755
1-801-298-5358
Fax 1-801-298-5468
Website address: http://www.heritagequest.com.

[Note: Prices and Phone Numbers subject to change]

Appendix 2

Turkey Town Treaty of 1817.
July 8, 1817. | 7 Stat., 156 | Proclamation, Dec. 26, 1817

Articles of a treaty concluded, at the Cherokee Agency, within the Cherokee nation, between major general Andrew Jackson, Joseph McMinn, governor of the state of Tennessee, and general David Meriwether, commissioners plenipotentiary of the United States of America, of the one part, and the chiefs, head men, and warriors, of the Cherokee nation, east of the Mississippi river, and the chiefs, head men, and warriors, of the Cherokees on the Arkansas river, and their deputies, John D. Chisholm and James Rogers, duly authorized by the chiefs of the Cherokees on the Arkansas river, in open council, by written power of attorney, duly signed and executed, in presence of Joseph Sevier and William Ware.

WHEREAS in the autumn of the year one thousand eight hundred and eight, a deputation from the Upper and Lower Cherokee towns, duly authorized by their nation, went on to the city of Washington, the first [141] named to declare to the President of the United States their anxious desire to engage in the pursuits of agriculture and civilized life, in the country they then occupied, and to make known to the President of the United States the impracticability of inducing the nation at large to do this, and to request the establishment of a division line between the upper and lower towns, so as to include all the waters of the Hiwassee river to the upper town, that, by thus contracting their society within narrow limits, they proposed to begin the establishment of fixed laws and a regular government: The deputies from the lower towns to make known their desire to continue the hunter life, and also the scarcity of game where they then lived, and, under those circumstances, their wish to remove across the Mississippi river, on some vacant lands of the United States. And whereas the President of the United States, after maturely considering the petitions of both parties, on the ninth day of January, A. D. one thousand eight hundred and nine, including other subjects, answered those petitions as follows: "The United States, my children, are the friends of both parties, and, as far as can be reasonably asked, they are willing to satisfy the wishes of both. Those who remain may be assured of our patronage, our aid, and good neighborhood. Those who wish to remove, are permitted to send an exploring party to reconnoiter the country on the waters of the Arkansas and White rivers, and the higher up the better, as they will be the longer unapproached by our settlements, which will begin at the mouths of those rivers. The regular districts of the government of St. Louis are already laid off to the St.

Francis.

"When this party shall have found a tract of country suiting the emigrants, and not claimed by other Indians, we will arrange with them and you the exchange of that for a just portion of the country they leave, and to a part of which, proportioned to their numbers, they have a right. Every aid towards their removal, and what will be necessary for them there, will then be freely administered to them; and when established in their new settlements, we shall still consider them as our children, give them the benefit of exchanging their peltries for what they will want at our factories, and always hold them firmly by the hand."

And whereas the Cherokees, relying on the promises of the President of the United States, as above recited, did explore the country on the west side of the Mississippi, and made choice of the country on the Arkansas and White rivers, settled themselves down upon United States lands, to which no other tribe of Indians have any just claim, and have duly notified the President of the United States thereof, and of their anxious desire for the full and complete ratification of his promise, and, to that end, as notified by the President of the United States, have sent on their agents, with full powers to execute a treaty, relinquishing to the United States all the right, title, and interest, to all lands of right to them belonging, as part of the Cherokee nation, which they have left, and which they are about to leave, proportioned to their numbers, including, with those now on the Arkansas, those who are about to remove thither, and to a portion of which they have an equal right agreeably to their numbers.

Now, know ye, that the contracting parties, to carry into full effect the before recited promises with good faith, and to promote a continuation of friendship with their brothers on the Arkansas river, and for that purpose to make an equal distribution of the annuities secured to be paid by the United States to the whole Cherokee nation, have agreed and concluded on the following articles, viz:

ARTICLE 1. The chiefs, head men, and warriors, of the whole Cherokee nation, cede to the United States all the lands lying north and east of the following boundaries, viz: Beginning at the high shoals of the Appalachy river, and running thence, along the boundary line between the Creek and Cherokee nations, westwardly to the Chatahouchy river; [142] thence, up the Chatahouchy river, to the mouth of Souque creek; thence, continuing with the general course of the river until it reaches the Indian boundary line, and, should it strike the Turrurar river, thence, with its meanders, down said river to its mouth, in part of the proportion of land in the Cherokee nation east of the Mississippi, to which those now on the Arkansas and those about to remove there are justly entitled.

ARTICLE 2. The chiefs, head men, and warriors, of the whole Cherokee nation, do also cede to the United States all the lands lying north and west of the following boundary lines, viz: Beginning at the Indian boundary line that runs from the north bank of the Tennessee river, opposite to the mouth of Hywassee river, at a point on the top of Walden's ridge, where it divides the waters of the Tennessee river from those of the Sequatchie river; thence, along the said ridge, southwardly, to the bank of the Tennessee river, at a point near to a place called the Negro Sugar Camp, opposite to the upper end of the first island above Running Water Town; thence, westwardly, a straight line to the mouth of Little Sequatchie river; thence, up said river, to its main fork; thence, up its northernmost fork, to its source; and thence, due west, to the Indian boundary line.

ARTICLE 3. It is also stipulated by the contracting parties, that a census shall be taken of the whole Cherokee nation, during the month of June, in the year of our Lord one thousand eight hundred and eighteen, in the following manner, viz: That the census of those on the east side of the Mississippi river, who declare their intention of remaining, shall be taken by a commissioner appointed by the President of the United States, and a commissioner appointed by the Cherokees on the Arkansas river; and the census of the Cherokees on the Arkansas river, and those removing there, and who, at that time, declare their intention of removing there, shall be taken by a commissioner appointed by the President of the United States, and one appointed by the Cherokees east of the Mississippi river.

ARTICLE 4. The contracting parties do also stipulate that the annuity due from the United States to the whole Cherokee nation for the year one thousand eight hundred and eighteen, is to be divided between the two parts of the nation in proportion to their numbers, agreeably to the stipulations contained in the third article of this treaty; and to be continued to be divided thereafter in proportion to their numbers; and the lands to be apportioned and surrendered to the United States agreeably to the aforesaid enumeration, as the proportionate part, agreeably to their numbers, to which those who have removed, and who declare their intention to remove, have a just right, including these with the lands ceded in the first and second articles of this treaty.

ARTICLE 5. The United States bind themselves, in exchange for the lands ceded in the first and second articles hereof, to give to that part of the Cherokee nation on the Arkansas as much land on said river and White river as they have or may hereafter receive from the Cherokee nation east of the Mississippi, acre for acre, as the just proportion due that part of the nation on the Arkansas agreeably to their numbers; which is to commence on the north side of the Arkansas river, at the mouth of Point Remove or Budwell's Old Place; thence, by a straight line, northwardly, to strike Chataunga mountain, or the hill first above Shield's Ferry on White river, running up and between said rivers for complement, the banks of which rivers to be the lines; and to have the above line, from the point of beginning to the point on White river, run and marked, which shall be done soon after the ratification of this treaty; and all citizens of the United States, except Mrs. P. Lovely, who is to remain where she lives during life, removed from within the bounds as above named. And it is further stipulated, [143] that the treaties heretofore between the Cherokee nation and the United States are to continue in full force with both parts of the nation, and both parts thereof entitled to all the immunities and privilege which the old nation enjoyed under the aforesaid treaties; the United States reserving the right of establishing factories, a military post, and roads, within the boundaries above defined.

ARTICLE 6. The United States do also bind themselves to give to all the poor warriors who may remove to the western side of the Mississippi river, one rifle gun and ammunition, one blanket, and one brass kettle, or, in lieu of the brass kettle, a beaver trap, which is to be considered as a full compensation for the improvements which they may leave; which articles are to be delivered at such point as the President of the United States may direct: and to aid in the removal of the emigrants, they further agree to furnish fiat bottomed boats and provisions sufficient for that purpose: and to those emigrants whose improvements add real value to their lands, the United States agree to pay a full valuation for the same, which is to be ascertained by a commissioner appointed by the President of the United States for that purpose, and paid for as soon after the ratification of this treaty as practicable. The boats and provisions promised to the emigrants are to be furnished by the agent on the Tennessee river, at such time and place as the emigrants may notify him of; and it shall be his duty to furnish the same.

ARTICLE 7. And for all improvements which add real value to the lands lying within the boundaries ceded to the United States, by the first and second articles of this treaty, the United States do agree to pay for at the time, and to be valued in the same manner, as stipulated in the sixth article of this treaty; or, in lieu thereof, to give in exchange improvements of equal value which the emigrants may leave, and for which they are to receive pay. And it is further stipulated, that all these improvements, left by the emigrants within the bounds of the Cherokee nation east of the Mississippi river, which add real value to the lands, and for which the United States shall give a consideration, and not so exchanged, shall be rented to the Indians by the agent, year after year, for the benefit of the poor and decrepit of that part of the nation east of the Mississippi river, until surrendered by the nation, or to the nation. And it is further agreed, that the said Cherokee nation shall not be called upon for any part of the consideration paid for said improvements at any future period.

ARTICLE 8. And to each and every head of any Indian family residing on the east side of the Mississippi river, on the lands that are now, or may hereafter be, surrendered to the United States, who may wish to become citizens of the United States, the United States do agree to give a reservation of six hundred and forty acres of land, in a square, to include their improvements, which are to be as near the centre thereof as practicable, in which they will have a life estate, with a reversion in fee simple to their children, reserving to the widow her dower, the register of whose names is to be filed in the office of the Cherokee agent, which shall be kept open until the census is taken as stipulated in the third article of this treaty. Provided, That if any of the heads of families, for whom reservations may be made, should remove therefrom, then, in that case, the right to revert to the United States. And provided further, That the land which may be reserved under this article, be deducted from the amount which has been ceded under the first and second articles of this treaty.

ARTICLE 9. It is also provided by the contracting parties, that nothing in the foregoing articles shall be construed so as to prevent any of the parties so contracting from the free navigation of all the waters mentioned therein.

ARTICLE 10. The whole of the Cherokee nation do hereby cede to the United States all right, title, and claim, to all reservations made to Doublehead and others, which were reserved to them by a treaty made and entered into at the city of Washington, bearing date the seventh of January, one thousand eight hundred and six.

ARTICLE 11. If. It is further agreed that the boundary lines of the lands ceded to the United States by the first and second articles of this treaty, and the boundary line of the lands ceded by the United States in the fifth article of this treaty, is to be run and marked by a commissioner or commissioners appointed by the President of the United States, who shall be accompanied by such commissioners as the Cherokees may appoint; due notice thereof to be given to the nation.

ARTICLE 12. The United States do also bind themselves to prevent the intrusion of any of its citizens within the lands ceded by the first and second articles of this treaty, until the same shall be ratified by the President and Senate of the United States, and duly promulgated.

ARTICLE 13. The contracting parties do also stipulate that this treaty shall take effect and be obligatory on the contracting parties so soon as the same shall be ratified by the President of the United States, by and with the advice and consent of the Senate of the United States.

In witness of all and every thing herein determined, by and between the before recited contracting parties, we have, in full and open council, at the Cherokee Agency, this eighth day of July, A. D. one thousand eight hundred and seventeen, set our hands and seals.

Andrew Jackson,
Joseph McMinn,
D. Meriwether, United States Commis'rs.
Richard Brown, his x mark,
Cabbin Smith, his x mark,
Sleeping Rabbit, his x mark,
George Saunders, his x mark,
Roman Nose, his x mark,
Currobe Dick, his x mark,
George Lowry,
Richard Taylor,
Walter Adair,
James Brown,
Kelachule, his x mark,
Sour Mush, his x mark,
Chulioa, his x mark,
Chickasautchee, his x mark,
The Bark of Chota, his x mark,
The Bark of Hightower, his x mark,
John Walker, his x mark,
Big Half Breed, his x mark
Going Snake, his x mark,
Leyestisky, his x mark,
Ch. Hicks,
Young Davis, his x mark,
Souanooka, his x mark,
The Locust, his x mark,
Beaver Carrier, his x mark,
Dreadful Water, his x mark,
Chyula, his x mark,
Ja. Martin,
John McIntosh, his x mark,

Katchee of Cowee, his x mark,
White Man Killer, his x mark,
Arkansas chiefs:

Toochalar, his x mark,
The Glass, his x mark,
Wassosee, his x mark,
John Jolly, his x mark,
The Gourd, his x mark,
Spring Frog, his x mark,
John D. Chisholm,
James Rogers,
Wawhatchy, his x mark,
Attalona, his x mark,
Kulsuttchee, his x mark,
Tuskekeetchee, his x mark,
Chillawgatchee, his x mark,
John Smith, his x mark,
Toosawallata, his x mark,

In presence of

J. M. Glassel, secretary to the commission,
Thomas Wilson, clerk to the commissioners,
Walter Adair,
John Speirs, interpreter, his x mark,
A. McCoy, interpreter,
James C. Bronaugh, hospital surgeon, U.S. Army,
Isham Randolph, captain First Redoubtables,
Wm. Meriwether,
Return J. Meigs, agent Cherokee Nation.

Appendix 3

Treaty of New Echota, 1835-36.
Dec. 29, 1835. | 7 Stat., 478. | Proclamation, May 23, 1836.

Articles of a treaty, concluded at New Echota in the State of Georgia on the 29th day of Decr. 1835 by General William Carroll and John F.. Schermerhorn commissioners on the part of the United States and the Chiefs Head Men and People of the Cherokee tribe of Indians.

WHEREAS the Cherokees are anxious to make some arrangements with the Government of the United States whereby the difficulties they have experienced by a residence within the settled parts of the United States under the jurisdiction and laws of the State Governments may be terminated and adjusted; and with a view to reuniting their people in one body and securing a permanent home for themselves and their posterity in the country selected by their forefathers without the territorial limits of the State sovereignties, and where they can establish and enjoy a government of their choice and perpetuate such a state of society as may be most consonant with their views, habits and condition; and as may tend to their individual comfort and their advancement in civilization.

And whereas a delegation of the Cherokee nation composed of Messes. John Ross Richard Taylor Danl. McCoy Samuel Gunter and William Rogers with full power and authority to conclude a treaty with the United States did on the 28th day of February 1835 stipulate and agree with the Government of the United States to submit to the Senate to fix the amount which should be allowed the Cherokees for their claims and for a cession of their lands east of the Mississippi river, and did agree to abide by the award of the Senate of the United States themselves and to recommend the same to their people for their final determination.

And whereas on such submission the Senate advised "that a sum not exceeding five millions of dollars be paid to the Cherokee Indians for all their lands and possessions east of the Mississippi river."

And whereas this delegation after said award of the Senate had been made, were called upon to submit propositions as to its disposition to be arranged in a treaty which they refused to do, but insisted that the same "should be referred to their nation and there in general council to deliberate and determine on the subject in order to ensure harmony and good feeling among themselves."

And whereas a certain other delegation composed of John Ridge Elias Boudinot Archilla Smith S. W. Bell John West Wm. A. Davis and Ezekiel West, who represented that portion of the nation in favor of emigration to the Cherokee country west of the Mississippi entered into propositions for a treaty with John F. Schermerhorn commissioner on the part of the United States which were to be submitted to their nation for their final action and determination:

And whereas the Cherokee people at their last October council at Red Clay, fully authorized and empowered a delegation or committee of twenty persons of their nation to enter into and conclude a treaty with the United States commissioner then present, *at that place or elsewhere* and as the people had good reason to believe that a treaty would then and there be made or at a subsequent council at New Echota which the commissioners it was well known and understood, were authorized and instructed to convene for said purpose; and since the said delegation have gone on to Washington city, with a view to close negotiations there, as stated by them notwithstanding they were officially informed by the United States commissioner that they would not be received by the President of the United States; and that the Government would transact no business of this nature with them, and that if a treaty was made it must be done here in the nation, where the delegation at Washington last winter *urged that it should be done for the purpose of promoting peace and harmony among the people;* and since these facts have also been corroborated to us by a communication recently received by the commissioner from the Government of the United States and read and explained to the people in open council and therefore believing said delegation can effect nothing and since our difficulties are daily increasing and our situation is rendered more and more precarious uncertain and insecure in consequence of the legislation of the States; and seeing no effectual way of relief, but in accepting the liberal overtures of the United States.

And whereas Genl William Carroll and John F. Schermerhorn were appointed commissioners on the part of the United States, with full power and authority to conclude a treaty with the Cherokees east and were directed by the President to convene the people of the nation in general council at New Echota and to submit said propositions to them with power and authority to vary the same so as to meet the views of the Cherokees in reference to its details.And whereas the said commissioners did appoint and notify a general council of the nation to convene at New Echota on the 21st day of December 1835; and informed them that the commissioners would be prepared to make a treaty with the Cherokee people who should assemble there and those who did not come they should conclude gave their assent and sanction to whatever should be transacted at this council and the people having met in council according to said notice.

Therefore the following articles of a treaty are agreed upon and concluded between William Carroll and John F. Schermerhorn commissioners on the part of the United States and the chiefs and head men and people of the Cherokee nation in general council assembled this 29th day of Decr 1835.

ARTICLE 1. The Cherokee nation hereby cede relinquish and convey to the United States all the lands owned claimed or possessed by them east of the Mississippi river, and hereby release all their claims upon the United States for spoliations of every kind for and in consideration of the sum of five millions of dollars to be expended paid and invested in the manner stipulated and agreed upon in the following articles But as a question has arisen between the commissioners and the Cherokees whether the Senate in their resolution by which they advised " that a sum not exceeding five millions of dollars be paid to the Cherokee Indians for all their lands and possessions east of the Mississippi river" have included and made any allowance or consideration for claims for spoliations it is therefore agreed on the part of the United States that this question shall be again submitted to the Senate for their consideration and decision and if no allowance was made for spoliations that then an additional sum of three hundred thousand dollars be allowed for the same.

ARTICLE 2. Whereas by the treaty of May 6th 1828 and the supplementary treaty thereto of Feb. 14th 1833 with the Cherokees west of the Mississippi the United States guarantied and secured to be conveyed by patent, to the Cherokee nation of Indians the following tract of country " Beginning at a point on the old western territorial line of Arkansas Territory being twenty-five miles north from the point where the territorial line crosses Arkansas river, thence running from said north point south on the said territorial line where the said territorial line crosses Verdigris river; thence down said Verdigris river to the Arkansas river; thence down said Arkansas to a point where a stone is placed opposite the east or lower bank of Grand river at its junction with the Arkansas; thence running south forty-four degrees west one mile; thence in a straight line to a point four miles northerly, from the mouth of the north fork of the Canadian; thence along the said four mile line to the Canadian; thence down the Canadian to the Arkansas; thence down the Arkansas to that point on the Arkansas where the eastern Choctaw boundary strikes said river and running thence with the western line of Arkansas Territory as now defined, to the southwest corner of Missouri; thence along the western Missouri line to the land assigned the Senecas; thence on the south line of the Senecas to Grand river; thence up said Grand river as far as the south line of the Osage reservation, extended if necessary; thence up and between said south Osage line extended west if necessary, and a line drawn due west from the point of beginning to a certain distance west, at which a line running north and south from said Osage line to said due west line will make seven millions of acres within the whole described boundaries. In addition to the seven millions of acres of land thus provided for and bounded, the United States further guaranty to the Cherokee nation a perpetual outlet west, and a free and unmolested use of all the country west of the western boundary of said seven millions of acres, as far west as the sovereignty of the United States and their right of soil extend:

Provided however That if the saline or salt plain on the western prairie shall fall within said limits prescribed for said outlet, the right is reserved to the United States to permit other tribes of red men to get salt on said plain in common with the Cherokees; And letters patent shall be issued by the United States as soon as practicable for the land hereby guarantied."

And whereas it is apprehended by the Cherokees that in the above cession there is not contained a sufficient quantity of land for the accommodation of the whole nation on their removal west of the Mississippi the United States in consideration of the sum of five hundred thousand dollars therefore hereby covenant and agree to convey to the said Indians, and their descendants by patent, in fee simple the following additional tract of land situated between the west line of the State of Missouri and the Osage reservation beginning at the southeast corner of the same and runs north along the east line of the Osage lands fifty miles to the northeast corner thereof; and thence east to the west line of the State of Missouri; thence with said line south fifty miles; thence west to the place of beginning; estimated to contain eight hundred thousand acres of land; but it is expressly understood that if any of the lands assigned the Quapaws shall fall within the aforesaid bounds the same shall be reserved and excepted out of the lands above granted and a pro rata reduction shall be made in the price to be allowed to the United States for the same by the Cherokees.

ARTICLE 3. The United States also agree that the lands above ceded by the treaty of Feb. 14 1833, including the outlet, and those ceded by this treaty shall all be included in one patent executed to the Cherokee nation of Indians by the President of the United States according to the provisions of the act of May 28 1830. It is, however, agreed that the military reservation at Fort Gibson shall be held by the United States. But should the United States abandon said post and have no further use for the same it shall revert to the Cherokee nation. The United States shall always have the right to make and establish such post and military roads and forts in any part of the Cherokee country, as they may deem proper for the interest and protection of the same and the free use of as much land, timber, fuel and materials of all kinds for the construction and support of the same as may be necessary; provided that if the private rights of individuals are interfered with, a just compensation therefor shall be made.

ARTICLE 4. The United States also stipulate and agree to extinguish for the benefit of the Cherokees the titles to the reservations within their country made in the Osage treaty of 1825 to certain half-breeds and for this purpose they hereby agree to pay to the persons to whom the same belong or have been assigned or to their agents or guardians whenever they shall execute after the ratification of this treaty a satisfactory conveyance for the same, to the United States, the sum of fifteen thousand dollars according to a schedule accompanying this treaty of the relative value of the several reservations.

And whereas by the several treaties between the United States and the Osage Indians the Union and Harmony Missionary reservations which were established for their benefit are now situated within the country ceded by them to the United States; the former being situated in the Cherokee country and the latter in the State of Missouri. It is therefore agreed that the United States shall pay the American Board of Commissioners for Foreign Missions for the improvements on the same what they shall be appraised at by Capt. Geo. Vashon Cherokee subagent Abraham Redfield and A. P. Chouteau or such persons as the President of the United States shall appoint and the money allowed for the same shall be expended in schools among the Osages and improving their condition. It is understood that the United States are to pay the amount allowed for the reservations in this article and not the Cherokees.

ARTICLE 5. The United States hereby covenant and agree that the lands ceded to the Cherokee nation in the forgoing article shall, in no future time without their consent, be included within the territorial limits or jurisdiction of any State or Territory. But they shall secure to the Cherokee nation the right by their national councils to make and carry into effect all such laws as they may deem necessary for the government and protection of the persons and property within their own country belonging to their people or such persons as have connected themselves with them: provided always that they shall not be inconsistent with the constitution of the United States and such acts of Congress as have been or may be passed regulating trade and intercourse with the Indians; and also, that they stall not be considered as extending to such citizens and army of the United States as may travel or reside in the Indian country by permission according to the laws and regulations established by the Government of the same.

ARTICLE 6. Perpetual peace and friendship shall exist between the citizens of the United States and the Cherokee Indians. The United States agree to protect the Cherokee nation from domestic strife and foreign enemies and against intestine wars between the several tribes. The Cherokees shall endeavor to preserve and maintain the peace of the country and not make war upon their neighbors they shall also be protected against interruption and intrusion from citizens of the United States, who may attempt to settle in the country without their consent; and all such persons shall be removed from the same by order of the President of the United States. But this is not intended to prevent the residence among them of useful farmers mechanics and teachers for the instruction of Indians according to treaty stipulations.

ARTICLE 7. The Cherokee nation having already made great progress in civilization and deeming it important that every proper and laudable inducement should be offered to their people to improve their condition as well as to guard and secure in the most effectual manner the rights guarantied to them in this treaty, and with a view to illustrate the liberal and enlarged policy of the Government of the United States towards the Indians in their removal beyond the territorial limits of the States, it is stipulated that they shall be entitled to a delegate in the House of Representatives of the United States whenever Congress shall make provision for the same.

ARTICLE 8. The United States also agree and stipulate to remove the Cherokees to their new homes and to subsist them one year after their arrival there and that a sufficient number of steamboats and baggage-wagons shall be furnished to remove them comfortably, and so as not to endanger their health, and that a physician well supplied with medicines shall accompany each detachment of emigrants removed by the Government. Such persons and families as in the opinion of the emigrating agent are capable of subsisting and removing themselves shall be permitted to do so; and they shall be allowed in full for all claims for the same twenty dollars for each member of their family; and in lieu of their one year's rations they shall be paid the sum of thirty-three dollars and thirty-three cents if they prefer it. Such Cherokees also as reside at present out of the nation and shall remove with them in two years west of the Mississippi shall be entitled to allowance for removal and subsistence as above provided.

ARTICLE 9. The United States agree to appoint suitable agents who shall make a just and fair valuation of all such improvements now in the possession of the Cherokees as add any value to the lands; and also of the ferries owned by them, according to their net income; and such improvements and ferries from which they have been dispossessed in a lawless manner or under any existing laws of the State where the same may be situated.

The just debts of the Indians shall be paid out of any monies due them for their improvements and claims; and they shall also be furnished at the discretion of the President of the United States with a sufficient sum to enable them to obtain the necessary means to remove themselves to their new homes, and the balance of their dues shall be paid them at the Cherokee agency west of the Mississippi. The missionary establishments shall also be valued and appraised in a like manner and the amount of them paid over by the United States to the treasurers of the respective missionary societies by whom they have been established and improved in order to enable them to erect such buildings and make such improvements among the Cherokees west of the Mississippi as they may deem necessary for their benefit. Such teachers at present among the Cherokees as this council shall select and designate shall be removed west of the Mississippi with the Cherokee nation and on the same terms allowed to them.

ARTICLE 10. The President of the United States shall invest in some safe and most productive public stocks of the country for the benefit of the whole Cherokee nation who have removed or shall remove to the lands assigned by this treaty to the Cherokee nation west of the Mississippi the following sums as a permanent fund for the purposes hereinafter specified and pay over the net income of the same annually to such person or persons as shall be authorized or appointed by the Cherokee nation to receive the same and their receipt shall be a full discharge for the amount paid to them viz: the sum of two hundred thousand dollars in addition to the present annuities of the nation to constitute a general fund the interest of which shall be applied annually by the council of the nation to such purposes as they may deem best for the general interest of their people. The sum of fifty thousand dollars to constitute an orphans' fund the annual income of which shall be expended towards the support and education of such orphan children as are destitute of the means of subsistence. The sum of one hundred and fifty thousand dollars in addition to the present school fund of the nation shall constitute a permanent school fund, the interest of which shall be applied annually by the council of the nation for the support of common schools and such a literary institution of a higher order as may be established in the Indian country.

And in order to secure as far as possible the true and beneficial application of the orphans' and school fund the council of the Cherokee nation when required by the President of the United States shall make a report of the application of those funds and he shall at all times have the right if the funds have been misapplied to correct any abuses of them and direct the manner of their application for the purposes for which they were intended. The council of the nation may by giving two years' notice of their intention withdraw their funds by and with the consent of the President and Senate of the United States, and invest them in such manner as they may deem most proper for their interest. The United States also agree and stipulate to pay the just debts and claims against the Cherokee nation held by the citizens of the same and also the just claims of citizens of the United States for services rendered to the nation and the sum of sixty thousand dollars is appropriated for this purpose but no claims against individual persons of the nation shall be allowed and paid by the nation. The sum of three hundred thousand dollars is hereby set apart to pay and liquidate the just claims of the Cherokees upon the United States for spoliations of every kind, that have not been already satisfied under former treaties.

ARTICLE 11. The Cherokee nation of Indians believing it will be for the interest of their people to have all their funds and annuities under their own direction and future disposition hereby agree to commute their permanent annuity of ten thousand dollars for the sum of two hundred and fourteen thousand dollars, the same to be invested by the President of the United States as a part of the general fund of the nation; and their present school fund amounting to about fifty thousand dollars shall constitute a part of the permanent school fund of the nation.

ARTICLE 12. Those individuals and families of the Cherokee nation that are averse to a removal to the Cherokee country west of the Mississippi and are desirous to become citizens of the States where they reside and such as are qualified to take care of themselves and their property shall be entitled to receive their due portion of all the personal benefits accruing under this treaty for their claims, improvements and *per capita;* as soon as an appropriation is made for this treaty.

Such heads of Cherokee families as are desirous to reside within the States of No. Carolina Tennessee and Alabama subject to the laws of the same; and who are qualified or calculated to become useful citizens shall be entitled, on the certificate of the commissioners to a preemption right to one hundred and sixty acres of land or one quarter section at the minimum Congress price; so as to include the present buildings or improvements of those who now reside there and such as do not live there at present shall be permitted to locate within two years any lands not already occupied by persons entitled to pre-emption privilege under this treaty and if two or more families live on the same quarter section and they desire to continue their residence in these States and are qualified as above specified they shall, on receiving their pre-emption certificate be entitled to the right of pre-emption to such lands as they may select not already taken by any person entitled to them under this treaty.

It is stipulated and agreed between the United States and the Cherokee people that John Ross James Starr George Hicks John Gunter George Chambers John Ridge Elias Boudinot George Sanders John Martin William Rogers Roman Nose Situwake and John Timpson shall be a committee on the part of the Cherokees to recommend such persons for the privilege of pre-emption rights as may be deemed entitled to the same under the above articles and to select the missionaries who shall be removed with the nation; and that they be hereby fully empowered and authorized to transact all business on the part of the Indians which may arise in carrying into effect the provisions of this treaty and settling the same with the United States. If any of the persons above mentioned should decline acting or be removed by death; the vacancies shall be filled by the committee themselves. It is also understood and agreed that the sum of one hundred thousand dollars shall be expended by the commissioners in such manner as the committee deem best for the benefit of the poorer class of Cherokees as shall remove west or have removed west and are entitled to the benefits of this treaty. The same to be delivered at the Cherokee agency west as soon after the removal of the nation as possible.

ARTICLE 13. In order to make a final settlement of all the claims of the Cherokees for reservations granted under former treaties to any individuals belonging to the nation by the United States it is therefore hereby stipulated and agreed and expressly understood by the parties to this treaty—that all the Cherokees and their heirs and descendants to whom any reservations have been made under any former treaties with the United States, and who have not sold or conveyed the same by deed or otherwise and who in the opinion of the commissioners have complied with the terms on which the reservations were granted as far as practicable in the several cases; and which reservations have since been sold by the United States shall constitute a just claim against the United States and the original reserve or their heirs or descendants shall be entitled to receive the present value thereof from the United States as unimproved lands. And all such reservations as have not been sold by the United States and where the terms on which the reservations were made in the opinion of the commissioners have been complied with as far as practicable, they or their heirs or descendants shall be entitled to the same. They are hereby granted and confirmed to them—and also all persons who were entitled to reservations under the treaty of 1817 and who as far as practicable in the opinion of the commissioners, have complied with the stipulations of said treaty, although by the treaty of 1819 such reservations were included in the uncoded lands belonging to the Cherokee nation are hereby confirmed to them and they shall be entitled to receive a grant for the same. And all such reserves as were obliged by the laws of the States in which their reservations were situated, to abandon the same or purchase them from the States shall be deemed to have a just claim against the United States for the amount by them paid to the States with interest thereon for such reservations and if obliged to abandon the same, to the present value of such reservations as unimproved lands but in all cases where the reserves have sold their reservations or any part thereof and conveyed the same by deed or otherwise and have been paid for the same, they their heirs or descendants or their assigns shall not be considered as having any claims upon the United States under this article of the treaty nor be entitled to receive any compensation for the lands thus disposed of. It is expressly understood by the parties to this treaty that the amount to be allowed for reservations under this article shall not be deducted out of the consideration money allowed to the Cherokees for their claims for spoliations and the cession of their lands; but the same is to be paid for independently by the United States as it is only a just fulfillment of former treaty stipulations.

ARTICLE 14. It is also agreed on the part of the United States that such warriors of the Cherokee nation as were engaged on the side of the United States in the late war with Great Britain and the southern tribes of Indians, and who were wounded in such service shall be entitled to such pensions as shall be allowed them by the Congress of the United States to commence from the period of their disability.

ARTICLE 15. It is expressly understood and agreed between the parties to this treaty that after deducting the amount which shall be actually expended for the payment for improvements, ferries, claims, for spoliations, removal subsistence and debts and claims upon the Cherokee nation and for the additional quantity of lands and goods for the poorer class of Cherokees and the several sums to be invested for the general national funds; provided for in the several articles of this treaty the balance whatever the same may be shall be equally divided between all the people belonging to the Cherokee nation east according to the census just completed; and such Cherokees as have removed west since June 1833 who are entitled by the terms of their enrollment and removal to all the benefits resulting from the final treaty between the United States and the Cherokees east they shall also be paid for their improvements according to their approved value before their removal where fraud has not already been shown in their valuation.

ARTICLE 16. It is hereby stipulated and agreed by the Cherokees that they shall remove to their new homes within two years from the ratification of this treaty and that during such time the United States shall protect and defend them in their possessions and property and free use and occupation of the same and such persons as have been dispossessed of their improvements and houses; and for which no grant has actually issued previously to the enactment of the law of the State of Georgia, of December 1835 to regulate Indian occupancy shall be again put in possession and placed in the same situation and condition, in reference to the laws of the State of Georgia, as the Indians that have not been dispossessed; and if this is not done, and the people are left unprotected, then the United States shall pay the several Cherokees for their losses and damages sustained by them in consequence thereof. And it is also stipulated and agreed that the public buildings and improvements on which they are situated at New Echota for which no grant has been actually made previous to the passage of the above recited act if not occupied by the Cherokee people shall be reserved for the public and free use of the United States and the Cherokee Indians for the purpose of settling and closing all the Indian business arising under this treaty between the commissioners of claims and the Indians.

The United States, and the several States interested in the Cherokee lands, shall immediately proceed to survey the lands ceded by this treaty; but it is expressly agreed and understood between the parties that the agency buildings and that tract of land surveyed and laid off for the use of Colonel R. J. Meigs Indian agent or heretofore enjoyed and occupied by his successors in office shall continue subject to the use and occupancy of the United States, or such agent as may be engaged specially superintending the removal of the tribe.

ARTICLE 17. All the claims arising under or provided for in the several articles of this treaty, shall be examined and adjudicated by such commissioners as shall be appointed by the President of the United States by and with the advice and consent of the Senate of the United States for that purpose and their decision shall be final and on their certificate of the amount due the several claimants they shall be paid by the United States. All stipulations in former treaties which have not been superseded or annulled by this shall continue in full force and virtue.

ARTICLE 18. Whereas in consequence of the unsettled affairs of the Cherokee people and the early frosts, their crops are insufficient to support their families and great distress is likely to ensue and whereas the nation will not, until after their removal be able advantageously to expend the income of the permanent funds of the nation it is therefore agreed that the annuities of the nation which may accrue under this treaty for two years, the time fixed for their removal shall be expended in provision and clothing for the benefit of the poorer class of the nation and the United States hereby agree to advance the same for that purpose as soon after the ratification of this treaty as an appropriation for the same shall be made. It is however not intended in this article to interfere with that part of the annuities due the Cherokees west by the treaty of 1819.

ARTICLE 19. This treaty after the same shall be ratified by the President and Senate of the United States shall be obligatory on the contracting parties.

In testimony whereof, the commissioners and the chiefs, head men, and people whose names are hereunto annexed, being duly authorized by the people in general council assembled, have affixed their hands and seals for themselves, and in behalf of the Cherokee Nation.

I have examined the foregoing treaty, and although not present when it was made, I approve its provisions generally, and therefore sign it.Wm. Carroll,
J. F. Schermerhorn.
Major Ridge, his x mark, [L. S.]
James Foster, his x mark, [L. S.]
Tesa-ta-esky, his x mark, [L. S.]
Charles Moore, his x mark, [L. S.]
George Chambers, his x mark, [L. S.]
Tah-yeske, his x mark, [L. S.]
Archilla Smith, his x mark, [L. S.]
Andrew Ross, [L. S.]
William Lassley, [L. S.]
Cae-te-hee, his x mark , [L. S.]
Te-gah-e-ske, his x mark, [L. S.]
Robert Rogers, [son of John and Sarah] [L. S.]
John Gunter, [L. S.]
John A. Bell, [L. S.]
Charles F. Foreman, [L. S.]
William Rogers, [son of John and Sarah] [L. S.]
George W. Adair, [L. S.]
Elias Boudinot, [L. S.]
James Starr, his x mark, [L. S.]
Jesse Half-breed, his x mark, [L. S.]

Signed and sealed in presence of—
Western B. Thomas, secretary.
Ben. F. Currey, special agent.
M.Wolfe Batman, first lieutenant, sixth U. S. infantry, disbursing agent.
Jon. L. Hooper, lieutenant, fourth Infantry.
C. M Hitchcock, M. D., assistant surgeon, U.S.A.
G. W. Currey,
Wm. H. Underwood,
Cornelius D. Terhune,
John W. H. Underwood.
In compliance with instructions of the council at New Echota, we sign this treaty.
Stand Watie,
John Ridge.
March 1, 1836.
Witnesses:
Elbert Herring,
Alexander H. Everett,
John Robb,
D. Kurtz,
Wm.Y. Hansell,
Samuel J. Potts,
Jno. Litle,
S. Rockwell.

Dec. 31, 1835. | 7 Stat., 487.

Whereas the western Cherokees have appointed a delegation to visit the eastern Cherokees to assure them of the friendly disposition of their people and their desire that the nation should again be united as one people and to urge upon them the expediency of accepting the overtures of the Government; and that, on their removal they may be assured of a hearty welcome and an equal participation with them in all the benefits and privileges of the Cherokee country west and the undersigned two of said delegation being the only delegates in the eastern nation from the west at the signing and sealing of the treaty lately concluded at New Echota between their eastern brethren and the United States; and having fully understood the provisions of the same they agree to it in behalf of the western Cherokees. But it is expressly understood that nothing in this treaty shall affect any claims of the western Cherokees on the United States.

In testimony whereof, we have, this 31st day of December, 1835, hereunto set our hands and seals.
James Rogers, (Seal)
John Smith, his x mark, (Seal)
Delegates from the western Cherokees.
Test:
Ben. F. Currey, special agent.
M. W. Batman, first lieutenant, Sixth Infantry,
Jno. L. Hooper, lieutenant, Fourth Infantry,
Elias Boudinot.

Article 20

The United States do also hereby guarantee the payments of all unpaid just claims upon the Indians, without expense to them, out of the proper funds of the United States, for the settlement of which a cession or cessions of land has or have been heretofore made by the Indians in Georgia. Provided the United States or the State of Georgia has derived benefit from the said cession or cessions of land without having made payment to the Indians therefore.-It is hereby however further agreed and understood, that if the Senate of the United States disapproves of this article it may be rejected with-out impairing any other provision of the treaty, or affecting the Indians in any manner whatever.

[Signed] A. McCoy ,Clk
[Signed] W.B. Thomas, Secry

In compliance with the unanimous request of the Committee of the Cherokee Nation in General council assembled, it is consented and agreed by the Commissioner on the part of the United States that the foregoing shall be added as a supplemental article to the Treaty under the express condition and stipulation that if the President or Senate of the United States disapprove of this article it may be rejected without impairing any other provision of this treaty or affecting the Indians in any manner whatever.

[Signed] J.F. Schermerhorn

March 1, 1836. | 7 Stat., 488. | Proclamation, May 23, 1836

Supplementary articles to a treaty concluded at New Echota, Georgia, December 29, 1835, between the United States and Cherokee people.

Andrew Jackson, President of the United States. To all and singular to whom these presents shall come, - Greeting:

WHEREAS the undersigned were authorized at the general meeting of the Cherokee people held at New Echota as above stated, to make and assent to such alterations in the preceding treaty as might be thought necessary, and whereas the President of the United States has expressed his determination not to allow any pre-emptions or reservations his desire being that the whole Cherokee people should remove together and establish themselves in the country provided for them west of the Mississippi river.

ARTICLE 1. It is therefore agreed that all the pre-emption rights and reservations provided for in articles 12 and 13 shall be and are hereby relinquished and declared void.

ARTICLE 2. Whereas the Cherokee people have supposed that the sum of five millions of dollars fixed by the Senate in their resolution of— —day of March, 1835, as the value of the Cherokee lands and possessions east of the Mississippi river was not intended to include the amount which may be required to remove them, nor the value of certain claims which many of their people had against citizens of the United States, which suggestion has been confirmed by the opinion expressed to the War Department by some of the Senators who voted upon the question and whereas the President is willing that this subject should be referred to the Senate for their consideration and if it was not intended by the Senate that the above-mentioned sum of five millions of dollars should include the objects herein specified that in that case such further provision should be made therefor as might appear to the Senate to be just.

ARTICLE 3. It is therefore agreed that the sum of six hundred thousand dollars shall be and the same is hereby allowed to the Cherokee people to include the expense of their removal, and all claims of every nature and description against the Government of the United States not herein otherwise expressly provided for, and to be in lieu of the said reservations and pre-emptions and of the sum of three hundred thousand dollars for spoliations described in the 1st article of the above-mentioned treaty. This sum of six hundred thousand dollars shall be applied and distributed agreeably to the provisions of the said treaty, and any surplus which may remain after removal and payment of the claims so ascertained shall be turned over and belong to the education fund. But it is expressly understood that the subject of this article is merely referred hereby to the consideration of the Senate and if they shall approve the same then this supplement shall remain part of the treaty.

ARTICLE 4. It is also understood that the provisions in article 16, for the agency reservation is not intended to interfere with the occupant right of any Cherokees should their improvement fall within the same. It is also understood and agreed, that the one hundred thousand dollars appropriated in article 12 for the poorer class of Cherokees and intended as a set-off to the pre-emption rights shall now be transferred from the funds of the nation and added to the general national fund of four hundred thousand dollars so as to make said fund equal to five hundred thousand dollars.

ARTICLE 5. The necessary expenses attending the negotiations of the aforesaid treaty and supplement and also of such persons of the delegation as may sign the same shall be defrayed by the United States.

In testimony whereof, John F. Schermerhorn, commissioner on the part of the United States, and the undersigned delegation have hereunto set their hands and seals, this first day of March, in the year one thousand eight hundred and thirty-six.

Andrew Ross, [L. S.]
William Rogers, [L. S.]
John Gunter, [L. S.]
John A. Bell, [L. S.]
Jos. A. Foreman, [L.S.]
Robert Sanders, [L. S.]
Elias Boudinot, [L. S.]
Johnson Rogers,[son of John and Sarah] [L. S.]
James Starr, his x mark, [L. S.]
Stand Watie, [L. S.]
John Ridge, [L. S.]

J. F. Schermerhorn.
Major Ridge, his x mark, [L. S.]
James Foster, his x mark, [L. S.]
Tah-ye-ske, his x mark, [L. S.]
Long Shell Turtle, his x mark, [L. S.]
John Fields, his x mark, [L. S.]
James Fields, his x mark, [L. S.]
George Welch, his x mark, [L. S.]
James Rogers, [L. S.]
John Smith, his x mark.[L. S.]

Witnesses:
Elbert Herring,
Thos. Glascock,
Alexander H. Everett,
Jno. Garland, Major, U. S. Army,
C. A. Harris,
John Robb,
Wm. Y. Hansell,
Saml. J. Potts,
Jno. Litle,
S. Rockwell.

Signed and sealed in presence of
Western B. Thomas, Secy
Ben F. Currey, Special Agent
M. Wolf Balenan
Jno L. Hopper
C.M. Hitchcock, M.D.
G.W. Currey
Wm. H. Underwood
Cornelius D. Terhune
John W.H. Underwood

In compliance with Instructions of the Council at New Echota we sign this Treaty - March 1st, 1836

[Signed] Stand Watie
[Signed] John Ridge

Schedule and estimated value of the Osage half-breed reservations within the territory ceded to the Cherokees west of the Mississippi, (referred to in article 5 on the foregoing treaty,) viz:

Augustus Clamont one section				$6,000
James	"	"	"	1,000
Paul	"	"	"	1,300
Henry	"	"	"	800
Anthony	"	"	"	1,800
Rosalie	"	"	"	1,800
Emilia D, of Mihanga				1,000
Emilia D, of Shemianga				1,300
				$15,000

I hereby certify that the above schedule is the estimated value of the Osage reservations, as made out and agreed upon with Col. A. P. Choteau who represented himself as the agent or guardian of the above reserves.
March 14, 1835[1836] [signed] J. F. Schermerhorn.

Ratification of Treaty

In the Senate of the U S
May 18th, 1836

Resolved, (two thirds of the Senate present concurring) That the senate do advise and consent to the ratification of the treaty between the United States of America and the Cherokee Indians concluded at New Echota the 29th day of December, 1835, together with the Supplementary articles thereto dated the first day of March one thousand Eight hundred and thirty six, with the following amendments thereto:

Article 17 lines 2 and 3, Strike Out the words, "by General William Carroll and John F. Schermerhorn, or "-

In the 4th line of the same article after the word "State," insert by an with the advice and consent of the Senate of the United States.

Strike out the 20th Article which appears as a Supplemental article.

Attest. Walter Lowell, Secretary

Now therefore be it known that I Andrew Jackson President of the United

States of America having seen and considered the said Treaty, and also the Supplementary Articles thereunto annexed, do, in pursuance of the advice and consent of the Senate, as expressed in their resolution of the eighteenth day of May, one thousand eight hundred and thirty-six, accept, ratify, and confirm the same, with the following amendments thereto, as expressed in the aforesaid Resolution of the Senate . . . .

In testimony whereof I have caused the Seal of the United States to be hereunto affixed, having signed the same with my hand.

Done at the City of Washington, this twenty third day of May, in the year of our Lord one thousand eight hundred and thirty-six, and of the Independence of the United States the Sixtieth.

[Signed] Andrew Jackson
By the President
[Signed] John Forsyth
Secretary of State

Index